The Early Years of Television and the BBC

Jamie Medhurst

EDINBURGH
University Press

Edinburgh University Press is one of the leading university presses in the UK. We publish academic books and journals in our selected subject areas across the humanities and social sciences, combining cutting-edge scholarship with high editorial and production values to produce academic works of lasting importance. For more information visit our website: edinburghuniversitypress.com

© Jamie Medhurst, 2022, 2019

Edinburgh University Press Ltd
The Tun – Holyrood Road
12 (2f) Jackson's Entry
Edinburgh EH8 8PJ

First published in hardback by Edinburgh University Press 2022

Typeset in Ehrhardt MT Pro by
Cheshire Typesetting Ltd, Cuddington, Cheshire, and
printed and bound by CPI Group (UK) Ltd
Croydon, CR0 4YY

A CIP record for this book is available from the British Library

ISBN 978 0 7486 3786 7 (hardback)
ISBN 978 1 3995 0411 9 (paperback)
ISBN 978 1 3995 0412 6 (webready PDF)
ISBN 978 1 3995 0413 3 (epub)

The right of Jamie Medhurst to be identified as author of this work has been asserted in accordance with the Copyright, Designs and Patents Act 1988 and the Copyright and Related Rights Regulations 2003 (SI No. 2498).

Contents

List of Figures   iv
Acknowledgements   v

1. Introduction   1
2. Early Television Developments   13
3. Enter the BBC   32
4. From Experiment to Service: 1929–1932   56
5. A Service and Two Rivals: 1932–1935   77
6. Preparing for the High-Definition Service   109
7. The BBC Television Service: 1936–1939   134
8. Conclusions   176

Bibliography   180
Index   190

Figures

4.1	Lance Sieveking with his 'fading board' and Val Gielgud rehearsing *The Man with the Flower in His Mouth*	61
4.2	*The Man with the Flower in His Mouth* cast and production staff in the Baird Television studio in Long Acre	62
5.1	The Baird 30-line scanner installed in Studio BB, Broadcasting House in 1932	79
5.2	The television studio at 16 Portland Place, March 1934	90
5.3	The television control room, 16 Portland Place, April 1935	91
5.4	Josephine Baker in Studio BB, Broadcasting House, October 1933	92
5.5	Cartoon that appeared in the *Daily Mirror* on 6 June 1932	99
6.1	Leslie Mitchell and Elizabeth Cowell in the Alexandra Palace make-up room with Mary Allen	117
6.2	Musings from *Punch*, 9 September 1936	124
7.1	Studio B – the Baird Studio – in Alexandra Palace, August 1936	135
7.2	Jasmine Bligh with an Emitron camera at Alexandra Palace	135
7.3	An Emitron camera being set up by the mobile television unit, in preparation for the Coronation procession in May 1937	145
7.4	One of the last programmes to be broadcast on pre-war television, *The Zoo*, an outside broadcast from Regent's Park Zoo, 31 August 1939	154
7.5	The BBC Gardener, C. H. Middleton, broadcasting from Radiolympia in September 1938	158

Acknowledgements

This book took a long time to come to fruition – longer than I had originally hoped and expected. In fact, two of my children were born and another grew up and got married during the research and writing.

Firstly, I would like to thank most sincerely my academic colleagues who have listened to seminar and conference papers on the topic and have offered constructive and friendly advice, and have basically kept me going academically over the years: Professor Malcolm Baird, Professor David Hendy, Emerita Professor Michele Hilmes, Professor Cathy Johnson, Professor Kate Lacey, Professor Rachel Moseley, Dr Kate Murphy, Professor Helen Wheatley, Dr Amanda Wrigley and Professor John Wyver. Colleagues and former colleagues at Aberystwyth University (in particular Professor Simon Banham, Dr Kate Egan, Professor Anwen Jones, Dr Kim Knowles, Dr Paul Newland and Professor Dame Elan Closs Stephens) have also been extremely helpful and supportive. Thanks to students over the years on my 'Television History' module for allowing me to indulge myself and try out some ideas. My colleagues in the Entangled Media Histories research network, in particular Professor Hugh Chignell, Dr Marie Cronqvist, Dr Christoph Hilgert, Dr Kristin Skoog and Dr Hans-Ulrich Wagner, have also been a source of inspiration and help – thank you/danke/tack!

Dr Donald F. McLean, Honorary Lecturer at Aberystwyth University, and Emeritus Professor Tom O'Malley, my former colleague and mentor, have gone above and beyond the call of duty in talking with me incessantly about early television and providing valuable feedback on draft chapters and answering obscure technical questions. I have benefited enormously from their wisdom and guidance. Thank you. Suffice to say that any remaining errors are mine alone.

This book would not have seen the light of day had it not been for the support of archive and library staff. Huge debts of gratitude go in particular to staff in the Hugh Owen Library at Aberystwyth University, and in the National Science and Media Museum (formerly the National Media Museum) in Bradford, colleagues at the History of Advertising Trust (who hold the Selfridges Archives), staff at the Marconi Archive in the Bodleian Library at the University of Oxford (the Marconi Archive), staff at the British Postal Museum and Archive in London (for the archives of the General Post Office (GPO)), staff at the National Archives in Kew, and staff at the wonderful and priceless BBC Written Archives Centre in Caversham. Louise North, Archivist at WAC, deserves a special mention for answering emails, unearthing obscure files, checking all the WAC quotations in detail (and in so doing saving me from embarrassment!) and generally being a superstar – many thanks, Lou! Thanks also to Andrew Martin in BBC Archive Development for allowing me access to his invaluable and comprehensive list of Baird Television and BBC programmes transmitted between 1929 and 1939, and to the BBC Photo Library for permission to use photographs. Many thanks also to Clare Colvin, archivist at the Royal Television Society, for her invaluable help with the RTS archives, and to Simon Vaughan, archivist of the Alexandra Palace Television Society, for allowing me to access the invaluable resources of the APTS and for answering obscure questions late at night about early television. I would also like to thank Robert Seatter, Head of BBC History, for allowing access to the BBC Oral History Collection.

I am grateful to the BBC, the Alexandra Palace Television Society Archive, the *Punch* Cartoon Library/Topfoto and Mirrorpix/Reach Licensing for permission to reproduce photographs. I am also grateful to the BBC for permission to use BBC Written Archives material and the BBC Oral History Collection. BBC copyright content reproduced courtesy of the British Broadcasting Corporation. All rights reserved.

Thanks also to Gillian Leslie, Richard Strachan, Bekah Dey and Sam Johnson at Edinburgh University Press for their tremendous patience in answering all my questions (and there were many) and flexibility in allowing me to extend the deadline for this book several times as a result of two periods of paternity leave and two periods as Head of Department.

I was fortunate to receive a British Academy Small Research Grant (2008), an Aberystwyth University Research Fund grant (2008) and funding for an early broadcasting research network from the Arts and Humanities Research Council (2010–12), all of which helped during the research for this book. I am extremely grateful to these organisations for their support.

Finally, I must thank my family, who have lived with this project for far too long. Thank you for believing in me and in my ability to write this book and for being interested in the project (or at least, pretending to be interested). Masses of love and thanks to my best friend and wife, Ceris, my three fantastic children, Alice, Leif and Henry, and wonderful son-in-law Jack. I'm sorry for all the times I couldn't come out to play football, go on picnics, help in the garden, or play on the Xbox – I promise to make it up to you and will even learn how not to destroy things in Minecraft. In the meantime, I dedicate this book of 'boring television history' – Leif's words, not mine – to you.

A part of Chapter 6 was previously published as '"What a Hullabaloo!" Launching BBC Television in 1936 and BBC2 in 1964', *Journal of British Cinema and Television* 14: 2 (2017), 264–82, and a part of Chapter 7 was previously published as 'Mea Maxima Culpa: John Reith and Television', *Media History* 25: 3 (2019), 292–306. Many thanks to the editors of these journals for permission to reproduce material here.

For
Ceris, Alice, Leif, Henry and Jack

CHAPTER 1

Introduction

Television. Not a nice word. Greek and Latin mixed. Clumsy. (C. P. Scott)[1]

On 26 January 1926, the Scottish inventor John Logie Baird demonstrated his experimental television equipment to members of the Royal Institution at his laboratory in Long Acre, central London. Ten years later, on 2 November 1936, the world's first regular high-definition television service was launched from the BBC studios at Alexandra Palace in north London, and ten years after that, on 7 June 1946, the service resumed, having been closed down for the duration of the Second World War. By the time the next decade had passed, the BBC's monopoly on television broadcasting had been broken by the advertising-funded public service broadcaster, Independent Television (ITV), heralding the beginning of the dominance of television as mass communication medium. In the space of forty years, television developed from a laboratory-based experiment to a medium of information, education and entertainment.

The origins of this book can be traced back to a research visit to the BBC's Written Archives Centre in Caversham in 2006. Having completed research on another book, I had some time to spare and so happened to come across BBC files relating to the Baird Television Company. Although I was familiar with John Logie Baird, I was not, at that point, aware of the full extent of the BBC's involvement with the introduction and development of a television service in the 1920s and 1930s. Further research opened up a fascinating set of debates around politics, technology, public service, commerce and business – and strong personalities. It also highlighted tensions between the government, the broadcaster (the BBC) and the fledgling radio and television manufacturing industry. Furthermore, the research led me to a discourse around early perceptions of the potential uses of television and, more importantly perhaps, made me reconsider the widely-circulated narrative that John Reith, the British Broadcasting Company's Managing Director and then the British

Broadcasting Corporation's first Director-General, despised television and would have nothing to do with it. I also encountered a discourse around national identity and 'Britishness' which emerged at various points in the narrative history. This book will address these issues through a detailed chronology and historical narrative based not only on revisiting some of the major secondary sources but also on original archival work. Each chapter of the book will also draw out some of the key themes or critical issues that emerge from the history.

The book traces the development of television during what I have called its 'early years', that is, between 1926 when Baird first demonstrated his television system in public to 1939, when the outbreak of the Second World War forced the closure of the BBC's fledgling regular television service. I have not attempted to write a fully comprehensive history of television – for such a task would be nigh-on impossible. Neither is it a history which focuses on John Logie Baird and his pioneering television work, although inevitably, from the British and international perspective, Baird is a major figure. Indeed, Asa Briggs argued that the relationship between Baird and the BBC is one of the main themes of television history in the 1930s.[2] Others have written extensively on Baird's contribution to the development of television in Britain and beyond, and while drawing on their work, I do not aim to replicate it.[3]

The focus of this book is on the BBC's relationship with television and the ways in which the BBC responded to, and eventually embraced, the medium. While the book examines the development of the medium primarily through the lens of the Corporation it also considers the BBC's relationship with government, the radio industry, and its listeners and viewers. The book is what some might term an institutional history. There are references to programmes and audiences, but these are generally within the context of thinking about the BBC engaging with television as an institution. It is not a 'social history' in the way that, for example, Joe Moran's history of television is a history of viewers' engagement with television (see below). Neither is it a technical history, or a book which focuses on the ways in which technology helped shape the development of television. Again, technology is discussed in broad terms, but not in the way that others have done. I provide examples of these later in this chapter.

In focusing on the BBC, I have written extensively about the period of the 1932–5 television service provided by the BBC. This is a period that Asa Briggs, in his history of the BBC, overlooked, and yet, while 'experimental' in many ways (and therefore subject to the possibility of neglect), the first service laid the foundations for the high-definition service which began in 1936 and pushed low-definition television as far as it would go within the confines of limited band width. In addition, it also offers a revised version of the commonly-held view that the Corporation's Director-General, John Reith, would have nothing to do with television. As discussed in Chapter 6, a more nuanced stance must be taken when considering Reith's relationship with the new medium.

Sources and methodology

This book is the result of a detailed historical study of the BBC's relationship with early television, framed by existing secondary source material and informed and deepened by an extensive and systematic examination of a wide range of archive material.

Two works written in the immediate post-war period provided a useful context for early television from the perspective of former BBC employees. Maurice Gorham's *Broadcasting and Television since 1900* and John Swift's *Adventure in Vision: The First Twenty-Five Years of Television* provide insights of those directly involved with early television. Gorham was given the task of heading the television service when it resumed after the Second World War, while Swift was a journalist on *Radio Times*, responsible for the television diary. Both provide details of early television developments at the BBC, and Swift usefully provides a good deal of first-hand information on the 1932–5 service together with studio plans from the pre- and post-war periods. More recently, Mark Aldridge's study of the early years of television in Britain, *The Birth of British Television: A History*, published in 2012, is a valuable study of the early development of television drawing on a range of archival material. My work differs in two respects. Firstly, the archival base is wider (in terms of the material consulted in the BBC Written Archives, for example). Also, Aldridge argued that it was not a foregone conclusion that the BBC would take responsibility for a television service. However, I would suggest that it was only the BBC which had the resources and infrastructure at the time to provide a public service of television. Television needed the BBC if it was to 'take off' in a meaningful way.

No historical study of television in Britain can be undertaken without recourse to Asa Briggs' monumental history of the BBC. For the purposes of this book, the penultimate chapter of Volume II has provided a foundation for my work on the pre-war period. Briggs' focus is on the institutional history of the BBC and I feel that I can align my work to his in this sense. As mentioned above, however, Briggs fails to discuss the BBC's 30-line service under Eustace Robb, which he may have considered too experimental to be of value. As a balance to Briggs's work, Joe Moran's social and cultural history of television, *Armchair Nation: An Intimate History of Britain in Front of the TV*, focuses on the viewer's experience of watching television throughout the twentieth century.

A number of works on the technical aspects of early television have informed my own work, although, as I state in the next chapter, this is not a detailed technical history of early television. Russell Burns' *British Television: The Formative Years* is a detailed account of early television developments while Albert Abramson's *The History of Television, 1880 to 1941* focuses on developments in the USA, Britain and beyond. Brian Winston's work on media technology – in particular his chapters on mechanical television and electronic television – are illuminating and valuable in understanding how television technology developed and adapted in the early years.[4] Doron Galili's excellent *Seeing by Electricity: The Emergence of Television, 1878–1939* published in 2020 is not just a technology-focused account of the origins and early development of what came to be known as television, but is a study which engages with the cultural, economic, social and political contexts in which television developed. Although the book has a US bias in terms of coverage, it also offers insights into the development of television on the international stage. One of the landmark books relating to early television development is Jason Jacobs' *The Intimate Screen: Early British Television Drama* published in 2000. Drawing on a wide range of archival sources, including studio camera floor plans, Jacobs countered the common belief that pre-war and immediate post-war television drama was no more than 'photographed stage plays' and argued that the early television drama producers devised innovative productions using a variety of techniques.

In addition to a growing body of scholarly work on early television in book and journal article form, there are a number of sources which record personal memories of the pre-war and immediate post-war period. One of these is Bruce Norman's *Here's Looking at You: The Story of British Television 1908–1939* which tells the story of the early development of television through interviews with executives, engineers, performers and other artistes involved in pre-war television. Cecil Madden's autobiography, *Starlight Days: The Memoirs of Cecil Madden: Wartime Radio and Television in the 1930's*, gives a personal view from the BBC's first television Programme Controller and producer at Alexandra Palace from 1936 onwards. Finally, Andrew Martin's *Sound and Vision: Television from Alexandra Palace*, published by Kaleidoscope after this book had been completed, will be an indispensable guide to all television programmes broadcast between 1929 and 1939. The painstaking work of gathering information from *Radio Times*, the Programme-as-Broadcast (PasB) documentation and other sources will undoubtedly provide a key source for researchers working on pre-war television in the future. I am grateful to Andrew for providing me with a pre-publication version of the work, which has been an enormous help.

Although John Reith left the BBC in 1938, his involvement in the development of television up to this point was an area of research that I wanted to study in some detail. There are a number of biographies of Reith, including Andrew Boyle's *Only the Wind Will Listen: Reith of the BBC* and Ian McIntyre's *The Expense of Glory: A Life of John Reith*, but neither book discusses Reith in the context of television. Charles Stuart's edited *The Reith Diaries* does not feature television and it requires a visit to the BBC Written Archives in Caversham to consult the transcripts of the original diaries in order to discover diary entries referring to television. Reith's daughter's account of her father's life, *My Father: Reith of the BBC*, does include reference to television, although I have questioned her assertions in Chapter 7 when discussing Reith's relationship with the medium. Finally, Reith himself refers only briefly to television in his 1949 autobiography, *Into the Wind*, where he noted that the coverage of the Coronation of King George VI and Queen Elizabeth in May 1937 was 'successful' and had gone well. He also noted that he had, much to the delight of the Earl Marshal, refused to let television cameras broadcast from inside Westminster Abbey during the ceremony.[5]

Given the focus of this book on the BBC's relationship with television from the mid-1920s up to the outbreak of the Second World War, the main archive for primary sources was the BBC's Written Archives Centre in Caversham. I worked through files containing correspondence with, and documentation on, the Baird Television Company, Marconi-EMI and other vested interests in television, television development and policy, together with minutes of the BBC's Control Board and Governors. The book therefore reflects the BBC's engagement with television on a strategic as well as an operational level. The transcript of Lord Reith's diaries was also scrutinised for references to television (which are there, though comparatively small in number) and the special collections of Cecil Madden and Sydney Moseley (Baird's friend and the Baird Television Development Company's de facto publicist) were also interrogated. The British Postal Museum and Archive in London, which houses the General Post Office (GPO) Archive, proved to be a very valuable source of information. The GPO was the government department with responsibility for Wireless Telegraphy under the 1904 Act, and as it was responsible for wireless reception licences it was almost by default that it took on the responsibility for overseeing the development of television on behalf of the government. The files held at the archive shed light on government policy towards television but also show how the GPO often acted as a mediator between the Baird Television Company and the BBC during the late 1920s and the first half of the 1930s. The GPO Archive also contained documents relating to the various Television Advisory Committees and the Selsdon Committee on television (1934). The National Archives in Kew held information on Cabinet-level discussions about television's development in the early period while the Selfridges Archive (at the History of Advertising Trust archive in Norwich) provided information on Baird's early demonstrations of television in that store in April 1925. The Marconi Archive at the University of Oxford was useful in terms of setting the context and background for television developments from the perspective of a major communications company, while the Royal Television Society archive in London held transcripts of interviews with some of early television's pioneers. It also provided me with an account of the early days of the Television Society itself, which had been established in 1927 to foster and encourage amateur and scientific interest in the new invention. Finally, the record of parliamentary debates, Hansard, was able to shed some light on debates within Parliament and gave me some memorable quotations (e.g. Sir Harry Brittain's description of television as 'a very tiresome invention'[6]).

Other sources of information included contemporary literature, such as *The Television Girl* written by the novelist Gertie S. de Wentworth-James in 1928, and contemporary films such as *Elstree Calling* (dir. André Charlot, Jack Hulbert, Paul Murray, Alfred Hitchcock, 1930). The journals on radio and television provided a fascinating insight into the growing amateur interest in television in the late 1920s and throughout the 1930s, and radio broadcasts (held in the British Library in London) in the second half of the 1930s allowed me to listen to contemporary views on the infant medium. Finally, the archives of the Alexandra Palace Television Society and the BBC Oral History Collection hold some unique material relating to all aspects of television in the pre-war period, including oral histories recording the testimony of those involved in early television.

Challenges in writing television history

For anybody writing the history of early television, one of the main issues is the lack of visual material – the programmes – upon which any television service is based. What we often have, therefore, is the 'context' without the 'text'. As John Caughie has noted:

> While cinema historians have a continuous, though incomplete, history of films from the 1890s, television has a pre-history in which programmes themselves do not exist in recorded form ... This makes the recovery of the early history of television form and style an archaeological, rather than a strictly historical, procedure.[7]

Likewise, Gill Branston has argued that '[i]magery of archaeological excavation can be eloquent in evoking the fragility and difficulty, as well as the pleasure, of making argument and proof in historical enquiry',[8] while Paddy Scannell and David Cardiff, referring to their own work on broadcasting and society in the pre-war period, talk of how 'shattered fragments allow a conjectural piecing together of what the whole must have been like'.[9] In their cultural history of technology and science, Hård and Jamison state: 'History ... is a process of recollecting, by which we try to make a coherent story out of disparate pieces of evidence.'[10] In terms of primary source material, while there is no visual record of the programme material as broadcast from the 1936–9 service period, and only fragments of what was transmitted during the 1932–5 service period (thanks to the pioneering work of Donald F. McLean), there is a good deal of written documentation in various archives to allow the historian to put together a reasonably comprehensive picture as noted above. A number of the methodological and historiographical challenges facing television historians were brought together in an excellent collection edited by Helen Wheatley, *Re-Viewing Television History: Critical Issues in Television Historiography*, published in 2007. One of the challenges, which I hope I have addressed (and hope I have overcome), is a teleological one – the problem of looking back from one's contemporary standpoint today and seeing things only from today's perspective. As Wheatley writes in her introduction, 'viewing, or re-viewing or analysing television from the present frequently produces a reading of television's texts, and its production and viewing practices, as being quaint, or somewhat limited or rather off in some way'.[11] My own contribution to Wheatley's volume focused on an oft-forgotten Welsh ITV company which operated for ten months between 1962 and 1963. The title of the chapter began with the phrase 'Piecing together' as the process of writing a history of that company, gathering information from a variety of primary and secondary sources, with no programme material remaining, was akin to creating a jigsaw, or putting together a narrative interpretation of something which in televisual terms had long gone. The same process has been deployed for this book in researching this fascinating and foundational period in British television history.

One final challenge – and this could be true for any author – was not to include *everything* I knew about the topic. With historical research in particular, I believe that there is a danger of cramming every last piece of archival research into the finished product, or even to continue to research without ever drawing a line and acknowledging that the material that one has systematically 'harvested' from a range of archives and secondary sources is enough for one to be able to write a comprehensive and engaging narrative and analysis. There are probably gaps in this history and every single aspect of early television may not be covered to the reader's satisfaction, and for this I apologise. However, as I have noted elsewhere in this introduction, I am focusing on a particular aspect and looking at early television from the BBC's perspective.

Structure

Chapter 2 begins with a brief outline of television's prehistory, noting some of the technological achievements, all of which provide a backdrop to John Logie Baird's now famous advertisement in *The Times* on 27 June 1923, which simply stated: 'Seeing by Wireless. Inventor of apparatus wishes to hear from someone who will assist (not financially) in making working model. Write Box S686, The Times, E.C.4.'[12] The focus of the remainder of this chapter is on the early experimental stages of television. The key points in this period are the experiments with machine-scanned television in 1923 and 1924, the first public demonstration of a prototype television in Selfridges, London in April 1925 and Baird's further experiments with his ventriloquist's dummy, 'Stookie Bill', in October 1925. The chapter continues with the development of electronic television systems in the USA by Farnsworth and Everson and the first public demonstration of television to members of the Royal Institute in London by Baird on 26 January 1926. Alongside these technical developments run parliamentary debates, sparked by questions which themselves had been prompted by newspaper reports of television experiments in the UK and USA. The final section of the chapter provides a bridge with the following chapter and focuses on the relationship between Baird, the GPO and the BBC. In order to progress his television experiments, Baird needed the support of the BBC (for frequencies to broadcast on outside of laboratory conditions).

The first official record of the BBC's consideration of television came in June 1927, and this is the starting point of Chapter 3. The period from then until the summer of 1929 is characterised by intensified pressure and debates between these three key players, and what this section does is to explore the reasons for the BBC's reluctance to fully embrace television as a medium. The role of individuals such as Oliver Hutchinson and Sydney Moseley within the Baird Company and Peter Eckersley and Noel Ashbridge in the BBC is discussed – and all of this against a wider changing and increasingly volatile economic backdrop.

Chapter 4 focuses on the period between September 1929 and July 1932 which saw the BBC collaborate with the Baird Company on an experimental 30-line television service. This collaboration came about after a period of pressure not only from the Baird Company but also from the government, which was aware of the potential damage the BBC's rejection of Baird's advances might cause should Baird (perceived in the press as the inventor of a *British* invention) be forced into liquidation through lack of a way of reaching a potential audience. While the period brought the tensions between the public service ideals of the BBC into direct conflict with the commercial imperatives of Baird's company, it was also a period of significant developments and landmarks, such as the broadcasting of the first television drama in July 1930. This came only months after synchronised sound on television finally became possible with the opening of the Brookman's Park transmitter in March 1930. Prior to this the sound and vision signals were transmitted on different frequencies with a two-minute delay between them. By early 1931, fewer than 1,000 television sets had been sold, although there may well have been many more constructed by hand by amateur enthusiasts. This chapter also marks a shift from reluctance to an agreement on the part of the BBC to provide its own experimental television service on the Baird system from August 1932 onwards.

The BBC's 30-line television service is the subject of Chapter 5. Beginning in August 1932, with the launch of the service from an adapted studio in Broadcasting House, London, this chapter traces the emergence of the Marconi-EMI company as a potential competitor in the television stakes in the early 1930s, a development which marked a change in the British broadcasting environment. The period covered by this chapter is characterised by intense (and often heated) discussions between the Baird Television Company, EMI and the BBC. The Post Office's involvement is worthy of note, particularly in the context of the discourses which pitted Baird's 'Britishness' against 'EMI's' 'Americanness'. For example, the BBC's decision to install EMI equipment in Broadcasting House, London in February 1933 caused alarm at the Baird Company. Secondly, the chapter focuses on internal debates within the BBC as to what might constitute a television service should the government decide (a) that television should be developed further and (b) that the BBC was the best organisation to be responsible for this. There is evidence of disagreement or uncertainty as to the nature of such a service, with debates ranging from whether or not it should essentially be a 'home cinema' service to the inadequacy of studio-based programming. The final section of the chapter focuses on the 1934 Selsdon Committee and the report which was published in January 1935, recommending that the BBC be allowed to develop a high-definition pubic television service. This, in turn, led to the demise of the 30-line low-definition service, much to the dismay of an increasing number of enthusiasts.

The focus of Chapter 6 is on the preparations for the high-definition BBC television service which ran between 1936 and 1939. Although the BBC's service commenced on 2 November 1936, the first broadcasts were actually made from Alexandra Palace especially for the Radio Exhibition at Olympia in London between 26 August and 5 September that year. The chapter concludes with the official opening ceremony in November 1936.

Chapter 7 explores the three years of the pre-war television service. This most productive period witnessed several 'firsts', including the televising of the Coronation of George VI in May 1937 and major sporting events such as the Wimbledon tennis tournament in June 1937 and the Oxford–Cambridge Boat Race and the FA Cup Final in April 1938. The television service ended abruptly on 1 September 1939 upon the outbreak of war. The chapter considers the influence of film, radio and theatre on early programming while also acknowledging the emergence of a new style or grammar of television that was being developed. Responses to the programming from members of the public and newly-appointed television critics are also discussed in this chapter and the chapter concludes with an analysis of what was achieved during this early period – my argument being that the service laid the foundations and set the overarching framework for television programming for decades.

Chapter 8, the concluding chapter, draws together some of the key issues which arise during the pre-war television period and notes that the service, which was suspended for the duration of the Second World War, was re-launched in June 1946.

Within these chapters, themes and critical issues that characterise the period under consideration are discussed; for example, the early perceptions of television – how television was conceived, imagined and thought of. Links with telephony (drawing on the work of Gabriele Balbi, for example)[13] can be useful in understanding how early television was conceived, as can futuristic/utopian portrayals of television in film and literature (e.g. *The Television Girl* from 1928, where television is akin to videophone). Fears of television are also explored (e.g. the use of television as surveillance), as are concerns over the displacement of other activities such as radio listening, theatre-going, sport, cinema, etc. Contemporary wireless journals and magazines, where the discourse was predominantly technical and scientific, also provide an insight into how television was perceived in its formative years, the focus being on (a) the ability to see at a distance, rather than any conception of a *service* of any kind and (b) being able to see events as they happen – the immediate and 'here and now'. I also consider some of the popular discourses on television in the press and in trade journals, in particular those around national identity and pride. The book, therefore, explores the BBC's relationship with early television within wider political, social, cultural, economic and technological contexts.

Written on the eve of the 1936 Radio Exhibition, the editorial of *The Listener*, 26 August 1936, led with a story about the BBC television service being exhibited and demonstrated for the first time at Olympia. The article pondered the future role of television in national life. Though generally positive, it ended on a cautionary note:

> The chance of having eyes as well as ears in every home in communication with the outside world is tremendously exciting. Imagination, dwelling on the possibilities of television, is justly fired and imagination is often right in the long run. But we shall be wise to dilute it, for the present, with a dose of caution.[14]

The following chapters will, I hope, reflect that excitement which surrounded the advent of television, but also highlight the initially cautious approach adopted by the BBC in the early years of the medium's development.

Notes

1. Kenneth Adam, *The Listener*, 7 July 1955, p. 19. Over the years, these words have been re-structured to form a sentence which is now used widely: 'Television? The word is half Latin and half Greek. No good can come of it.' I am very grateful to Tom May, doctoral student at Northumbria University, for his help with discovering the source of this quotation.
2. Asa Briggs, *The History of Broadcasting in the United Kingdom. Volume II. The Golden Age of Wireless* (Oxford: Oxford University Press, 1995), p. 485.
3. See Russell Burns, *John Logie Baird, Television Pioneer* (London: IEE, 2000); Donald F. McLean, *Restoring Baird's Image* (London: IEE, 2000); Antony Kamm and Malcolm Baird, *John Logie Baird: A life* (Edinburgh: National Museums of Scotland, 2002). Early works on Baird include Ronald F. Tiltman, *Baird of Television: The Life Story of John Logie Baird* (London: Seeley Service, 1933) and Sydney Moseley, *John Baird: The Romance and Tragedy of the Pioneer of Television* (London: Odhams Press, 1952). Among the most comprehensive and illuminating sources is Donald F. McLean,

The Dawn of Television Remembered – the John Logie Baird Years: 1923–1936. Audio CD. Published by the author in 2005 as a product of a Royal Television Society (RTS) Shiers Trust grant, it is a detailed history of the early years of television from (primarily) a technical perspective. It contains, among other things, excerpts of interviews with engineers and early television entertainers from the RTS archive but also includes rare restored footage from the 1932–5 BBC television service which used Baird's equipment.
4. Brian Winston, *Media, Technology and Society: A History – from the Telegraph to the Internet* (London: Routledge, 1998).
5. J. C. W. Reith, *Into the Wind* (London: Hodder & Stoughton, 1949), pp. 280–1.
6. *House of Commons Debates [HC Deb] 12 April 1927 vol 205 c192*.
7. John Caughie, 'Before the Golden Age: Early Television Drama' in John Corner (ed.), *Popular Television in Britain: Studies in Cultural History* (London: BFI, 1991), pp. 24–5.
8. Gill Branston, 'Histories of British Television' in Christine Geraghty and David Lusted (eds), *The Television Studies Book* (London: Hodder Arnold, 1998), p. 52.
9. Paddy Scannell and David Cardiff, *A Social History of British Broadcasting. Volume One: 1922–1939* (Oxford: Blackwell, 1991), p. xiii.
10. Mikael Hård and Andrew Jamison, *Hubris and Hybrids: A Cultural History of Technology and Science* (London: Routledge, 2005), p. 293.
11. Helen Wheatley (ed.), *Re-Viewing Television History: Critical Issues in Television Historiography* (London: I. B. Tauris, 2007), p. 10.
12. *The Times*, 27 June 1923.
13. Gabriele Balbi, 'Studying the Social History of Telecommunications', *Media History*, 15:1 (2009), 85–101.
14. *The Listener*, 26 August, p. 376.

CHAPTER 2

Early Television Developments

The history of the development of television is a fascinating story of numerous small advances by many individuals towards the ultimate goal, some brilliant ideas by a few creative geniuses which can now be seen to be of vital and continuing importance, and the occasional pursuit of a blind alley of development with all the heart-break that entailed … It seems very doubtful whether even the most optimistic and far-sighted of the pioneers had any clear vision of what, in the fullness of time, was to be achieved.[1]

This chapter outlines some of the key developments in the history of television prior to the BBC's initial recorded interest in television in 1927. While the focus of this book is the BBC's relationship with television in its early years, it is useful to explore the background and understand that television developed as a technology and a medium in a period of shifting political, economic, social and cultural contexts, not only in Britain but internationally. Detailed histories of the early technology, and the ways in which the specific technology of television developed, have been written by, among others, Burns, Abramson, Winston and McLean,[2] and I will draw on these works and others in this chapter. However, this chapter will not be a detailed technical history – the aforementioned provide this in greater detail and with greater authority. The chapter will, however, consider technical developments and developments in technology within a social and cultural context. The chapter draws on primary source material from the archives of the General Post Office, the BBC, Selfridges, the Marconi Company, and the specialist journals that began to offer their readers insights into the new technology. The three key questions framing this chapter and the next are:

> How did television develop in the way it did and who was involved in its development? When did the BBC become involved in television? Why, when it did engage with television, was the Corporation reluctant to embrace the new technology, only doing so eventually under pressure from government?

The origins of television

When considering the origin or beginning of television, the precise starting point is difficult, even impossible, to locate.[3] The American historian Richard W. Hubbell has argued that aspirations to television can be traced all the way back to ancient Egyptians and Assyrians,[4] while Philip Sewell notes that '[t]elevision had been imagined in the form of crystal balls, magic eyes, and super telescopes for centuries, if not millennia, prior to the nineteenth century'.[5] Abramson states, in a chapter on what he calls the 'archaeology and prehistory of television', that the invention of the magic lantern in 1671, which in turn was a stimulus in developing the film industry in the late nineteenth and early twentieth centuries, also sowed the seeds for the desire to see instantaneously at a distance.[6] Knut Hickethier argues along the same lines that there are three periods to television's early history: from the middle of the seventeenth century to around 1880 (television's prehistory, where discoveries are made but television as concept had not been conceived); from 1880 until 1910 (at which point inventors are thinking about transmitting pictures at a distance and 'television' is beginning to be discussed, although the exact form and shape is not clear at this point); and then from around 1910 until 1933 (when technological developments led to individual inventors and large companies becoming fully invested in the idea of television – although, as will be explored later in this book, the precise nature or idea of what 'television' actually meant was still unclear).[7] According to Brian Winston, 'by the First World War, the dream of television was over thirty years old'.[8] The excitement which followed the advent of the telephone in the late nineteenth century, and the realisation of the photo-sensitive properties of selenium by Willoughby Smith, a telegraph engineer, in 1873, led to speculation over what 'telescopy' might look like:

> The invention of television is ... embedded in the cultural context of the leading European industrialised countries of the nineteenth and twentieth centuries. That cultural context must also be seen as embedded in the process of modernisation occurring in western societies. Television is both the result of, and the means to express, and industrial and cultural efforts towards modernisation, and has strongly promoted this mission throughout the second half of the twentieth century.[9]

William Uricchio argues that talk of the televisual can truly begin with the coming of Alexander Graham Bell's telephone in 1876: 'The telephone sparked an anticipatory interest in visual systems that could share the instrument's ability to link distant locations point to point in real time.'[10] Writing in 1893, Scottish scientist John Munro discussed the possibility of sending images at a distance using light and electricity, comparing the scientific potential with that of the telephone transmitting sound. Striking a very positive note, and basing his remarks on experiments and scientific understanding at the time, he wrote that 'we may be justified in entertaining hopes that someday a means will be found of transforming a luminous image into electricity, and after transmitting that to a distance, reproducing the original image'. Furthermore:

> Lovers will be able to see each other, while conversing at a distance. Doctors will examine their patient's tongues in another town. The drama will be 'switched on' to private houses; and on Sundays and holidays even the poor will be able to enjoy a visual trip to wherever their main fancy may incline. In hot weather a man will be able to refresh himself with a glimpse of the Alpine glaciers, or the icebergs of the Arctic Circle, and in the rigours of a north-east wind he may taste the pleasures of imagination, by gloating over the palms and orchids of the tropics. Think of paying your shilling for a view of the geysers of the Yellowstone, or an eruption of Vesuvius, or a peep at the Yosemite Falls![11]

By the early years of the twentieth century, and prompted by experiments using electricity, predictions were being made by a number of scientists in Europe of seeing pictures (still and moving) at a distance. Responding to a letter from Shelford Bidwell in the journal *Nature* on 4 June 1908, the Scottish scientist Alan Archibald Campbell-Swinton put forward a suggestion for an electronic (rather than mechanical) television system.[12] Although the contents of the letter fell on deaf ears, a presidential address at the Röntgen Society in 1911 and a publication of his ideas in 1924 led to an interest in experimentation and exploration in television by electronic means which bore fruit – as discussed in Chapter 3 – in the 1930s.[13]

There was a definite interest in the potential of seeing at a distance among the population at large in the early years of the twentieth century. In February 1910, the *Cardiff Times* published an article on 'Marvels of the Future'. Developments in wireless telegraphy in the USA, together with the discovery of telephotography in 1906 by the Munich physicist Professor Arthur Korn, had 'foreshadowed the distant possibility of an even more marvellous discovery – that of television or seeing at distance'. The article had a clear sense of what television would be: 'this instantaneous reproduction upon a distant screen of the moving features of a living face – the gestures, expressions, and attitudes of a person far away'. The article also referred to Ernest Ruhmer, a German physicist who had been experimenting in the field of telephony and wireless telegraphy in the early years of the century and who had made apparatus (using selenium cells) 'which actually solves the problem of seeing at a distance'.[14] Two months later the *Merthyr Express* reported on a spiritualist society meeting which had discussed the 'new discoveries every day' in the physical sciences, 'some of them so sensational in character, such as wireless television'.[15] It is quite easy to see why Briggs commented that 'people were prepared for television long before the apparatus or the programmes were available'[16] and why Donald F. McLean has argued: 'Though the desire for television is simple and ages old, the development of it is complex, immersed in detail and above all recent.'[17]

Britain in the inter-war years

While the inter-war years – the 1920s and 1930s – have been characterised as decades of depression, high unemployment and general decline (hence Richard Overy's use of the phrase 'The Morbid Years' as the title of his book on the period[18] and descriptions of the 1930s as 'The Devil's Decade'[19]), there is evidence, as Stephen Constantine has argued, that 'interwar Britain was for most people on balance a period of improving living standards'.[20] There were certainly *periods* of depression, but the British economy was not as badly affected by the depression as the German and American economies. As Martin Pugh has argued, from the consumer's point of view, the rising real value of wages led to a boom in housing, leisure activities and motoring.[21] One explanation for the growth in the economy was the investment made in new technology after the First World War. Michael Law notes that Britain's obsession with technology, which can be traced back to the middle of the nineteenth century, was accelerated by the impact of the Great War.[22] 'New' industries emerged in areas such as chemicals, plastics, electrical engineering, new consumer goods and manufacturing.

At the same time, the 'old', heavy industries of coal and steel became leaner and adopted new technology in their operations. As a result, the working classes working in these industries were hit by unemployment. It was, as Stephen Constantine argues, a 'comparatively prosperous but socially unequal' society by the end of the 1930s.[23] Increased prosperity paved the way for an increasingly affluent mass consumer society, one in which leisure pursuits and activities grew. As earnings improved and the number of working people eligible for paid holidays increased, there was more disposable income to spend on household goods (part of the shift to the domestic focus for leisure activities).

It also led to a more homogeneous national culture, crossing class and regional divides. The BBC played its role in the creation of a mass public and the radio service in the inter-war period provided that focal point for a shared culture, be it news, comedy or a national occasion.[24] In addition to the radio, the cinema was one of the most important forms of popular culture during the inter-war period. By 1934, there were around four thousand cinemas in Britain, with an average weekly attendance of 20 million by 1939. Just as radio transcended class and gender boundaries, so cinema-going offered a common experience to all classes.[25]

Radio and the BBC

The period following the Great War (1914–18) resulted in a renewed interest in science and technology – partly as a result of the use of telegraphy and wireless communication during the conflict – as did a belief that they could benefit humankind during peacetime.[26] One of the most striking advances in communication was the advent of domestic radio in the 1920s. A recital by the Australian opera singer Dame Nellie Melba on 15 June 1920, from the Marconi Company's Chelmsford base, is considered to be the starting point for radio in Britain. Sponsored by the *Daily Mail*, it was a high-profile experiment which helped spark an interest in radio broadcasting and reception and started growing public interest in the development of radio as an entertainment medium. The *Daily Mail* also sponsored concerts in The Hague (in The Netherlands), which it advertised to its British readers.[27] Despite the growing interest, the British government announced in November 1920 that concerts being broadcast from the Marconi transmitter in Chelmsford would be terminated, for fear that the signals should interfere with 'legitimate' communications (i.e. military). Nevertheless, the fuse had been lit, and across the country, wireless clubs and societies were established by amateurs with an interest in this new mode of communication – and they needed something to which to listen. Increased pressure on the government in the early 1920s eventually led to the Marconi Company being permitted to broadcast for short periods of time from Writtle near Chelmsford in February 1922. Marconi was not the only organisation to get involved in experimental radio broadcasts. Companies such as Metropolitan-Vickers, the General Electric Company (GEC) and the Western Electric Company had been experimenting with broadcasting in London, Birmingham and Manchester. With a total of six companies broadcasting and with limited frequencies, the General Post Office wished to avoid unfettered competition. Yet it did not wish to operate a broadcasting service itself or be seen to show favouritism to one company in particular in awarding a licence. The solution was to create a broadcasting company – the British

Broadcasting Company – made up of all six companies, in the form of a monopoly.[28] The BBC, under the leadership of General Manager John Reith, began broadcasting in November 1922 from Marconi House on the Strand in London, moving to Savoy Hill the following year.[29] Over the following eighteen months, BBC stations opened across the UK in cities such as Manchester, Glasgow, Cardiff and Birmingham, initially providing programming from London but with some regional variation.

From the outset, broadcasting in Britain operated within a public service framework. As the service had to share the airwaves with the military and emergency services, a shortage of frequencies meant that the scarce resources had to be utilised in the national interest. A similar rationale was behind the broadcasting services in Belgium and Denmark, for example. Broadcasting was viewed as a public utility, and the mandate to develop it as a national service in the public interest came from the state. This was in contrast to the model in the USA. Although the broadcaster David Sarnoff had referred to broadcasting as a public service in a speech in 1922, drawing attention to its potential to inform, educate and entertain the nation, broadcasting development took the commercial as opposed to the state-controlled, public service path.[30] Although it would be unfair to argue that the broadcast media in the USA developed in a completely chaotic and unregulated manner, there were fewer restrictions than in the UK.

Reith interpreted public broadcasting by developing a set of principles that were to dominate British broadcasting for decades. This Reithian approach to public broadcasting in the early days of radio broadcasting was based on four tenets. First, the need to protect broadcasting from commercial pressures was safeguarded by creating an assured source of funding (a licence fee for all those who owned wireless sets). Second, the service was to be provided for the whole nation regardless of the geographic location of the listener. This policy of a universal service was achieved, third, by the establishment of a national programme (broadcast from London) and, fourth, by a regional programme from selected cities across the UK (including Cardiff and Birmingham). Radio soon established itself in British households, and between March 1929 and March 1933 the number of those holding a licence (which was a legal requirement for owning a wireless set and which provided the funding for the service) doubled. By 1935, 98 per cent of the population could listen to the BBC and by the outbreak of war in 1939 the GPO had issued over 9 million licences.[31] This, then, was the context for the emergence of television.

John Logie Baird

One cannot write the history of early television in Britain without reference to John Logie Baird. Born in 1888, the son of a Scottish minister, he was responsible for creating a public awareness of, and interest in, television, and while some have argued that his mechanical system of television was 'doomed to failure',[32] he did, nevertheless, demonstrate the potential value of television as a public service and, more importantly, ensure that the BBC took television seriously in the early 1930s. As Maurice Gorham, former Head of Television at the BBC, wrote:

> Baird was a brilliant pioneer, an inventor rather than a scientist ... Within a few years he progressed from televising moving images over wires from one room to another in his Soho workshop to televising from London to New York, televising in colour, televising the Derby in a cinema on a big screen. Often he was heading up blind alleys ... but his achievements undoubtedly hastened the coming of television, and patriotic pride in his pioneering achievements aroused strong support for the idea of making Britain the first country in the world where television could be seen in the home.[33]

Much has been written about Baird and his early experiments with television, as noted in Chapter 1. His interest in television can be traced back to 1903 when the idea of producing television – seeing at a distance – first occurred to him,[34] and Russell Burns suggests that an article in the 11 November 1922 edition of *Wireless World and Radio Review* fired Baird's interest.[35] Whenever the spark was ignited, it was while recuperating from illness in Hastings in 1923 that Baird set to work to pick up on his earlier idea of seeing at a distance.[36] Baird's advertisement in *The Times* on 23 June 1923 noting that he was seeking non-financial support for his work into 'Seeing by Wireless' heralded the beginning of his pioneering work in television. Operating from his flat, and later in a makeshift workshop and laboratory in Hastings, Baird worked with the minimum of finance and mainly on his own to achieve his goal of transmitting images at a distance. An application for a patent was submitted by Baird and his financial backer Wilfred Day, a wireless shop owner from London, on 26 July 1923 for 'A system of transmitting views, portraits and scenes by telegraphy or wireless telegraphy' and granted as Patent 19,173/23.[37] One of the earliest accounts of his work was published by Baird himself in May 1924 in *The Wireless World and Radio Review*. The article informed readers of Baird's experiments, and while he admitted that the early apparatus had resulted in 'only crude outline images', he was now using apparatus which was 'capable of giving a certain amount of detail'.[38] Various tests and demonstrations continued during 1924, and in November that year Baird moved his television apparatus to 22 Frith Street in Soho, London.

The basic premise of Baird's system was the scanning of a scene using a Nipkow disc, so-called after its inventor, the German Paul Nipkow, in 1884. The disc scanned one image on each rotation and for 30-line television (which operated in Britain between 1926 and 1935) there would be thirty apertures (which were holes or lenses) distributed equally around the disc. Light cells were also used but amplification of the signal was poor as the electronics were not far enough advanced at this time. Because of the poor sensitivity of the light cells the only images that could be produced initially were 'shadowgraphs' without any tonal quality or grading.[39]

Baird published a 'follow-up' article in *The Wireless World and Radio Review* early in 1925 stating that the apparatus was constructed 'purely for experimental purposes' and could only transmit simple objects (such as the letter H). A moving hand could be transmitted but resulted in a blur, and a face 'with careful focussing' could just about be seen, albeit as a white oval shape with dark patches for the eyes.[40]

At the same time, experiments were being undertaken by the American Telephone and Telegraph (AT&T) Company in the USA. Unlike Baird, who was essentially a lone inventor in the early years at least, AT&T had at its disposal a team of scientists and laboratory resources. In 1924 still pictures were transmitted over telephone wires and a photoradiogram was transmitted from London to New York by the Marconi Wireless Telegraph Company and RCA.[41]

The first major public demonstration of television took place in April 1925. George Selfridge Jr., owner of Selfridge's store in Oxford Street, London, invited Baird to set up a display and demonstration of television in the store. Selfridge's connection with broadcasting went back to the beginning of the British Broadcasting Company. The Company had asked for the transmitters for the 2LO station to be located on the roof of the store and the twin towers were erected and began transmitting in April 1925. It was fitting, therefore, that during the same month Selfridge should host Baird to demonstrate the new marvel of science, television. In February 1925, Selfridge had tracked Baird down to his Soho laboratory having heard of the experiments being undertaken. He was given a demonstration and viewed crude images in a 'televisor'. Taken aback by what he saw, he offered Baird £20 a week to demonstrate the apparatus three times daily in the store and Baird agreed. Shop assistants handed out leaflets ('Selfridge's Present the First Public Demonstration of Television') to those members of the public who were curious, which explained what television was:

> It means the INSTANTANEOUS transmission of a picture so that the observer at the 'receiving' end can see, to all intents and purposes, what is a cinematographic view of what is happening at the 'sending' end ... The apparatus here is demonstrated ... 'in the rough' ... but it does, undoubtedly, transmit an instantaneous picture. The picture if flickering and defective, and at present only simple pictures can be sent successfully; but Edison's first phonograph announced that 'Mary had a little lamb' ... and yet, from that first result has developed the gramophone of today ... We should perhaps explain that we are in no way financially interested in this remarkable invention; the demonstrations are taking place here only because we know that our friends will be interested in something that should rank with the greatest inventions of the century.[42]

The leaflet gives a fascinating insight into Selfridge's view of this new invention. It was not a cheap commercial publicity stunt and the store would not benefit financially, although it could attract customers who would not normally enter the shop. There is an honesty in the description of the image quality and the leaflet, to borrow a common phrase today, manages the expectations of those who came to see the display. Yet, at this time, the wonder did not necessarily stem from the transmission of identifiable or 'real' images. The curiosity and excitement derived from the fact that pictures – still or moving – could be sent from one place to another.[43] The word 'instantaneous' was capitalised so as to highlight the immediacy and 'liveness' of the new invention and this would be one of the 'selling points' of television. It was not a recorded medium, it was not cinema or film (despite the use of the word 'cinematographic'). This would be a medium which, in due course, would provide a window onto the world and it was this vision which drove television developments and influenced the discourse around television in the 1920s and 1930s. The comparison with Edison and the first phonograph is interesting, and intimates that from simple beginnings great things will develop. Clearly, George Selfridge Jr. realised the potential in television: 'It is a link between all peoples of the world. Great good can come of it', he is reported to have told his Sales Manager.[44] After three weeks, the pressure of the demonstrations, together with what Gordon Honeycombe described as 'his distaste for public performance', resulted in Baird returning to the laboratory. At this point, Briggs notes that Baird 'passed yet again into the twilight world of insecurity', Selfridges having only provided a three-week period for him and the Marconi Company and newspapers generally being uninterested in his work.[45] With limited financial backing from family and friends, Television Limited was registered as a company on 11 June 1925.[46]

Four months later, on 2 October 1925, Baird achieved what he had been trying to achieve: the world's first television image. The ventriloquist's dummy used for experiments, Stookie (or Stooky) Bill, appeared on the screen not as a black and white blur, but with tonal detail. Despite such a significant achievement, it was three months before Baird gave a public demonstration of television. T. H. Bridgewater, who worked with Baird from 1928 onwards and later became Chief Engineer at the BBC, suggests that in Baird's mind, going public could compromise all his research and there was a genuine fear that some of the larger wireless concerns – effectively his rivals – would 'steal' his ideas.[47] The stimulus for this period of innovation, creativity, speculation and enterprise was the desire to be the first to devise a television system – effectively to win the race for television – and it was this 'race' that was to influence and impact upon the way in which the government, the GPO, the Baird companies and the BBC interacted in the period 1926 to 1929.

The GPO's first direct encounter with Television Ltd came at the beginning of 1926 when Captain Oliver Hutchinson, the company's Business Manager, wrote to the Postmaster-General informing him that the company had completed and patented a machine 'with which vision can be transmitted instantaneously by wireless'. The letter went on to state that the company wished to apply for a licence to broadcast from London, Glasgow, Manchester and Belfast. Hutchinson noted that, in fact, no licence was necessary to transmit vision, but that the application would be submitted 'to keep ourselves in order'.[48] This last point was picked up on by the GPO solicitor, who noted that the law surrounding 'vision' was unclear as to whether or not still or moving pictures were covered by law under the terms of the 1904 Wireless Telegraphy Act (a matter which still being discussed at the time of the Selsdon Committee in 1934 – see Chapter 5).[49] Hutchinson sent a further letter on 11 January informing the GPO that 500 receiving sets were being made for clients and therefore the company was seeking clarification that no objections were being raised. The GPO had clearly been taken by surprise, and there is no obvious explanation for the company's decision to commence production of sets before a licence had been granted or a demonstration provided of what television was capable of doing, and without (presumably) any material to broadcast. The only possible explanation was a desire to sell sets to make money. The GPO responded on 13 January stating that the Postmaster-General was unable to come to a decision at this point due to a lack of information.[50]

A major turning point came on 26 January 1926, when Baird demonstrated his television system to members of the Royal Institution, the world's first public demonstration of 'true' television. The demonstration, which appears to have had the dual purpose of gaining publicity for the television experiments but also aiming for a seal of approval or a mark of respectability from an august organisation, took place at Baird's laboratory in Soho, and according to Baird, visitors had to 'climb three flights of narrow stone stairs and then to stand in a narrow, draughty passage, while batches of six at a time were brought into the two tiny attic rooms which formed my laboratory'.[51] There has been some discussion as to whether the visitors were shown Baird's flying-spot technique (where a camera emits a very thin beam of light across the subject in a darkened room which is then scanned), or the floodlit studio method, where the subject sat under floodlights which emitted an almost unbearable amount of heat. Donald F. McLean, who has studied the 1926 demonstration in detail, argues that the latter formed the basis of the Soho demonstration to the Royal Institution.[52] The only newspaper invited to report on the demonstration was *The Times*, a decision made on the basis of not wanting any unscrupulous press interests to 'steal' information on the apparatus being shown. Further demonstrations were organised once other newspapers and specialist magazines heard of the development. The response was mixed, from those who saw the great potential in this new scientific discovery, to those who were less sanguine and questioned the benefits of television.[53] Baird himself typed some notes on the day of the demonstration: 'It sees through brick walls and around corners. to whatever distance sounds can be broadcast the televisor can send vision ... The long looked for sequence to listening in has now arrived – our prying eyes can now follow our listening ears.'[54]

Although details of the January demonstration are few and far between, a report by an engineer at the Gas, Light and Coke Company, E. G. Stewart, provides an insight into what the visitors may have seen. Stewart was invited to a demonstration in Soho in April 1926. The television transmitter (camera) was in one room and the receiver (and audience) in another. Baird declined to show the inside of his apparatus, which reflected the secretive nature of his work and the fact that he feared some sort of industrial espionage: 'He has definitely decided to give a minimum of information upon the details of construction and operation to anyone.'[55] Stewart discussed the progress of television with Hutchinson, who informed him that the company would soon be selling sets (in wooden cases the size of a large suitcase with a space to receive pictures of 2 inches x 1½ inches) to the public for £30. These would then be attached to existing wireless sets to receive the pictures. The report also noted that the experiments were receiving support from companies such as General Electric (GEC) which were supplying Baird with lamps, batteries and other equipment. Interestingly, Hutchinson appears to have informed Stewart of the company's negotiations with the government, the BBC and cinema interests regarding television. While the GPO had been approached earlier in the year (see above), the BBC certainly was not involved in any kind of discussion about television until the following year. As to Stewart's overall assessment of what he saw, his view was that 'at the present time the image resulting is appreciably lacking in detail and so can have but little practical application'. He noted his concern at Baird's aspiration to put television sets on the market in the present state of development, something which Stewart saw as a mistake and 'error of judgement' for three reasons: the apparatus gave crude images which were not necessarily pleasant to view and only a small field of view was possible (e.g. the face). Also, while an initial market could be found, formed of enthusiasts and those who marvelled at the new discovery, the public would soon want to see rapid improvement and, if this were not not forthcoming, might turn their backs on television. Finally, any contemporary personalities or celebrities whom the public might wish to see on the small screen would be unlikely to be tempted to be seen on television, due to the very poor reproduction of images. Yet the report ends on an upbeat note, with a recognition of the 'likely importance' of television in the future.[56]

Nevertheless, the demonstration and the publicity surrounding it prompted the GPO to contact Hutchinson on 30 January to inform him that the Postmaster-General would be willing to grant a licence for two wireless stations at a cost of £3 per station 'for purely experimental purposes' on the 150–200 medium wavelength.[57] No experimental broadcasts were permitted during broadcasting hours. Despite this offer, Hutchinson contacted the GPO on 4 February claiming that the invention of television was of enormous importance and that it was 'practically out of the experimental stage'. This was a remarkable claim. As noted above, while the response to television was positive on the whole, and while people saw the *potential* of television (although in what ways was not clear at this stage), to state so boldly that it was out of the experimental stage was quite extraordinary. However, the next part of Hutchinson's conversation with the GPO revealed the main reason for such a statement. The Baird Company needed the agreement of the GPO before a public service could be sanctioned – although it is unclear as to what Hutchinson meant by a 'public service' in this context – and Baird and Hutchinson were short of money for further development and therefore needed to raise capital on prospects for the invention. What he (Hutchinson) required was a concession or a promise of a public service. The GPO's short response was that it could not commit at this stage.[58] A further letter from Hutchinson to the GPO followed on 21 June pressing for a response and another on 29 June. The latter informed the Secretary of the GPO of the financial losses being incurred by Television Ltd, but more importantly noted that the company had received a 'tempting offer' from a 'powerful American syndicate' for the television apparatus. The letter stated that while the company *wanted* to keep control of television in Britain, if facilities for the advancement of the new system were being withheld then there would be no other option but to take it elsewhere. On 5 July, the GPO made a decision, possibly in the light of the threat implied in Hutchinson's letter. The Postmaster-General was now in a position to grant permission to install transmitting stations at Motograph House in Upper St Martin's Lane in London (the company had moved there from Frith Street in February 1926). Discussion ensued over the maximum wattage of the stations, with the GPO and Television Ltd finally agreeing on 250 watts maximum for both stations on 200 metres on the medium wavelength. In a letter from the GPO Secretary to Television Limited on 15 July, the wattage issue was confirmed, as was a warning that the transmissions stations were purely for experimental purposes and that if there were any question of a permanent service then the wavelength would be revoked.[59] On 10 August 1926, the 2TV (Motograph House) and 2TW (Harrow) licences were issued by the GPO and almost immediately, on the strength of this decision, Television Ltd put televisors on the market. A version of these events appeared in the *Sunday News* on 13 February 1927 under the headline 'Ultimatum to P.M.G.'. The story quoted Hutchinson as stating that neither he nor Baird was keen to present the television rights to a powerful foreign rival, yet both were 'disgusted by the continual obstruction with which Government Departments met their request for a broadcasting license [sic] and other essential facilities'.[60]

By the end of 1926, television was an accomplished fact if we take television to mean the transmitting of moving images over a distance, instantaneously, with a degree of shading. Television had emerged from the laboratory and in was now in the public domain. Increasing numbers of articles on television were appearing in journals devoted to wireless technology, with forty-five articles appearing on Baird's activities alone.[61] Yet, it was still very experimental and Shiers refers to the sheer 'fantasy' of Oliver Hutchinson's notion of selling mass-produced receivers.[62] Nevertheless, the major battle to get television to a wider public through regular transmissions was to come in the three years that followed, but, as Shiers has argued, in 1926, for the time being at least, 'television belonged to John Logie Baird'.[63]

The following year, 1927, saw further advances in television. In April 1927, the Baird Television Development Company (BTDC) was established with an authorised capital of £125,000 and with a remit 'to develop commercially the Baird television and other inventions'.[64] With Sir Edward Manville (chair of the Daimler Company) as its chair, the BTDC signalled that '[t]elevision had passed from its experimental stage into the arena of high finance and business speculation'.[65] Baird, according to Bridgewater, 'was no longer the lone, struggling, impecunious, dedicated experimenter'. He now headed a laboratory with an increasing number of staff and was, to quote Bridgewater, 'on the crest of a wave'.[66] An increasing number of articles on television were appearing in wireless journals and lectures and demonstrations of television systems were gathering apace in Britain and elsewhere.[67]

On 7 April 1927, Bell Telephone Laboratories of American Telephone and Telegraph (AT&T) demonstrated their television system under the direction of Dr Herbert E. Ives and Dr Frank Gray. Pictures were sent from Washington DC to New York City by wire and there was a further wireless demonstration from Whippany in New Jersey to New York City. The main event in the broadcast was a speech by Herbert Hoover, US Secretary of Commerce, followed by Vaudeville acts. The demonstration was deemed an outstanding success by those present and, as Abramson notes, it was 'the best demonstration of a mechanical television system ever made to this time'.[68] Crucially, it demonstrated that television could be achieved over a great distance – in this case over 250 miles. Images were produced using a Nipkow-based system with a 50-line picture at 18 pictures per second.[69]

The demonstration, notable as it was, had international impact. In a question in the House of Commons on 12 April 1927, five days after the Bell/AT&T experiments, Sir Harry Brittain, Conservative MP for Acton, asked the Postmaster-General whether his attention had been drawn to the results of television experiments in the USA and whether or not any research of a similar kind was being undertaken in the UK. In a brief answer, the Assistant Postmaster-General, Viscount Wolmer, said that the answer to both was 'Yes'. Brittain then went on to ask 'Will the noble Lord be very careful about encouraging what may prove to be a very tiresome invention?', to which Wolmer answered: 'The Post Office is bound to accept all inventions which may be for the service of the community, whether they are tiresome or not.'[70]

The demonstration took Baird and his financial backers by surprise. He immediately set to work on a demonstration of television at a greater distance of 438 miles – from London to Glasgow. On 24 May 1927, Baird successfully transmitted pictures over a landline from Long Acre to the Central Hotel in Glasgow, thus staging a major publicity event which once again gave him the 'edge' in the race for television.[71] Events such as these attracted great interest from the press on both sides of the Atlantic. Between 1927 and 1933, for example, *The New York Times* published 477 stories about mechanical television, with interest increasing as television stations appeared in major cities; 111 stories were published in 1928 and 109 in 1929.[72]

If television had 'arrived', then thoughts turned increasingly to what to do with it. In the June 1927 edition of *Popular Radio* Thomas Elway posed the questions which were on many minds: 'What shall we do with television?' and 'Will television be a useful aid to mankind or an annoyance or merely a scientific toy?' While acknowledging the limitations placed on developments by technology, the article contained musings on the purposes to which television might be put. Drawing on the work that had been, and was being, undertaken by Baird in Britain and Charles F. Jenkins and Herbert Ives in the USA, the article suggests possible uses in the fields of medicine (a patient in one room surrounded by doctors and nurses and a consultant three thousand miles away observing), criminology (criminal 'line-ups' in Boston, New York, Washington, Philadelphia and Chicago being watched by the police forces in these cities) and education (university lectures being televised to students).[73]

In September 1927, Baird delivered a lecture at the meeting of the British Association (now the British Science Association) in Leeds. In the lecture, he referred to the achievement of what he called 'true television' for the first time in October 1925, when the head of his dummy, 'Stookie Bill', had been televised with shading, grading and detail at his Long Acre laboratory. He also talked about the demonstration of television to members of the Royal Institution on 26 January 1926. Proposing a vote of thanks, Association member W. G. W. Mitchell (who went on to become editor of the world's first television journal, *Television*) also proposed the formation of a society for enthusiasts and scientists, 'whose sole interest would be the study and development of problems associated with television, noctovision and phonovision and even photo-telegraphy and allied subjects'. The meeting unanimously agreed to the establishment of a society.[74]

The brief, therefore, was wide. Television was still in the laboratory stage and was being explored alongside Baird's interests in a night-vision system and a recording disc – the 'true' use or purpose to which television could be put was still up in the air. The Society aimed to offer a common meeting ground for assisting and advising amateur television enthusiasts and to host lectures for all those – professionals and others – with an interest in television. A founding document, 'Formation of a Society', also referred to the link with John Logie Baird:

> Although the Society now formed was not to exploit Mr Baird's system of Television [sic], but any inventor was at liberty to put forward his ideas for consideration and acceptance by the Society, yet so far ... the impetus created in forming this society was the outcome of the success directly attendant on the achievements by Mr Baird in the art of television and his demonstrations to the British Association at the meeting in Leeds.[75]

Up until this point, television had primarily been the preserve of the Baird Television Development Company, the GPO, some sections of the press, and an ardent group of enthusiasts who formed the Television Society. The turning point came in mid-1927, when the BBC first acknowledged the presence of television, although, as the next chapter shows, acknowledging was a far cry from welcoming and embracing.

Notes

1. John Bray, *Innovation and the Communications Revolution: From the Victorian Pioneers to Broadband Internet* (London: IEE, 2002), p. 95.
2. R. W. Burns, *British Television: The Formative Years* (London: Peter Peregrinus, 1986); Albert Abramson, *The History of Television, 1880 to 1941* (Jefferson: McFarland, 1987); Brian Winston, *Media Technology and Society. A History: From the Telegraph to the Internet* (London: Routledge, 1998); Donald F. McLean, *Restoring Baird's Image* (London: IEE, 2000).
3. The term 'television' was first coined by the Russian scientist Constantin Perskyi, whose paper 'Television by means of electricity' was delivered at the International Electricity Congress in Paris in August 1900. See Abramson, *The History of Television*, p. 23.
4. Robert W. Hubbell, *4000 Years of Television: The Story of Seeing at a Distance* (New York: G. P. Putnams and Sons, 1942), pp. 16–17.
5. Philip W. Sewell, *Television in the Age of Radio: Modernity, Imagination, and the Making of a Medium* (New Brunswick, NJ: Rutgers University Press, 2014), p. 3.
6. Abramson, *The History of Television*, pp. 1–9.
7. Knut Hickethier, 'Early TV: Imagining and Realising Television' in Jonathan Bignell and Andreas Fickers (eds), *A European Television History* (Oxford: Blackwell, 2008), p. 56.
8. Winston, *Media Technology and Society*, p. 91.
9. Hickethier, p. 56.
10. William Uricchio, 'Television's First Seventy-Five Years: The Interpretive Flexibility of a Medium in Transition' in Robert Kolker (ed.), *The Oxford Handbook of Film and Media Studies* (Oxford: Oxford University Press, 2008), p. 289.

11. John Munro, *The Romance of Electricity* (London: Religious Tract Society, 1893), pp. 300–1.
12. 'Letters to the Editor', *Nature*, 18 June 1908, p. 15.
13. McLean, *Restoring Baird's Image*, p. 31.
14. *Cardiff Times*, 12 February 1910, 4.
15. *Merthyr Express*, 19 March 1910, 11.
16. Asa Briggs, *The History of Broadcasting in the United Kingdom. Volume II. The Golden Age of Wireless* (Oxford: Oxford University Press, 1995), p. 14.
17. McLean, *Restoring Baird's Image*, p. 11.
18. Richard Overy, *The Morbid Age: Britain between the Wars* (London: Penguin, 2009).
19. Andrew Thorpe, *Britain in the 1930s: The Deceptive Decade* (Oxford: Blackwell, 1992), p. 3.
20. Stephen Constantine, *Social Conditions in Britain 1918–1939* (London: Routledge, 2006), p. 13.
21. Martin Pugh, *We Danced All Night: A Social History of Britain between the Wars* (London: Vintage, 2009), viii.
22. Michael John Law, *1938: Modern Britain. Social Change and Visions of the Future* (London: Bloomsbury, 2018), p. 6.
23. Constantine, *Social Conditions*, p. 45.
24. Ibid., p. 43.
25. Thorpe, *Britain in the 1930s*, p. 107.
26. George Shiers, *Early Television: A Bibliographic Guide to 1940* (New York and London: Garland, 1997), p. 61.
27. Seán Street, *Crossing the Ether: British Public Service Radio and Commercial Competition 1922–1945* (Eastleigh: John Libbey, 2006), p. 41.
28. An authoritative account of the establishment of the BBC can be found in Asa Briggs, *The History of Broadcasting in the United Kingdom. Volume I. The Birth of Broadcasting* (Oxford: Oxford University Press, 1995). For a detailed account of the similarities and differences in the establishment of radio in Britain and the USA, see Michele Hilmes, *Network Nations: A Transnational History of British and American Broadcasting* (London: Routledge, 2012).
29. Robert Graves and Alan Hodge described the BBC's headquarters at Savoy Hill as 'lively and informal' (Robert Graves and Alan Hodge, *The Long Weekend: A Social History of Great Britain, 1918–1939* (London: Hutchinson, 1940), p. 90).
30. For a detailed study of this, see Michele Hilmes, *Radio Voices: American Broadcasting 1922–1952* (Minneapolis: University of Minnesota Press, 1977).
31. Asa Briggs, *The History of Broadcasting in the United Kingdom. Volume II. The Golden Age of Wireless* (Oxford: Oxford University Press, 1995), p. 235.
32. See e.g. Bray, p. 100.
33. Maurice Gorham, *Broadcasting and Television since 1900* (London: Andrew Dakers, 1952), pp. 115–16.

34. Malcolm Baird (ed.), *Television and Me: The Memoirs of John Logie Baird* (Edinburgh: Mercat Press, 2004), p. 19.
35. Burns, p. 8. The article in question was Nicolas Langer, 'A Development in the Problem of Television', *Wireless World and Radio Review* Vol. 11, No. 6, 197–201, which addressed, among other things, Professor Arthur Korn's television experiments.
36. Antony Kamm and Malcolm Baird, *John Logie Baird: A Life* (Edinburgh: National Museums of Scotland, 2002), p. 31.
37. RTS Archive Box 5 File 5/1.
38. John Logie Baird, 'An Account of Some Experiments in Television', *The Wireless World and Radio Review*, 7 May 1924, 153–5.
39. Donald F. McLean, 'The Achievement of Television: The Quality and Features of John Logie Baird's System in 1926, *International Journal for the History of Engineering and Technology* Vol. 84, No. 2 (2014), 230. I am grateful to Don for many a conversation regarding the technical aspects of Baird's system and a very detailed description of Baird's early equipment can be found in his book *Restoring Baird's Image* and in Russell Burns' *British Television: The formative years*.
40. John Logie Baird, 'Television: A Description of the Baird System by Its Inventor', *The Wireless World and Radio Review*, 21 January 1925, 153–5. Interestingly, the title of this article refers to Baird as the 'inventor' of television, an issue which is explored in the conclusion of this chapter.
41. Shiers, *Early Television*, p. 79.
42. Selfridges Archive. SEL 1157. Original capitalisation.
43. This theme is developed by Wendy Davis in 'Television's *Liveness*: A Lesson from the 1920s', *Westminster Papers in Communication and Culture* Vol. 4, No. 2 (2007), 36–51.
44. Gordon Honeycombe, *Selfridges: Seventy-Five Years. The Story of the Store 1909–1984* (London: Selfridges, 1984), p. 57. Selfridge's went on to establish the world's first television sales department, selling the Baird televisor in February 1928 for £6 10s 1d.
45. Briggs, II, p. 486.
46. Ray Herbert, *Seeing by Wireless: The Story of Baird Television*. 2nd edn ([…]: PW Publishing, 1997), p. 10.
47. T. H. Bridgewater, 'Baird and Television', *Journal of the British Kinematography, Sound and Television Society* 49 (1967), 64.
48. POST 33/3853. Letter dated 4 January 1926.
49. Briggs, II, p. 540.
50. POST 33/3853.
51. Sydney Moseley, *John Baird: The Romance and Tragedy of the Pioneer of Television* (London: Odhams Press, 1952), p. 76.
52. McLean, 'The Achievement of Television', 241.
53. Ibid., 242.
54. RTS Archive Box 5 File 24: 'The Televisor', 26 January 1926.

55. BBC WAC S69: Special Collections. The Gas, Light and Coke Co. 1926.
56. Ibid.
57. POST 33/3853.
58. Ibid.
59. Ibid.
60. POST 33/2515B. A GPO note on file next to the cutting notes that 'Captain Hutchinson's memory must be failing' and offers an alternative chronology and version of events, ending with a reference to a 'campaign of lies' on the part of Television Limited.
61. Shiers, *Early Television*, p. 84.
62. Ibid., p. 80.
63. George Shiers, 'Television 50 Years Ago', *Journal of Broadcasting*, Vol 19, No. 4 (1975), 396.
64. Burns, p. 73.
65. Briggs, II, p. 488.
66. Bridgewater, 65.
67. Shiers, pp. 104–5.
68. Abramson, p. 101.
69. McLean, *Restoring Baird's Image*, p. 46.
70. *House of Commons Debates*, vol. 205, col. 191–2, 12 April 1927. Brittain, a press journalist and founder member of the Empire Press Union, may have had professional grounds to fear the new invention. However, his view of television had clearly changed over a decade later, as he was interviewed on the 200th edition of the television service's flagship programme, *Picture Page*, on 15 December 1938. See L. M. Gander, 'Picture Page', *Radio Times*, 13 January 1939, 6.
71. McLean, *Restoring Baird's Image*, pp. 46–7.
72. James R. Walker, 'Old Media on New Media: National Popular Press Reaction to Mechanical Television', *Journal of Popular Culture* Vol. 25, No. 1 (1991), 24.
73. Thomas Elway, 'What Shall We Do With Television?', *Popular Radio* Vol. 11, No. 6 (June 1927), 519–22, 579.
74. Royal Television Society (RTS) Archive Box 5 File 5/3.
75. RTS Archive Box 1, File 4: 'Formation of a Society'.

CHAPTER 3

Enter the BBC

The first mention of television in the BBC's official meetings came on 15 June 1927 in the form of a short (but prophetic) minute from the Corporation's Board of Governors meeting: 'The Director-General referred to television experiments which, he said, had not so far been regarded as sufficiently satisfactory to justify the support of the Corporation. Developments were being carefully watched.'[1] In many ways these two sentences set the tone for the BBC's engagement with the new technology/medium over the next two years. In his report to the Board on 13 July 1927, Reith noted that the Baird Television Development Company (BTDC) had expressed a feeling that the BBC's attitude towards television had been 'rather obstructive', and added, 'from one point of view perhaps it has'. By his own admission, the BBC, said Reith, did not want to be too closely associated with television at such an early or experimental phase. The Corporation did not want to give the impression that the process (television) was more advanced that it actually was. He was 'afraid also that directly or indirectly B. B. C. co-operation might be made the means of raising more capital from the public' on the part of the Baird Company. The BBC had agreed, he informed the Governors, to give facilities after programme hours on the understanding that these were experimental or scientific investigations only and that no publicity was to be given by the Baird Company to this co-operation.[2] The BBC's station was used on three occasions for these experimental transmissions, and tests were made for reception and field strength. However, an intervention from the Postmaster-General had brought these transmissions to an abrupt end, much to the annoyance of Oliver Hutchinson, who met with F. W. Phillips from the GPO on 25 July. Once again, Hutchinson mentioned that BTDC had been approached by an American company, named this time as AT&T, and that it wanted the rights to the television equipment. The company had also been offered £100,000 for the option of picture rights on behalf of Wannamaker's broadcasting station in New York. Phillips was unimpressed by this. Firstly he noted that the BBC was not licensed to carry out experimental television broadcasts or to loan its stations for experimental purposes. Secondly, the GPO could not allow the BBC to grant facilities to one company which could not reasonably be granted to others on equal terms. Finally, Phillips was concerned over the publicity which might be generated by experimental broadcasts (in conjunction with the BBC) and the possibility of this publicity being exploited to sell television sets. Before any firm decisions could be made, GPO engineers would require a demonstration of television.[3] On the same day, the Secretary of the GPO, Sir Evelyn Murray, decided that he was inclined to the view that the use of BBC stations could be allowed for a limited period for experimentation *if* a GPO engineer was happy with progress on the overall quality of the Baird apparatus. A demonstration was arranged for 29 July 1927 but was postponed by Baird – a recurring theme over the next two years.[4]

By 1928, the Baird Television Development Company was working on a 30-line system with the picture scanning at 12½ frames per second. The company was also producing sets (televisors) for sale to the domestic market. At this point, Winston argues, the BBC viewed the Baird Company as an 'unwarranted upstart' and he found the Corporation's view to be justified: 'The fact remained that Baird's was a partial prototype and it represented the end of the line, just as the BBC claimed.'[5] 1928 was, in Briggs' words, a 'critical year' for television development,[6] and John Swift described 1928–9 as 'a year of bitter controversy in which Baird's supporters openly clashed with the BBC. There was agitation for official recognition and for the transmission of programmes.'[7] It is no coincidence that this was the year Baird met Sydney Moseley, a journalist who took it upon himself to take up Baird's cause and to berate those who doubted the genius of Baird and his television work – especially the BBC, and in particular the Corporation's Chief Engineer, Peter Eckersley. The year also saw the launch of the world's first journal dedicated to television. Under the editorship of Alfred Dinsdale, the Television Society's *Television* launched in March 1928, its aim, according to the editorial, being 'to keep interested members with up-to-date and authentic information upon this new branch of science'. Interestingly, the editorial also admitted that it could be accused of acting prematurely by devoting a journal 'solely to a subject which has as yet hardly emerged from the laboratory' – this more cautious approach was a far cry from the hyperbole of O. G. Hutchinson. And while not explicit at the outset, the journal acted as a publicity machine, or advocate at least, for the Baird television companies.[8]

Eckersley was the author of an undated memorandum (though Briggs suggests that it was published in 1928) headed 'Terms of Reference'.

The paper was in essence a policy statement on the BBC's position with regard to television. The statement acknowledged that television could be achieved in a limited way but that the present stage of development restricted it to laboratory conditions. Incorporating television transmissions into the general pattern of broadcasting would use wavelengths that could not be spared. Although the Baird companies and their supporters viewed the BBC as being 'obstructive and irrational', the statement is clear in its stance: 'It is the opinion of the B.B.C. supported by all competent and independent authorities, that to give further trials to the Baird system in its present stage would only mislead the public by sustaining unfounded hopes and claims.'[9] The statement also listed a series of issues to note in thinking about any demonstrations of television, including the limited vision achievable – faces held 'rigidly close' to the transmitter (camera). No televising of, for example, football matches, action, or topical events would be possible, and *these*, in Eckersley's mind, constituted 'real' television. Eckersley also noted that during television transmissions, those who did not wish to purchase television sets (the vast majority) would be denied 'ordinary broadcasting'. The paper concluded with a set of questions to be asked before viewing a demonstration. These included the lack of outside broadcast capabilities; the cost (would those viewing the demonstration be willing to pay £50 to see picture quality of the kind seen in the demonstration?); whether the apparatus in its current stage of development was capable of being used as widely as wireless apparatus; and whether laboratory experiments should continue until *service* conditions were attained. In summary, the policy to be followed was that if the BTDC could demonstrate pictures of a high enough quality then the BBC would consider broadcasting them. Yet, as Briggs points out, that would have been impossible on the wavelengths available to the company at the time.[10]

On 15 May 1928, the BBC's Control Board discussed the current situation regarding television:

> C.E. mentioned the sporadic attacks made on us for doing nothing about Television, and suggested some form of cover for the public eye, such as the appointment of a committee to investigate the matter (he already being thoroughly in touch, and being satisfied that there was nothing to be given to the public at this moment). It was decided finally that the matter should be covered by a series of three articles in the 'Radio Times' by experts, whose names were to be agreed between C.E. and A.C. (I).[11]

On 11 June Peter Eckersley wrote to Professor L. B. Turner from the University of Cambridge inviting him to write an article for *Radio Times*:

> The world is apt to go mad and it is the duty of experts to restrain enthusiasm which is based on insecure foundations ... My private feeling has been for a long time past that the public is being somewhat deceived as to the immediate possibilities of television. There is a theory that television is to all intents and purposes in a practical state of development, and can at any moment be put into actual service. People therefore have made speculative investments and considerable companies are being formed with this idea in view ... there are such fundamental difficulties in the way of the practical realisation of television that its introduction as a service must be postponed until some practical method is found which overcomes present difficulty.[12]

Eckersley wrote that he would like Turner to help 'clear up public misconception' by contributing an article and noted that Dr Eccles[13] and Professor Edward Appleton[14] had also been invited to contribute.

Meanwhile, the subject of television – and developments in Britain in particular – was becoming a topic of discussion more frequently during 1928 in Parliament. On 28 February, Cecil Malone, the Labour MP for Northampton, asked the Postmaster-General, Sir William Mitchell-Thomson, if he had taken any steps to 'keep in touch' with recent developments in television and whether or not he had considered applying existing radio legislation to the new invention. Mitchell-Thomson answered in the affirmative to both, adding that his technical advisers at the GPO were keen to underline the fact that television was still at an experimental stage.[15] The following month, Sir Harry Brittain asked the Postmaster-General what was being done to develop television in Britain and whether there had been any successful tests recently. The Postmaster-General responded noting that the wireless licences covering experimental transmissions had been issued to 'various people' and that tests had been carried out. However, the government was keen to emphasise again that 'the matter has not yet advanced beyond the experimental stage'.[16] It is quite possible that these two questions were prompted by landmark achievements (which also provided excellent publicity opportunities) by the BTDC. In February 1928, Baird succeeded in broadcasting across the Atlantic from London to New York, and the following month, he successfully broadcast from London to the SS Berengaria mid-Atlantic.[17]

Cecil Malone returned to television developments towards the end of May 1928 when he asked the Postmaster-General if the GPO was being kept informed of progress, and 'seeing that this invention must necessarily function in conjunction with the national broadcasting services [if] he proposes to amend the licence and agreement under which the British Broadcasting Corporation now functions so as to permit that body to employ television?'. The reluctance of the government to fully embrace television as a public service is clear in the answer given: 'I am advised that television is still in the experimental stage, and I do not think that the time has yet come to make arrangements for the provision of a public service.'[18] Malone pursued the subject again in June 1928, asking the government if any technicians or engineers from the GPO had seen a demonstration of television. The Postmaster-General confirmed that technical officers of the GPO had seen three demonstrations in the UK and one in the USA. He also stated that 'the company most active' in the UK – that is, the Baird Television Company – had agreed in September 1927 to give GPO engineers a further demonstration but this had not yet taken place. The implication was that the Company had not fulfilled its promise to do this.[19]

Reith's concern for the BBC's reputation in the eyes of the British public came to the fore in June 1928. In a letter to the GPO Secretary, Reith drew attention to an advertisement which had appeared in the *Evening News* of 21 June in which Baird televisors were being placed on the market. Reith argued that television was not yet in a state to offer a service and that the public would be misled by the advertisement. In a further letter to the GPO on 30 June, he stated:

> The advertisements appear to contain such palpable misrepresentations as to create a situation which the Corporation should not ignore, as the public is probably being led to expect an early inauguration of a 'Television' service in co-operation with the B.B.C.[20]

Reith requested that the Postmaster-General issue a statement disassociating the BBC from the advert, a request that was declined (although the GPO was content for the BBC to issue a statement itself). The timing of the advertisement coincided with the establishment of Baird International Television. The company, under the chairmanship of Lord Ampthill, was launched on 25 June 1928 to deal with the overseas activities of Baird Television, and by September that year a deal had been struck with the Dutch Government which would see Baird apparatus being used to develop television in The Netherlands.[21] Further advertisements appeared in the British press during August 1928 which prompted the GPO to write to the BTDC on 7 August reminding it that experimental work only was to be carried out from the 2TV and 2TW transmitters and that any other use was forbidden.[22] A. A. Campbell-Swinton had seen the advertisements, and wrote to Peter Eckersley at the BBC accusing Baird and Hutchinson of being 'rogues, clever rogues and quite unscrupulous, who are fleecing the ignorant public'.[23] Campbell-Swinton also wrote to *The Times* on the same matter on 21 August. 'Television as at present developed', he wrote, 'is not ready for general public use at all, and is not likely to be so for quite a long time.'[24] The only way forward in television, argued Campbell-Swinton, was the cathode ray tube and not 'moving parts'.

The debate over television intensified during the autumn of 1928. On 12 September, the Secretary of the GPO wrote to Reith to inform him that *if* the experiments being undertaken by Baird were satisfactory (measured by demonstration) then the Postmaster-General would allow the use of one of the BBC's stations for further experiments. Then, having waited since August 1927, the GPO was finally given a demonstration of television on 18 September between the Baird studio at Long Acre and the Engineers' Club some 600 yards away. Colonel A. S. Angwin of the Post Office, in a report of the demonstration, suggested that there was enough evidence to merit some form of experimental trial on a BBC station under normal broadcasting conditions.[25] On the other hand, another observer took a far less positive view of what he saw in his very detailed and descriptive report to W. Gladstone Murray, the Assistant Controller (Information) at the BBC:

> The Baird machine may be said to give a recognisable human head. It is curiously unlike any particular face. I suspect that the eyebrows were heavily made up. Only very slow movements are possible, anything of even normal speed producing a wild blurr [sic]. The impression is of a curiously ape like head, decapitated at the chin, swaying up and down in a streaky stream of yellow light. I was reminded of those shrunken heads favoured by such persons as Mr M. Hedges. Not even the collar or tie were visible, the effect being more grotesque than impressive.[26]

The observer went on to describe the reaction of those leaving the demonstration (or 'show' as he called it) noting that their faces 'showed neither excitement nor interest'. The image, he reported, held for 4½ minutes before requiring adjustment.[27]

Against this backdrop, the correspondence between the BTDC (in the form of Sydney Moseley) and the BBC (Murray) intensified. Writing on 13 September 1928, Moseley protested at the 'unfair attitude' which the BBC was adopting towards television. He referred to the BBC's decision to work on experiments with the American-based Wireless Pictures Ltd using the Fultograph method of transmitting still pictures and called for the Corporation to at least give a similar opportunity to a British company. Murray responded the same day, stating that the BBC was experimenting with Fultograph in order to test public demand.[28] He also took a swipe at the Baird Company's reluctance to show its apparatus to the BBC:

> I wonder if you realise that the company whose shares you were commending [to the public in a financial article which Gladstone Murray had read recently] have

refused to allow their apparatus to undergo the simple practical test offered them by the B.B.C.?[29]

On 21 September 1928, the *Daily Mail* reported that home-receiving Baird televisors were on show for the first time in commercial form. Two types of set were on show: combined radio and television sets, and television apparatus for those who already owned 'a powerful radio set'. The paper also stated that regular television broadcasts would commence in October by 'private enterprise'.[30] However, a letter in *The Times* a week later from a Norman Edwards in London poured cold water on the enthusiastic pronouncements. He congratulated A. A. Campbell-Swinton for doing a 'public service' in explaining the current state of television and agreed with him that there was too much misunderstanding about the potential value of television. 'Although interesting to the student, it can, in its present form, have but little interest from the public service utility point of view to the average listener-in.'[31]

By the end of September, such was the level of public and private debate that the BBC prepared a statement for any enquiries regarding television. It stated that the BBC would consider the possibility of broadcasting television experimentally *after* the Baird system had undergone tests. Any technical details of possible transmissions could not be discussed until the demonstration for BBC officials had taken place. Early the following month, Reith received a letter from BTDC asking for facilities to be given at one of the BBC stations for television purposes with a suggestion of a prior demonstration for the Corporation. Reith, in discussing the request at the 2 October meeting of the Control Board, stated that he had asked the GPO to insist on a demonstration and he would appeal to the Postmaster-General to decline the use of a BBC station if the demonstration was 'really bad'. He would reply to the Baird Company in the same way.

A demonstration of Baird television was arranged for BBC officials on 9 October 1928. On the eve of the demonstration, Peter Eckersley wrote a memorandum, 'Suggested attitude towards Television', which went to Reith, Carpendale and all members of the Control Board. The memo summarised his long-held views on television and included a number of points for members of the Control Board to consider during the demonstration. Eckerlsey predicted that they would see the head and shoulders of a person and that the quality of the image might be better than expected. However, he went on, would they be able to see the person in full length? Or more than one person? A game of football, or a liner arriving at Plymouth, or any topical event? If the answer to any of these was 'no' then Eckersley suggested that the BBC could reject any experimental broadcasts until the company *was* able to deliver on these. If the Control Board were to decide to go ahead with transmissions based on a head and shoulders, then an extra wavelength would be required and a wavelength would have to be 'sacrificed' for television. He summarised: 'I think to take up so much aether in the broadcasting band simply to give the small picture of the head and shoulders of a man to people who can afford £40 sets, is rather ridiculous.'[32] The memorandum continued to predict that the Post Office would 'let us down again' by insisting that further experimental work via a BBC station would be beneficial, and then the Corporation should insist on a special wavelength 'out in the country'. The BBC's Chief Engineer then drew parallels between the current state of television and another invention:

> If I were developing a fountain pen before fountain pens were invented, is it really thought advisable that I should distribute inadequate pens which occasionally wrote 'a. b. c.' and would not write anything else, to the public, in order to see if I could improve my fountain pen?[33]

The memo ended with a plea for the Control Board to think – would what they see at the demonstration constitute a *service*? He reminded members that only a minority would be able to afford television sets, and he questioned the artistic value of television. 'Is it not in fact', he ended, 'simply a publicity stunt?'[34]

With this memorandum fresh in their minds, the BBC's Control Board members saw the demonstration on 9 October 1928. On the basis of what they saw, the decision was taken not to undertake further collaboration with the Baird Company. In a memorandum reporting on the demonstration, Murray concluded that what they had seen was an interesting laboratory experiment and that 'the principle and practice of successful television ... have yet to be discovered and applied'. In considering the demonstration from the point of view of a potential service, he went on: 'Yesterday's demonstration would be merely ludicrous if its financial implications did not make it sinister. The demonstration considered in terms of service might well be considered an insult to the intelligence of those invited to be present ... the Baird method, therefore, is either an intentional fraud or a hopeless mechanical failure.'[35] There were no holds barred in his report. Murray accused BTDC of exercising political influence and forcing the GPO to make the BBC accept the demonstration the previous day. He also predicted that the Post Office would blame the BBC for any further obstruction to the development of television. The report ended by suggesting that the BBC issue a carefully considered statement expressing an interest in the new medium but waiting to see an improvement in results before doing anything else. The last thing the BBC wanted to be doing was to mislead the public into thinking that a television service was likely in the near future.

The Board of Governors agreed to a press announcement regarding television being published which stated that experimental transmissions through the BBC were 'inexpedient' but that the Corporation would be willing to reconsider its decision if and when developments in the television system justified it.[36] As expected, the Baird Company was outraged by this decision. The *Daily News and Westminster Gazette* reported that it had asked the BBC to explain its attitude to the public, the result of which was the aforementioned statement which noted that the demonstration has 'failed to fulfil the conditions which would justify trial through a B.B.C. station'. A Baird Company spokesman told the paper that they would not take the matter lying down, arguing that 'the ether is free to everybody' and that Baird Television had been shown to around 1,000 people daily at the September Radio Exhibition at Olympia.[37] *The Times*, on the other hand, agreed that the BBC's decision was 'probably justified' at this stage, but in prophetic tones talked of television soon being counted as a scientific mystery that would be transformed into a public toy. While expensive at first, television would soon go the way of the telephone and the gramophone and appeal to the masses, becoming 'a necessity of existence rather than a luxury plaything'.[38]

On 18 October 1928 Reith wrote to Murray. The Governors were keen for something on the BBC's position regarding television to go into *Radio Times*. The editor of the journal *World Radio* was also keen to publish something. In response to a similar memo from Reith dated 23 October 1928, Murray had written a response to Peter Eckersley (copied in to the correspondence) in his own handwriting: 'Perhaps you would care to refresh your memory before this is discussed at CB [Control Board] tomorrow. I am at present rather against any reference in our papers to a thing which doesn't exist, i.e., "Television"!'[39] Murray reiterated his views in a letter to Moseley on 22 October when he responded to a letter Moseley had sent Reith regarding some form of co-operation between the BTDC and the BBC. Any form of experimental co-operation at this stage, Murray argued, would be disastrous.[40]

When the Control Board next met, on 24 October, it was thought that the Postmaster-General might be put under pressure (from the Baird Company advocates) to do more for television. It was agreed that Reith should see the Postmaster-General to put forward the BBC's views on television and that Murray should write an article on the same lines, 'should an attack necessitate it'.[41] The result was a lengthy statement on the BBC's position regarding television and was written on 3 November. Citing leading scientists such as A. A. Campbell-Swinton and Oliver Lodge, the article argued that the best that could be said for the results thus far was that they were interesting laboratory experiments. In one of the BBC's key arguments against television, the article argued that by being available only to 'a minority of well-to-do listeners' as a 'mechanical toy', television would 'upset the democratic foundation of British broadcasting and disturb its basic tradition of the greatest good for the greatest number'.[42] The article highlighted some of the artistic and technical limitations of television before ending with a strong statement underlining the 'primary duties' of the BBC: 'To protect the efficiency and democratic nature of the broadcasting service from what might be, in practice, a serious menace'.[43]

Despite the BBC's clear reservations, increasing pressure from the government – as a result of increased pressure from the Baird Company and its proponents – was placed on the BBC to collaborate more positively in encouraging the development of television. On 14 November 1928 the BBC Chairman, the Earl of Clarendon, and Reith reported to the Corporation's Governors on a meeting with the Postmaster-General. Political pressure was clearly being applied on the BBC to allow the Baird Television Development Company to give a private demonstration from a BBC station. 'He [the Postmaster-General] added that in the event of this being declined, he would be obliged to give facilities to the Baird Company which might be repugnant to the Corporation.' The Board of Governors wanted to minute their surprise at the attitude of the government and had expected the support of the Postmaster-General in the general public interest. The Board agreed, however, to allow the use of a BBC station subject to conditions being settled by Reith and the Secretary of the General Post Office.[44] At the same meeting, Reith reported that the BBC's Controller of Programmes, Charles Carpendale, had seen an article in a recent edition of the *New York Times* in which it was argued that the publicity surrounding television had been 'overplayed' and that there was a long way to go before television would be up to the standard required for a service. Given the publicity surrounding television, Carpendale concluded, it was not unreasonable to believe that the public would expect results similar to that of sound broadcasting – but television was a long way behind sound in terms of quality and output.[45]

In a lengthy memorandum to BBC senior staff on 19 November, Murray referred to what he called a 'temporary interruption of hostilities' between the Corporation and the Baird Television Development Company. He had met with Sydney Moseley and Oliver Hutchinson earlier that day at Long Acre and had spent time listening to their grievances. Hutchinson reported that the GPO had sent engineers to see a demonstration and that he now understood that the Postmaster-General was inclined to agree to the use of one of the BBC stations for public tests of television. Hutchinson made several comments regarding the way in which the October demonstration had been handled, including the fact that the BBC's decision not to offer facilities for experimental broadcasts was issued to the press late at night. He also informed Murray that the Postmaster-General was concerned by the attitude of the BBC and that measures were in hand to address this. In response, Murray assured Moseley and Hutchinson that there were no hidden motives behind any of the BBC's decisions and that television was considered purely on its technical merits and its relationship to sound broadcasting. The BBC would be implementing its policy of resisting television while it was in its current state but would encourage its use once it had reached a stage where it could be considered a service.

Pressure continued to mount on the BBC to engage with television experiments in 1929. On 6 January, *The People* published a scathing attack on the Corporation under the headline 'Great Wireless Mystery'. Invoking patriotic language, the article said:

> the attitude of the B.B.C. in regard to this amazing British invention is absolutely incomprehensible ... What justification has the B.B.C. for denying the British public the same opportunities which are now open, or very soon will be open, to wireless enthusiasts in other parts of the world?[46]

A report on 'Television' to the BBC's Control Board in January 1929 noted the Postmaster-General's increasing frustration. He was, noted the report, 'finding it difficult politically to defend an entirely negative attitude towards television'. Although not suggesting that the BBC was wrong in its approach, he was keen to see television being tested under stringent conditions. It was agreed that a panel of independent judges – the Postmaster-General, Sir Evelyn Murray, the Secretary of the GPO, the BBC's Governors, the Director-General, the BBC's Controller and a number of Members of Parliament – would view a television demonstration. The Baird Company had agreed in principle though the fundamental condition of the demonstration was that it should be conducted with 'absolute secrecy'.[47]

On 26 January 1929, the Corporation received a letter from Cyril Andrew Craggy of York. He prefaced his comments by noting that he was a shareholder in Baird Television. Craggy had read in the press of the BBC's attitude towards television and the impression being given was that the BBC viewed the Baird Company as the new baby that 'has put the BBC's nose out of joint'. He accused the BBC of being opposed to television broadcasting and this had filled the public with 'wonder and amaze [sic]'. He argued that as other countries were already broadcasting television, 'then why not this, the home of the inventor', and continued that 'when aural radio was first generally broadcast it had not reached the standard of perfection that it has now reached, and the same applies to visional radio ... Mr Baird is not a charlatan but a scientist.' Finally, he argued that the attitude of the BBC towards Baird was akin to that of a 'sulky child'. The letter ended: 'I think the B.B.C. ... should come to attention and march along with Television from the start as reciprocatory [sic] comrades, for the public good.'[48] Murray responded to the latter on 30 January 1929:

> The B.B.C. is fully alive to the importance of encouraging and adopting inventions calculated to improve and widen the broadcasting service. You will readily understand, however, that the Corporation owes it to its listeners to be particularly careful to avoid arousing expectations which are likely to be unfulfilled. New ideas and inventions are constantly under review; as and when they reach a stage capable of general application, without dislocating the existing service, they are adopted. This is the rule which is applied to systems of television.[49]

On 7 February 1929 Murray wrote to Reith. There appeared, he suggested, to have been a subsidence of hostility on the part of the Baird Company 'and its agents' (possibly a reference to Sydney Moseley). However, Murray was concerned about certain aspects of the overall situation with regard to television. He pointed out that the Postmaster-General had informed the House of Commons of the secret demonstration of Baird equipment which was taking place on 27 February 1929. The President of the Board of Trade, on 5 February, again in Parliament, appeared to give substantial support to the Baird Company in answer to a question as to why a general meeting of the company had not taken place for more than eighteen months by explaining that a general meeting of shareholders had not taken place as negotiations were under way with the GPO and BBC for experimental broadcasts and only now was there something to report to shareholders. He also noted his concern that not only would this encourage Baird interests, but, by inference, it associated the BBC with Baird developments. Hinting at some tensions between the Corporation and government, he added that he would have liked the BBC to have had prior warning of this answer. Well-informed gossip in the Lobby, he went on, was clear that the BBC is under political pressure to change its policy towards television. After the 27 February demonstration, the BBC would need to be 'cautiously friendly to television', with a recommendation of some further action on the part of the BBC.[50] Reith was clearly annoyed that the Postmaster-General had divulged the fact of the proposed demonstration of the Baird system in the House of Commons. In his February 1929 report to the Board of Governors, he made clear his view that Baird wanted BBC backing for purely publicity purposes and to secure a deal in France to get his system used throughout Europe.[51]

On 27 March 1929, the GPO wrote to the Baird Television Development Company. The Postmaster-General had recently seen a television demonstration given by the Baird Company. While acknowledging it as a 'noteworthy scientific achievement', the decision was that television could not be accommodated within current broadcasting hours. The reason given was not so much the quality of the picture which, the GPO noted, could be improved further, but rather the limited scope of the object that could be shown on screen. That said, the Postmaster-General was keen to give the company facilities for 'continued and progressive experiments' and noted that a BBC station could be used outside of normal broadcasting hours for this purpose. The GPO's understanding was that the BBC was content to do this provided that it was understood that the facilities being granted were for experimental purposes only and that neither the Postmaster-General nor the BBC would accept responsibility for the quality of the transmissions. The aim would be to allow the Baird Company to improve upon the quality of the transmissions, and while the company would not be precluded from selling television sets that would need to be done on the basis that those buying sets were aware that they were buying at their own risk and that television as a transmitting and receiving system had not yet reached the stage of warranting a place during normal broadcasting hours.[52]

The following day, the *Evening News* published what was essentially an interview with Baird on the 'television age'. Baird envisaged a near future where people would sit at home in an armchair watching the Boat Race 'thrown on to a screen on the wall' and hear the roar of the crowd through a loudspeaker. He went on to say that the directors of the Baird Television Company had drawn up plans for a simple television service following the Postmaster-General's concession to allow the BBC to transmit television. Baird, as expected, had great expectations, stating that 'the impetus and encouragement of this B.B.C. concession will hasten the progress of television' and would give a much-needed boost to the radio industry.[53] Less than a month later, Oliver Hutchinson wrote to W. G. W. Mitchell, editor of *Television*, to inform him that 4,000 television sets were under construction and were being sold as complete units although there was also a plan to sell them as kits at some point in the future for those who wished to construct them from scratch (with 'preferential treatment' being given to Television Society members for these).[54]

In the meantime, the Baird Television Development Company was exploring options overseas. On 2 May 1929, Oliver Hutchinson wrote to Eckersley suggesting strongly that the delay in establishing television could lead to Britain losing out to another country:

> It has already been pointed out in a letter to the Postmaster General that the policy of the Baird companies in their negotiations for the exploitation of the foreign and colonial rights in the Baird inventions has been, and is now, to retain for the British companies control of the foreign and colonial companies already formed and intended to be formed, and the seeming delay in placing at our disposal broadcasting facilities here may have the effect of losing for the British companies and British interests control of Television in foreign and colonial countries.[55]

Hutchinson had been sent a translation from the Press Service of the Reichs-Runkunk-Gesellschaft (the Reich Broadcasting Corporation) which suggested that the German Broadcasting Service was not interested in 'winning the race' for the prestige of being the first to provide a television service, but that it wanted a suitable and reliable television system, which was why it was consulting with Baird, von Mihaly (the Hungarian television pioneer) and others.[56] On 15 May, Hutchinson wrote to Eckerlsey again, this time asking why the BTDC had not received confirmation of the broadcasting facilities to be put at the company's disposal following the Postmaster-General's agreement to this course of action.[57] It was not until 26 June that the BTDC received a letter from Charles Carpendale offering the use of the 2LO transmitter for very limited periods outside of normal broadcasting hours – three morning broadcasts of 15 minutes each on a weekly basis. Hutchinson refused this offer, and on 9 July, Lord Ampthill, Chairman of Baird International Television Ltd, and Sir Edward Manville, Chairman of the Baird Television Development Company, wrote to the Postmaster-General, H. B. Lees-Smith, to complain. They stated that the BBC had initially offered 2LO to be used between 11 p.m. and 12 a.m. for experimental broadcasts but were now offering the 15-minute slots. This, they argued, was insufficient for demonstrating the possibilities of the system and satisfying manufacturers that they might begin to construct and sell television receiving sets. The letter went on to complain about the negative attitude of BBC officials throughout the discussions:

> The privileged position conferred on the British Broadcasting Corporation ... had been used by the officials of that Company ... to hinder and delay the progress of a

system which is of national importance and which, if properly fostered, would create a new industry in this country to the great benefit of workers in the electrical trades.[58]

On 16 July 1929, Hutchinson wrote to the Postmaster-General in a clear attempt to garner favour and support for the Baird Television companies. He began by mentioning a conversation he had had with Labour cabinet member Clement Attlee, 'a brother officer' of Hutchinson's in the army. Hutchinson had been discussing his interest in television and the work of the Baird companies 'and the question of broadcasting in this country'. Attlee had suggested that Hutchinson contact Lees-Smith, and the letter contains a request for a meeting and a demonstration of television, underlining 'the urgency of the matter'.[59]

Writing to *The Times* in July 1929, A. A. Campbell-Swinton yet again sounded a note of caution – and offered a possible riposte to Baird – referring to what he called 'very absurd prognostications' about television. Arguing that mechanically-operated television could only transmit very simple pictures (e.g. a single human face which was just about recognisable), he went on:

> Now, however, in numerous publications, the public are being led to expect, in the near future, that, sitting at home in their armchairs, they will be able, with comparatively inexpensive apparatus, to witness moving images, approximating in quality to those of the Cinematograph, of actual events transmitted from television broadcasting stations.[60]

Campbell-Swinton, supported by Sir Oliver Lodge, the pioneer inventor in the field of wireless telegraphy, continued by underlining that mechanical devices could not achieve the high quality required and that the only way of improving the quality would be to dispense with 'moving parts' altogether. In reminding readers that the Postmaster-General still considered television to be in an experimental state in the UK and the US, Campbell-Swinton concluded: 'Thus both scientific theory and skilled experience join in the opinion that satisfactory television than can be broadcast on any reasonable scale still remains to be accomplished, and that this may take a long time.'[61]

Reith visited Sir Evelyn Murray at the GPO on 6 August to discuss the matter of experimental transmission hours, and on 12 August he officially offered an increase in hours to five 30-minute periods a day outside of normal broadcasting hours.[62] On 11 September, after a lengthy meeting at the BBC, both sides agreed on a statement to the press that confirmed the 30 September 1929 start date for the experimental transmissions, initially from the 2LO transmitter in Oxford Street and then transferring to the

Brookman's Park transmitter when that was ready. Transmissions were to be between 11.00 and 11.30 on weekday mornings. The object of the broadcasts was to allow the Baird Company to develop further the possibilities of television and to extend the scope and quality of the reproduction of images. The statement ended with a sentence which effectively removed any responsibility for the quality of transmissions or the results obtained on television sets from the Postmaster-General or the BBC.

Conclusions

Baird was not the only person working to achieve television. Contemporaries such as Charles F. Jenkins in the USA and others were experimenting and demonstrating, building on past achievements and nudging television forward towards the point where it would become a viable proposition. For example, the mechanical scanning device invented by Paul Nipkow in 1884 formed the basis of many of the early systems developed by a number of pioneers. There was, of course, a large measure of national pride which drove developments during the very early years of television, as has been shown in this chapter. Donald F. McLean summarises the point thus:

> Each country believes they have their own television pioneer(s). People in the US believe it was Jenkins, or Farnsworth, or Zworykin with support from Hungarian Tihanyi's patents. The Japanese believe it was Takayanagi. In Russia, Boris Rosing. In France, Belin and Barthelemy. Eastern Europe, von Mihaly. Germany, Karolus. In the UK we have the choice of Campbell-Swinton for concept and Baird for practical demonstration and harbinger of the television age.[63]

In a letter to Donald Flamm in 1984, Tony Bridgewater (who worked with Baird on the early television transmissions) wrote:

> I know you want me, and everyone else, to state that this first demonstration [on 26 January 1926] was the same thing as 'inventing' television. But as I have said before my understanding of the word implies a considerable degree of originality of conception as well as putting an idea to work. If we look at the case of Baird ... we find, as indeed he acknowledged, an obvious dependence on someone else's earlier proposal – in this case Nipkow's.

Yet Bridgewater was happy to acknowledge Baird as the first person to *demonstrate* television – just not to 'invent' it.[64] The fact that a number of countries (including Britain, the USA, France and Germany[65]) were investigating, developing and experimenting with television systems during the mid-to-late 1920s gave rise to a discourse around the notion of a 'race' for television, national pride and, in the case of Britain, a means of connecting what remained of the British Empire. For example, a meeting of the Baird Television Development Company in July 1927 discussed the AT&T television demonstration – 'a crude form of television' – between Washington and New York (around 200 miles) and compared it to Baird's demonstration between London and Glasgow over a distance of 430 miles. While the American demonstration had relied upon around a thousand people to undertake it, Baird's experiment involved only three people. The meeting concluded that the British system was 'greatly superior'.[66] Then in December 1928, N. B. Reynolds, one of the directors of *Television*, wrote an open letter to amateur television enthusiasts (readers of the journal) in which he demanded the broadcasting of 'British television ... this new wonder of science'. He referred to Baird as 'the only Britisher in the International Race for Television' and urged readers to sign a petition supporting his demand, 'and so help the British Empire to maintain the lead role she undoubtedly has today in this new triumph of scientific research and inventive genius'.[67] So, if Baird cannot be proclaimed *the* inventor of television, what was his contribution, particularly during the crucial years of experimentation? Donald F. McLean proffers this evaluation:

> Baird achieved what others had not. His innovation was in configuring and adapting existing methods and technology. His subsequent achievements were in pioneering and promoting wide-ranging imaging applications and, more thorough inspiration than invention, accelerating the development of broadcast television in Britain.[68]

There is no doubting the interest created by Baird's work. Between 1928 and 1930, the Baird Television Development Company kept a Visitors Book for those attending television demonstrations at Long Acre. The range of visitors is impressive, from British MPs to eminent scientists, and from all parts of the world. One of the first entries summed up the tone for the remainder of the book: 'The greatest invention of the age'.[69] What is clear from the entries is the sense of amazement and wonder at what the technology was able to achieve. More than one entry calls for television to be made public, to break free from the laboratory. James Brown, the Labour MP for South Ayrshire, for example, wrote: 'There are great possibilities in television. I think it has reached the stage when it should be given to the British public.' Another stated, 'Marvellous. It must not be withheld from the public any longer', and the Director of the Czechoslovakia Broadcasting Organisation considered television to be in a 'commercial' state. The book is striking also in terms of the number of overseas visitors who visited the laboratories. Members of the Tokyo Broadcasting station in Japan visited. along with representatives from

Australia, New Zealand and South Africa, Portugal, the Soviet Union, Sweden, India and Canada (four members of the Royal Commission on Radio Broadcasting visited on 4 February 1929). Given that many of the countries represented were part of the British Empire, it is worth noting the comment from a Frank Sorter: 'This will show us what we have all wanted to see – our overseas brethren of the Empire.' There were also a small number of comments which reflected on television in a less positive light, such as 'Where will it all end?' and 'Will anything remain hidden?'.[70]

The main reason for the desire to 'win' the race for television was an economic one. As noted in Chapter 2, the economic climate meant that any new invention would lead to industrial activity which would, in times of economic hardship, lead to a healthier balance sheet. If Britain were to establish a television industry, it could corner the export trade market and secure a position for itself as a world leader in television – the manufacture of sets, but also the programming which would drive that manufacture. It would also encourage new businesses to be established and, according to the Liverpool Journal of Commerce, 'help solve the unemployment question'.[71] This was made clear in the letter sent by Lord Ampthill and Sir Edward Manville to the Postmaster-General in July 1929. They stated that while Germany had begun to develop a public television service and receiving apparatus, potential manufacturers of television sets in Britain were impeded by the lack of progress. They were anxious to construct and sell sets, but only with the assurance of a daily broadcast service during ordinary hours for a number of years. If developed, argued Ampthill and Manville, 'a very large amount of employment wold be provided for British workpeople'.[72] Hutchinson made a similar point in a letter to the Postmaster-General around the same time. As a result of the German Post Office's support for television, manufacturers would be making sets in time for the Television Exhibition in Berlin at the end of August 1929 and the export market would then be captured by Germany, 'because of the ready facilities and whole hearted encouragement being attended them by the German government'.[73] The prestige that would follow the first nation to establish a television industry would be great. Television was, and still is, a business. Burton Paulu draws an interesting comparison between the early history of radio and television: 'in the United States and the United Kingdom much of the early radio broadcasting had been done by equipment manufacturers in order to stimulate receiver sales; and television's early experimental costs likewise were underwritten by forms wanting to sell sets'.[74] This commercial or business or industrial imperative certainly played a part in early television development. This, together with the pressure placed on the government by individuals associated with the

Baird Television Development Company (see below), might help explain the decision of the Postmaster-General to threaten the BBC in November 1928 if the Corporation did not collaborate with Baird. The economic imperative and the 'race for television' forced the government's hand, which in turn forced the BBC to work with Baird to develop television beyond the laboratory. Thus decisions were made within a complex set of political, economic and publicity-related processes.

One of the main criticisms aimed at the BBC during the early years of television's development was that the Corporation was very reluctant to engage with the new technology on any level and that, in later years, Reith, as Director-General, would have nothing to do with the medium, deliberately eschewing anything television-related. The latter point is discussed more fully in Chapter 7, but in terms of the initial response to the concept and practical application of television there are a number of reasons why the BBC took a less than positive stance.

From the outset there was a reluctance to fully embrace television due to a clash of ideals (public service vs commercial) between the Corporation and the Baird Company. In order to recoup money spent on items transmitted (albeit a very limited amount of items), the company had to sell television sets. In order to sell sets, the company had to ensure that enough interest was generated among a potential television audience. This partly explains the exaggerated claims made by the Baird Television Development Company and its associates in the press in 1926 and 1927. For example, in the *Daily Express* on 8 January 1926, Oliver Hutchinson wrote that 'for fifty years television has been the dream of scientists. Time and time again, statements have been made that their schemes were about to be realised. Yesterday it came true.'[75] The following day an article in the *Daily News* quoted Baird as saying that television had reached the stage of 'commercial proposition' and that home receiving sets were to be manufactured by the Baird Television Development Company.[76] According to Burns, Oliver Hutchinson knew that Baird was short of money for his work and was sure of encouraging interest from the public 'by making sweeping statements to a gullible public'.[77] In relation to this, Andreas Fickers, in his article on the presentation of television at Word Fairs in the 1930s, quotes Alva Johnston writing in the *Saturday Evening Post* during the New York World Fair in April 1939:

> Television has suffered from its own prophets. Broadcasting and the talking pictures had taken people by surprise; they resolved that television would not catch them off their guard. Back in the 20s it was taken for granted that television was only a year or two away. Warnings or difficulties had no effect ... The public was saturated with the wonders of science; miracles were commonplace.[78]

There is no doubt that the often wild and exaggerated claims made by Hutchinson and Moseley in particular, which found their way often into the popular press, added to the Corporation's wariness and concern over television. The fact that those associated with Baird often used publicity to promote the economic interests of the Baird Television Development Company and to try to pressure the BBC and the government into supporting television developments resulted in the Corporation taking a less than positive view of Baird and his work.

There was also an issue of reputation at stake. The BBC's sound broadcasting service had, by this point, made its mark on British society, and to have engaged wholeheartedly with an emerging and experimental technology at this stage would have been a risky step. This was particularly true when the low-definition, 30-line service had no *real* entertainment value beyond the marvel or wonder of seeing at a distance. In addition, as noted earlier in this chapter, Peter Eckersley and W. Gladstone Murray feared for the basic premise of the BBC – that of broadcasting democracy. Radio was available to all; television had the potential to be the toy of the rich.

The reasons given by the Corporation for its initial reluctance to engage related to commercial concerns, picture quality and overall reputation. However, the BBC had a monopoly on broadcasting during this time and was concerned at the prospect (however remote) of competition, albeit in a new and emerging medium. Writing in 1934, Sir Ambrose Fleming, President of the Television Society, criticised the BBC for its attitude towards television in the previous decade:

> It seems clear that their intention is to first squeeze out all rivalry or competition and by putting their present small television demonstration at inconvenient hours to prevent the public from obtaining television receivers other than those suitable for the reception of B.B.C. Television.[79]

It is also worth reiterating that radio was still in its infancy and nurturing an increasingly loyal audience. Diverting resources – financial and human – from sound broadcasting, which was proving popular, to developing a new invention which, in the BBC's view, had limited appeal would be a dereliction of duty.

The 1920s also produced a great deal of speculation as to what television could be and could achieve. Television entered the popular imagination at a time of scientific discovery and innovation; there was no *clear* sense of what exactly television was, or could do, and various predictions were made (right into the mid-1930s, as is discussed in Chapter 3). Writing in 1928, the editor of *Television* and supporter of Baird's work, Alfred Dinsdale, wrote:

> we shall one day be able to see as well as hear the man at the other end of the telephone line. We shall be able to see as well as hear what is going on in the studio of the broadcasting station; and instead of waiting for a verbal description in the newspapers of events of national importance, or listening to the sounds of it as broadcast, we shall be able to see a reproduction of the event on a screen as and while it is actually taking place.[80]

Much of this speculation was reflected in popular culture at the time, in literature and film, for example. This 'interval of uncertainty, when the new medium had arrived but nobody yet knew what it meant', as David Trotter calls it, saw the publication of the first British novel to feature television.[81] Written by Gertie de S. Wentworth-James (author of the bodice-rippers *Pink Purity* and *Crimson Caresses*), the book centres on a bachelor osteopath, Dr Bertrand Clegg. 'The osteopath went across to the side of the room where, standing on what looked like a large walnut box with a ground glass front (the Blair televisor) was the phone.' The novel refers to the 'Blair Televisor', a thinly-disguised reference to Baird's televisor, and when the receiver is removed (suggesting a telephone-like device) the face of the operator appeared on the screen. A misdialled number results in the face of a woman – the book's titular television girl – appearing on the screen, and not the intended recipient of the call, his badminton partner, Dick Clancaster. A romance begins and is conducted solely via the television, and it transpires that the woman is also an osteopath, and the two characters eventually meet and marry.[82]

The film industry also responded to the increasing public interest in television. The French film *L'inhumaine*, released in 1924, showed the main protagonist, a famous singer, using a television system to sing to her worldwide fans. Fritz Lang's dystopian *Metropolis* (1927) portrays a picture telephone device which allowed the city's ruler to communicate with the underground machine rooms, while the plot of the British film *The Third Eye*, directed by Maclean Rogers and released in 1929, revolved around thieves using a television system to discover safe combinations in banks. Another British film, *High Treason*, produced by Gaumont-British (who, in the 1930s, took over the Baird Television Company – see Chapter 4) and directed by Maurice Elvey, again portrayed television as a telephone with screen.

The period from the early 1920s up to September 1929 was a period of great creativity, innovation, hostility, hyperbole and innovation. The focus in this period was on the science and technology of the emerging medium rather than on the artistic or programming aspects – that would come in the 1929–35 period. Television itself moved from the laboratory to the studio, and while the programming of the Baird Television Company's service from 30 September 1929 onwards was experimental, it was, nevertheless, transmitted on a regular basis to a small but dedicated audience. This was no mean feat for a system which had, six years previously, been a pipe-dream in a Hastings attic.

Notes

1. BBC WAC R1/1/1: Board of Governors Minutes, 15 June 1927.
2. BBC WAC R1/63/1: DG's report for Board Meeting. This had been decided at the meeting of the Control Board on 21 June 1927.
3. POST 33/3853.
4. For example, demonstrations had been arranged for GPO engineers to view the television system on 9 August and 2 September 1927 but both had been postponed by the BTDC (POST 33/3853).
5. Brian Winston, *Media Technology and Society*, p. 96.
6. Briggs, II, p. 490.
7. John Swift, *Adventure in Vision: The First Twenty-Five Years of Television* (London: John Lehmann, 1950), p. 43.
8. *Television*, Vol. 1, No. 1 (1928), 7.
9. BBC WAC T16/42/1: TV Policy: Baird Television Co. Ltd.
10. Briggs, II, p. 492.
11. BBC WAC T16/214/1.
12. Ibid.
13. Dr William Eccles, an associate of Marconi, an expert in wireless technology, who was, in 1928, President of the Physical Society.
14. Professor Edward Appleton, Professor of Physics at King's College London.
15. *House of Commons Debates*, vol. 214, col. 207, 28 February 1928.
16. *House of Commons Debates*, vol. 214, col. 1717–8, 13 March 1928.
17. For a contemporary account see Alfred Dinsdale, *Television* (London: Television Press, 1928), pp. 155–60. For a detailed critical analysis of the transatlantic transmissions see Donald F. McLean, 'Seeing Across Oceans: John Logie Baird's 1928 Trans-Atlantic Television Demonstration', *Proceedings of the IEEE* Vol. 107, No. 6 (2019), 1, 206–18.
18. *House of Commons Debates*, vol. 217, col. 1679, 22 May 1928.
19. *House of Commons Debates*, vol. 218, col. 801, 12 June 1928.
20. POST 33/2525B
21. Burns, pp. 122–3.
22. POST 33/3853.
23. BBC WAC T16/42/1.
24. RTS Archive. Box 33. *The Times*, 21 August 1928.

25. Burns, p. 109.
26. BBC WAC T16/42/1: TV Policy (Baird).
27. Ibid.
28. See R. W. Burns, 'Wireless Pictures and the Fultograph', IEE Proceedings Vol. 128, No. 1 (1981), 78–88.
29. Ibid.
30. BBC WAC S2/5. Special Collection: Sydney Moseley Press Cuttings: Baird Television 1928–51. *Daily Mail*, 21 September 1928.
31. BBC WAC S2/5. *The Times*, 28 September 1928.
32. BBC WAC T16/42/1: TV Policy (Baird).
33. Ibid.
34. Ibid.
35. Ibid.
36. BBC WAC R1/1/1: Board of Governors Minutes.
37. BBC WAC S2/5. *Daily News and Westminster Gazette*, 18 October 1928.
38. BBC WAC S2/5. *The Times*, 19 October 1928.
39. BBC WAC T16/214/1: TV Policy: TV Development 1928–1936.
40. BBC WAC T16/42/1: TV Policy (Baird).
41. Ibid.
42. BBC WAC T16/214/1: TV Policy: TV Development 1928–1936. 'The Truth about Television'.
43. Ibid.
44. BBC WAC R1/1/1: Board of Governors Minutes.
45. BBC WAC R1/64/1: DG's report for Board Meeting on 14th November 1928.
46. BBC WAC T16/42/2: TV Policy (Baird).
47. Ibid.
48. Ibid.
49. Ibid.
50. Ibid.
51. BBC WAC R1/65/1: DG's report for Board Meeting.
52. RTS Archive Box 1 File 27.
53. BBC WAC S2/5. *Evening News*, 20 March 1929.
54. RTS Archive Box 3 File 1.
55. Ibid.
56. Ibid.
57. BBC WAC T16/42/2: TV Policy (Baird).
58. POST 33/3853.
59. Ibid.
60. BBC WAC S2/5. *The Times*, 20 July 1929.
61. Ibid.
62. Ibid.
63. 'The Dawn of TV: The Mechanical Era of British Television', <https://www.tvdawn.com/background/early-pioneers/> (last accessed 24 October 2019).

64. RTS Archive, Box 25 File 22.
65. See Hickethier, pp. 64–7.
66. RTS Archive, Box 5 File 5/4.
67. RTS Archive, Box 3 File 1.
68. McLean, 'The Achievement of Television', 230.
69. RTS Archive Box 7. Baird Television Ltd Visitors Book, 1928–30. Many of the entries are anonymous, with the signatory occasionally adding his or her name. Very few dates are given next to the comments though all were made between 1928 and 1930.
70. RTS Archive Box 7.
71. RTS Archive, Box 33. *Liverpool Journal of Commerce*, 27 May 1927.
72. POST 33/3853.
73. Ibid.
74. Burton Paulu, *Television and Radio in the United Kingdom* (Minneapolis: University of Minnesota Press, 1981), p. 46.
75. *Daily Express*, 8 January 1926. POST 33/2525B.
76. *Daily News*, 9 January 1926. POST 33/2515B.
77. Burns, p. 49.
78. Andreas Fickers, 'Presenting the "Window on the World" to the World. Competing Narratives of the Presentation of Television at the World's Fairs in Paris (1937) and New York (1939)', *Historical Journal of Film, Radio and Television* Vol 28, No 3 (2008), 306.
79. RTS Archive. Box 5 File 27.
80. Alfred Dinsdale, *Television* (London: Television Press, 1928), pp. 6–7.
81. David Trotter, *Literature in the First Media Age: Britain between the wars* (Cambridge, MA: Harvard University Press, 2013), p. 10.
82. Gertie de S. Wentworth-James, *The Television Girl* (London: Hurst & Blackett, 1928).

CHAPTER 4

From Experiment to Service, 1929–1932

This chapter will examine the period of low-definition, 30-line television service, provided by Baird Television on the BBC's transmitters from 30 September 1929. During these years, television developed from being an experiment hosted by a reluctant, or, in Ronald Coase's words, 'niggardly', BBC,[1] to the point where the Corporation provided a more regular television service from 1932 onwards, one that was watched by an increasing number of television enthusiasts. The key issues which dominated this period of television's development were: the often-complex dynamics between the Baird television companies and the BBC; developments internationally, in particular in Germany and the USA; the negotiation of the relationship between television, cinema, theatre and radio; and a notion of 'Britishness' which emerged within the context of a discourse around fears of Americanisation.

Baird Television and the BBC

On 30 September 1929 an experimental television service from the studio of the Baird Television Company in Long Acre began broadcasting using the BBC's London transmitter (2LO). The *Radio Times* entry for 11.00 a.m.–11.30 a.m. on the day showed that it was billed as an 'Experimental Television Transmission by the Baird Process' nestled between a wireless talk on 'How I Planned my Kitchen' and a programme of gramophone records.[2] This somewhat insignificant billing belied an important event – a culmination of years of experimentation, press interest and political lobbying (as discussed in Chapters 2 and 3). The opening broadcast consisted of a number of items, including speeches by John Logie Baird, Sydney Moseley and Sir Ambrose Fleming, a letter from Sir William Graham, the government's President of the Board of Trade (which was read out), and light entertainment provided by comedian Sydney Howard, singer Lulu Stanley and Connie King, Baird's secretary.[3] Unfortunately, sound and vision could not be transmitted simultaneously, as only one BBC transmitter – 2LO – was available. Therefore, each contributor had to speak or perform (sound only on the radio) and then repeat the speech or performance in order to be televised. While not ideal, the fact that pictures were being transmitted in real time, 'live', and were being viewed as they happened at a distance was enough to capture the imagination of a writer in *Amateur Wireless*, who stated that while there was yet much to be done in terms of television transmission, 'the present stage is highly creditable' and the fact that the BBC was now permitting broadcasts would 'undoubtedly hasten progress'.[4] The viewing experience may not have been the most satisfactory, but television had arrived, albeit in a very experimental form. Estimates of those who had either purchased a set or who had built a homemade televisor to attach to the wireless set vary, but Baird himself guessed that only around thirty or so people would have seen the first broadcast.[5]

Details of programme content during the very early years of experimental transmission are few and far between. However, we know that at this point, due to the bandwidth available, the 30-line picture on a small screen was very basic by today's standards, and yet was a major step forward in 1929/30. In a confidential report to the Marconi Wireless Telegraph Company in February 1930, Sir Ambrose Fleming praised Baird for being the first to transmit pictures of living and moving objects successfully. He also acknowledged the criticisms of people such as Peter Eckersley and A. A. Campbell-Swinton (see Chapter 3), but also remarked how 'wonderful' it was to see these moving images on a television receiver. Fleming also touched on a key aspect in television's development – that of Baird's work as a lone inventor as compared with the large research groups which were working on television in the USA. The final part of the report recommended that Marconi hold back from acquiring any rights in television at this stage, but rather that it should keep a watching brief on developments. At present, the public were not flocking to purchase sets as there was very little to see, and very few broadcasting hours.[6]

This was a major issue in the late 1920s and early 1930. The incentive to purchase a televisor – or, indeed, to build one from kits which were being sold to the public – was lacking. Beyond the initial excitement and wonder of watching something at home at the exact same time as it was being televised miles away, the limitations created by the mechanical television system in terms of artistes' movements, together with the bandwidth limitations, meant not only that the 30-line picture was of a very low definition but that the content itself lacked what we might today term 'televisual interest'. However, one problem – that of synchronised sound and vision – was eventually addressed in March 1930 when the BBC's

Brookmans Park transmitter was opened on 30 March, thus allowing both sound and vision to be transmitted simultaneously.

The BBC's *Yearbook* first referred to television in its 1930 edition. Restricting itself to a purely descriptive account, the *Yearbook* described television as 'a system, as yet in the experimental stage only, whereby a fixed or moving object is made visible at a distance by electronic means'.[7] In the same *Yearbook*, the entertainment critic Charles Morgan pondered the future of television within the wider context of entertainment. Beginning in a relatively positive register, he suggested:

> It is yet too early to speak in detail of the probable effect of television on entertainment. It is not impossible that the time may come when, without leaving his armchair, a man may be a seeing and hearing member of the audience in any playhouse, cinema or concert hall throughout the world.

However, the article went on to raise fears about the potential power of television:

> If this power is ever brought to mechanical perfection, there is little reason, except the desire to be gregarious, that anyone but a few should go in person to any place of entertainment again; from which it follows that, for want of a local audience, theatres, cinemas and concert halls may be closed down and all entertainment be concentrated in studios supported by an international organisation of televisionists. By this gigantic pooling of resources we might obtain the most wonderful entertainment the world has ever seen, but might alternatively, if the control fell into the wrong hands, see all entertainment debased to the level of international millions or used for the vilest propaganda.

The section on television ended with what might be seen as an argument for the BBC to be given primary responsibility for the development of television, based on its wireless reputation: 'The same danger, though in less degree, attended the first coming of wireless, and has been averted by raising wireless above commercial competition. The development of television will need to be watched with equal care.'[8] It might also have been a case of the Corporation arguing for the maintenance of a monopoly in broadcasting and ensuring that there was no competition from any potential rival company.

By April 1930, John Logie Baird had ensured that a television was installed in Downing Street, as a letter from the Labour Prime Minister, Ramsey MacDonald, to Baird attested:

> I must thank you very warmly for the television instrument you have put into Downing St. What a marvellous discovery you have made! When I look at the

transmissions I feel that the most wonderful miracle is being done under my eye. I congratulate you most heartily & send you my sincerest hopes for your further success. You have put something in my room which will never let me forget how strange is the world – and how unknown. Again & again I thank you. With kindest regards, yours very sincerely, J. Ramsay MacDonald.[9]

This was a major step in gaining support for television from the highest echelons of the British Establishment, although there had been previous attempts to engage Downing Street's interest in the new invention. For example, on 6 December 1928, Lord Angus Kennedy, Vice President of the Society, wrote to Stanley Baldwin (then Conservative Prime Minister) inviting him to a demonstration of television. He wanted the Prime Minister to see 'this new achievement of <u>British</u> scientific research and inventive genius'.[10] Kennedy also argued that television would be a means of cementing the British Empire (tapping into a discourse around the importance of being the first country to introduce television – see Chapter 3), be a humanising influence in the League of Nations, and have educational possibilities also. Downing Street sought the GPO's advice before responding to Kennedy. On 13 December, the GPO replied noting that the Television Society had been formed, essentially, to create and foster interest in the Baird television system. In the view of the technical officers at the Post Office, television was still in its experimental stage 'despite the extravagant claims made on its behalf in the press'.[11] As the BBC was not prepared to provide the use of a station (as the system was, in the Corporation's eyes, still not sufficiently advanced), the GPO saw no reason why the Prime Minister should attend the demonstration. If he did decide to attend, the GPO warned that his presence might be 'exploited for press misrepresentation'.[12]

The first television drama[13]

On 14 July 1930 at 3.30 p.m., the BBC broadcast Luigi Pirandello's *The Man with the Flower in His Mouth*, a joint production between the Corporation and the Baird Television Company. The idea for producing and broadcasting a play may have come from Sydney Moseley, who claimed that he had to persuade the BBC to accept the idea.[14] The minutes of the Control Board of 6 May 1930 suggest that the BBC agreed to the idea grudgingly, noting that while collaboration was 'desirable', the Baird Television Company should refrain from using the opportunity 'for undue publicity'.[15] Val Gielgud, the Corporation's Production Director, chose this one-act play – effectively a dialogue – as the first ever drama production on television in Britain, presumably as he was aware of the limitations imposed on the actors by the studio set-up.[16] Up until this point, television broadcasts had been relatively unambitious, mainly due to technical limitations – talks, singing, musical instrument performances, all quite static, but nevertheless entertaining for those watching. There was a good deal of interest in the broadcast before transmission. The actor V. C. Clinton-Baddeley, in an article on 'The Case for Wireless Drama' in *The Listener* on 11 June, was concerned that television would be a threat to radio drama, referring to it as 'the little devil at the bottom of the Pandora's Box of Savoy Hill'. He continued:

> Once that marvel is set free the present purpose of radio drama will be stultified, and the spirit voices that call insidiously down the many avenues of man's imagination, will be silenced to make a peep-show for the ingle-nooks of Suburbia.[17]

On a more positive note, however, the *Evening Herald* (Dublin) of 4 July looked forward in anticipation to this 'thoroughly interesting experiment' and suggested that it might even lead to an increase in demand for television sets.[18]

The play was broadcast from the Baird Television Company studio at 133 Long Acre in London on the medium wave band via the BBC's transmitter at Brookmans Park. Earle Grey played the man with the 'flower' (referring to the character's epithelioma), his wife was played by Gladys Young, and the other character was played by Lionel Millard. C. R. W. Nevinson, the war artist, painted the sets. It was billed in *Radio Times* and given a separate 'box' in the top middle of the National Programme page for Monday, 14 July, together with the following notice:

> Although television is as yet in the experimental stage, the Baird Television Company, in co-operation with the B.B.C., is this afternoon presenting the first production of a play by television. Care has been taken by the joint-producers of 'The Man with the Flower in his Mouth' to make full use of the limited scope for visual production as yet afforded by the invention, and those listeners who are able to hear and witness the play will find it by far the most interesting television transmission so far attempted.[19]

As noted in *Radio Times*, the play was adapted and produced by Lance Sieveking. Sieveking was a pioneering BBC radio producer, noted for his experimental and modernist productions in the late 1920s.[20] Writing in August 1930 in the Royal Television Society journal, *Television*, he wondered whether or not those watching appreciated the significance of the event and compared the 14 July celebrations of the Revolution in France with the 14 July 1930 revolution in television. Sieveking, however, acknowledged that producing the play was not unproblematic.

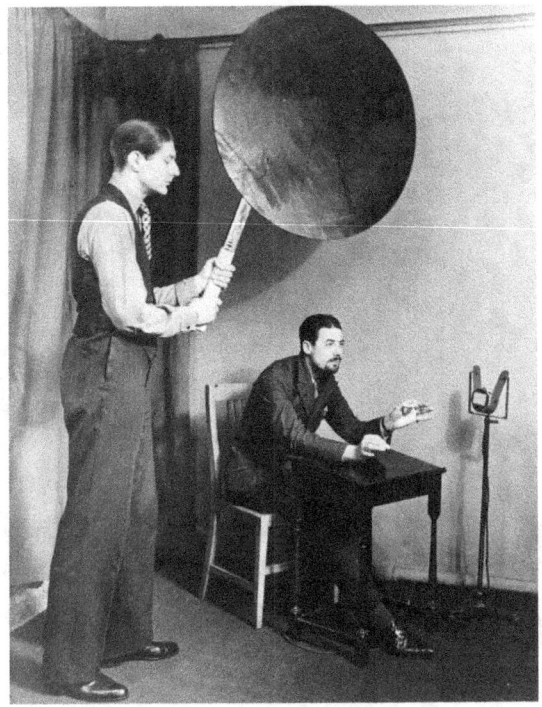

Figure 4.1 Lance Sieveking (left, producer) with his 'fading board' and (right, seated) Val Gielgud rehearsing *The Man with the Flower in His Mouth*, July 1930. BBC copyright.

The technical limitations – including a fixed camera resulting in limited movement for the actors – meant that the production team 'needed all the patience and ingenuity we could bring to it'. After what Sieveking considered to be a near-perfect production, he noted that '[a]t the end, Mr. Baird, Mr. Gielgud, Mr. Moseley and I looked at each other in silence'.[21] Although not recorded in the Programme as Broadcast (PasB) documentation, Sieveking gave a speech at the end of the production in which he thanked Val Gielgud and Sydney Moseley from the BBC and the Baird Company respectively. He also expressed his wish that this first television drama production would 'lead to greater things in the future' and ended by humming the first half of 'God Save the King'.[22] Desmond Campbell, an engineer at Baird Television, considered the production to be a pioneer effort, and never anticipated that within six years drama productions on the scale of those at Alexandra Palace would be undertaken.[23]

Although the exact numbers watching are impossible to gauge, we can be quite confident that it was hundreds (rather than thousands)

Figure 4.2 *The Man with the Flower in His Mouth* cast and production staff in the Baird Television studio in Long Acre, July 1930. Left to right: George Inns (the young boy), Lance Sieveking (producer), Gladys Young, Earl Grey, C. Denis Freeman (kneeling), Lionel Millard and Mary Eversley. BBC Copyright.

of enthusiasts who had either built or purchased 30-line televisors to watch a screen the size of a postcard. The *Sheffield Daily Independent* predicted on the day of transmission that this would be 'by far the most interesting television transmission so far attempted'.[24] A lengthy review in *The Times* the following day, 15 July 1930, highlighted the difficulties involved in producing the play – the cramped conditions of the studio, the small space in which the actors had to act, the need to keep movement to a minimum for fear of blurred pictures on the receiving end (for technical reasons), the need for a black-and-white chequered board to signify a change of scene. In a comment reminiscent of a school report's 'could do better', the review ended: 'The time for interest and curiosity is come, but the time for the serious criticism of television plays, as plays, is not yet.'[25] The broadcast was viewed across the UK. The *Belfast Newsletter* of 15 July welcomed the experiment, calling it 'a start in the right direction',[26] while the *Sheffield Daily Telegraph* heralded the production as 'another milestone'.[27] The August 1930 edition of *Television* received complimentary letters from around the country, including Newcastle, 'the North' and Chesterfield (where, apparently, 130 people, including schoolchildren, saw the play).[28]

The Control Board discussed the broadcast at its meeting on 22 July 1930. The production had provided material of interest to the Productions Department and to Baird Television Ltd,[29] and, the Control Board argued, it showed the willingness of the BBC to co-operate to the limits of Baird's system. However, the meeting concluded that 'no material technical progress has been made such as would justify our programme Branch co-operating any further; such co-operation, with attendant publicity, would mislead the public as to the possibilities of the system now or as now foreseen'. The main issues with the system as it stood were that only one figure was able to be televised, and that person could move very little. In addition, the focus was 'uncertain and variable'. As a result, the Board decided to withdraw from its involvement in programme content but agreed that the BBC would continue to support the Baird transmissions through engineering support only.[30]

The following day, *The Listener* reviewed the broadcast in its editorial. The journal noted that the production had broken new ground, that the producers had followed through on their desire not to merely '[transfer] old dramatic matter in to the new medium', but had shown that television had the potential 'to develop into rather more than a younger sister of wireless drama as we know it now'. At the same time, and unlike the article by Baddeley earlier that month, the journal took a more pragmatic view, and rather than proclaiming the death of radio drama underlined the strengths and advantages of the older medium: 'The great advantage which the present form of wireless drama has enjoyed is the freedom to move actors about like disembodied spirits. A man may be in a taxi in the Strand one moment and going over Niagara Falls in a barrel the next.' When actors could be seen as well as heard, 'we impose upon ourselves the restrictions of reality' although there was also a recognition that at present, television was a 'live' medium but that with time, and technical developments, it could 'conquer the time question and … rival the ordinary broadcast drama on its own ground … plays will be rehearsed, produced and acted months before they are broadcast.'[31] What the editorial did, possibly for the first time, was to give a foretaste of some of the key issues around both the enormous potential and, at the same time, the limitations of television as a medium for drama. These would only really be addressed when television moved from the low-definition 30-lines to a higher definition in 1936.

One of the most scathing reviews of the broadcast came from the former Chief Engineer of the BBC, P. P. Eckersley. Writing in *Popular Wireless* in

August 1930, he criticised every aspect of the production, in particular the sound and vision, complaining that watching a 2 inch by 3 inch screen which swayed made him feel sick. He also complained about the quality of the image and likened the main actor to a monkey with a plum in his mouth, such was the poor quality of the picture. Echoing many of the reservations he had harboured when on the staff of the BBC, Eckersley continued:

> It's all rather terrible. How sane people can put this kind of stuff over the ether, how the B.B.C. can allow itself to be party to it, makes me amazed. I believe, and have believed always, in speaking out about such things. Call it experimental, call it what you like, the putting the announcement of a television play in the paper must deceive the public into believing that they are to see something not very inferior to the talkies. The public should not be so deceived.[32]

Eckersley then repeated his belief that television broadcast with the existing wavelengths, allowing only 30-lines, had no future at all. He concluded the article by suggesting that the BBC should abandon the idea of supporting a public television service, should have nothing to do with television in its current state, and should allow Baird's company to continue experimenting on its own:

> Let the Baird Company leave the B B.C. out of it and start real experimenting with their own stations. I wish them luck if they would do that, but they will need more than my wishes even then. It is not that I would discourage their efforts, it is that public service does not enter the question at all today.[33]

The Baird Company continued to put pressure on the BBC to increase the level and nature of its support for television. On 10 September 1930 Sydney Moseley wrote to Murray at the BBC. Moseley wrote that he had just returned from Germany, where there was a great deal of interest in television from the German Post Office and the authorities:

> Don't you think it would be a fine gesture if the B.B.C. offered to help us further: (1) by giving us transmissions free of cost; (2) To extend or so alter the times of transmission as to give a greater number the opportunity of looking in.

He ended by noting that the Rundfunk (the German Post Office) wanted to develop television 'so that they shall lead the world'.[34] On 8 November, Lord Gainford (Vice-Chairman of BBC) wrote to Reith informing him of a conversation he had had with Lord Ampthill (Chair of Baird Television Ltd[35]). Ampthill argued that the BBC should take a more proactive role in promoting and developing television and Gainford had responded by saying that while the BBC wished to support the Empire and British trade, the Corporation's duty was 'to 3,200,000 listeners who paid 10s. to listen to programmes, and for us to deprive those people of one alternative programme for longer intervals than were now conceded was unreasonable'.[36] A further letter was sent by Ampthill to Gainford on 17 November. According to the letter, the company had been launched with the sole purpose of developing and improving John Logie Baird's inventions in Britain and across the world. While the BBC gave hours for transmission, these were inconvenient hours and were of no use in trying to sell the televisor which was on sale. Ampthill noted that information from Radio trade was that people would not buy television sets if programmes were on only during normal working hours or normal sleeping hours. He understood that the BBC would extend hours if there were evidence of public demand – but herein lay the problem. Without the hours being increased or put at more accessible times, the demand would not grow (beyond the faithful group of enthusiasts and inquisitive public). Ampthill appealed to Gainford on national and imperial grounds, but also the industrial grounds noted at the end of Chapter 2:

> The inventions we are developing are purely British and will if successfully developed provide increased trade and work for this country, and anything which will help to this end should receive special consideration at the present juncture. You may not be aware of the intense rivalry which exists between America and this country in matters of television, but I would like to stress the fact that the Radio interests there are using every effort to establish a position better than that occupied by this Company ...[37]

The Baird Company was at that time negotiating a deal for broadcasting facilities in Canada and hoped to be successful. A deal had already been struck in Germany, and there were indications that France and Australia were also interested in the Baird system. Ampthill ended by raising an 'Americanisation' fear, and argued that if Britain failed to lead the way in television developments then America could force its own television standards on the world. Lord Gainford replied on 9 December 1930 and stated again that the prime consideration for the BBC was a continuous service to millions of listeners. Anything that affected this had to be avoided 'if we would observe our tradition and practice'. Subject to this, though, the BBC was 'ready to assist meritorious invention and new enterprise, particularly when it is British'.[38]

Baird's dissatisfaction with what he saw as the BBC's 'unsympathetic attitude' towards television led to his requesting a meeting with the Postmaster-General, Hastings Lees-Smith. They met on 2 January 1931 and Baird outlined his grievance: that in addition to the BBC charging for the half-hour daily experimental transmissions from Brookmans Park, the Baird Television Company was paying for the cost of producing the programmes and incurring heavy expenditure in developing the television system itself. Shareholders were dissatisfied, according to Baird, and the company's funds were depleted. As a way of addressing this, Baird suggested that his company should get a percentage of the ten-shilling licence fee. The Postmaster-General insisted that this was a matter for the BBC to discuss with Baird but added that, if he felt that he was being treated unfairly by the Corporation, he could make representations to the General Post Office.[39] The likelihood of Baird approaching the BBC following his meeting with the Postmaster-General was raised at the Control Board meeting of 6 January 1931. The minutes also show that there was a discussion over the amount that the BBC was charging Baird for transmission, which apparently did not cover all expenses including BBC engineers' time and transport. It was suggested that the Corporation should now consider charging in the region of £25 per month.[40] At the meeting of the Control Board on 17 February, an article from the German newspaper *Berliner Tageblatt*, from 28 January, was read out. According to the newspaper, television experiments had been abandoned in America and also in Germany, more or less due to escalating costs. Interested parties were attempting to convince the public that the service was good and were also pressing for valuable broadcasting time in Germany. The article denounced this stance as not being in the public interest, but only in the interest of those with funds vested in the television companies. The Control Board noted (possibly with some satisfaction) that the article supported what had always been BBC policy.[41]

Although the BBC still adopted a cautious policy towards television, the televising of the Derby from Epsom on 3 June 1931 marked another step towards a more positive engagement with the new medium. Replacing the Nipkow disk with a more effective mirror drum scanner positioned near the finishing post, the first outside broadcast by the Baird Television Company relayed the excitement of the race to viewers (albeit with blurred, low-definition pictures). The newspapers heralded the event as a milestone in broadcasting and Baird himself noted that this showed the potential for further topical outside broadcasts.[42] Later that month, on 23 June, the Control Board was made aware that pressure would possibly be placed on the BBC to 'take over television organisation' in some form, although the minutes do not indicate from where the pressure would come (possibly the GPO?) or for what reason. Possibly as a direct result of this, and in a more positive tone, Gladstone

Murray wrote to Sydney Moseley on 12 August noting that the BBC was thinking about new ways of helping the Baird Company to expedite the progress of British television. 'The B.B.C. is naturally anxious that British television should retain and increase its margin of superiority.' He also stated that the BBC wanted to revisit the experimental transmission times and propose a better scheme. The Corporation also wanted to see a demonstration of the progress of television during the past year, and any new developments that had emerged from the research being carried out by the Baird Television Company. Moseley responded on the same day: 'I think it is vital in the interests of this country, that the one great force which is able to help it should come to an arrangements [sic] with the Baird Company to safeguard the interests of British television.'[43] However, despite the positive overtones, Baird felt it necessary to contact the Prime Minister, Ramsey MacDonald, on 24 September, complaining that despite the outwardly friendly stance, the BBC was 'inwardly hostile'. He quoted Moseley, who had returned from the USA and who compared the British situation unfavourably with the US, complaining of being 'impeded through entirely inadequate broadcasting facilities' while American television was being allowed to develop unfettered. Baird referred to a speech given by MacDonald where he had exhorted the public to 'buy British' and argued that unless the government were to take action with regard to television, 'big British industry and invention will fall into American hands'. This was, Baird underlined, an issue of national importance.[44] The following month, on 12 October, Noel Ashbridge, the BBC's Chief Engineer, attended a television demonstration at the Baird laboratories at Long Acre. In his report, he stated that it had been the best television he had seen thus far and that the picture had 'programme value'. While it was not ready to be developed commercially, he did think that television would soon be a viable proposal.[45] This was undoubtedly a turning point from the point of view of the BBC's engagement with television. Writing to Reith on 19 October, Murray stated that the BBC now had to take a strategic position and initiative over television. His view was that the BBC's Chief Engineer had to be satisfied that the conditions were satisfactory and, given the report from Ashbridge, he believed that the time had arrived and that the Corporation should now seize the opportunity to develop television. Murray's view was that the Baird Company should focus on its commercial operations, leaving the programming to the BBC.[46]

At a meeting of the Control Board on 27 October 1931 the discussion on television centred on memoranda from Ashbridge and Murray on a new method of showing television on a four-foot by two-foot screen. Although it was deemed to be 'unduly expensive' at the time, Reith thought it could be a possibility in two to five years' time. In general terms, Ashbridge and Murray noted that

> [their] feeling was that television, though still non-commercial, had got to a stage where we should make up our minds whether to co-operate wholeheartedly with the Baird system or see it disappear for lack of funds and opportunity, with the possibility of replacement by an American development at a later date.[47]

If the BBC failed to co-operate it could be accused of obstructing progress, and yet if it co-operated and there was a financial failure it might get blamed by the company's shareholders. In the end, a majority of the Board – backed by Reith – was in favour of co-operation with an agreement on finance that would reimburse the BBC should television become commercially viable. The co-operation would include: facilities for installation of apparatus at Broadcasting House by the Baird Company; suitable programme arrangements by the BBC in liaison with Baird Company; and BBC engineers controlling transmissions in co-operation with the Baird Company engineers. Programmes would be broadcast between 11.00 a.m. and 12.00 noon on weekday mornings and between 12.00 noon and 1.00 p.m. on Saturdays. Terms were agreed by the Baird Company, including a clause which would allow the BBC to continue to broadcast 'by other Television methods' should the Baird transmissions come to an end.[48] The significance of that clause would come to light in the years that followed.

Towards a BBC television service

Reflecting on the year that had just passed, the December 1932 edition of *Television* ventured to guess that 'the scholar of the future will associate 1932 with the beginning of a television service'.[49] The year saw a number of landmarks, including the appointment of the BBC's first television producer and first television engineers, the televising of the Derby to a cinema, and the inauguration of the first BBC Television Service in August 1932. It also saw more ambitious programming, culminating with the first televised pantomime in December, and an increase in the numbers of television viewers.

On 25 January 1932, F. W. Phillips, the GPO Assistant Secretary, wrote to Reith. He had received a letter from A. G. Church (of Baird Television) with a cutting from *The Times* (19 January 1932) noting that Germany was calling a conference with all interested parties to discuss the development of the television industry in that country. Phillips informed Reith that the Postmaster-General wanted to know whether the BBC thought it would be worth convening a similar conference in Britain. Ashbridge commented on the letter and stated clearly that the only meeting to be had was between the BBC and the Baird Company. Reith finally replied to Phillips on 12 February saying that while the BBC could see no advantage in holding such a conference, 'the view of the Corporation is that, although television is still in its experimental stage, enough progress has been made to justify the more active interest reflected by the new plan of co-operation'.[50] The response in many ways signals another step forward in the BBC's engagement with television. Noting that there had been regular experimental transmissions over the past two years, Reith went on to say that the Corporation had also 'taken the initiative in exploring ways in which television may be more actively developed'. Enclosed with Reith's response was a confidential memorandum on 'Television'. In it, the BBC intended to expand the hours of the experimental transmissions and expenditure had been approved for additional programmes of an hour (or two half-hours) on Saturdays and for two half-hours on other days. This would relieve some of the financial pressure on the Baird Company (highlighted by Baird in his meeting with the Postmaster-General in January 1931), although the Baird Company would meet the costs of any other transmissions. However, Baird no longer wished to broadcast in the mornings and so programmes would now be transmitted at 11.00 p.m. every weekday evening, 'the programmes being entirely a B.B.C. affair'. At the same time, the BBC wished to offer an assurance that the 30-line transmissions on the Baird system would continue until 31 March 1934 (although the length and nature of programmes could be altered during this period). The BBC would also retain the option of 'televising by any other system at any time', a reference, possibly, to the developing electronic system at EMI.[51]

On 29 March Ashbridge attended a television demonstration at the Baird Television laboratories in Long Acre. Others present included the Postmaster-General (now Howard Kingsley Wood) and the President of the Television Society, Sir Ambrose Fleming. Sydney Moseley, also present, suggested to Kingsley Wood that the BBC had been obstructive in the past but that relations had improved of late. Ashbridge, in his report of the demonstration to Reith, noted that he had to interject at various points to give the BBC's point of view. Nevertheless, the demonstration went well. The Postmaster-General was shown a home machine which was in development with a three-foot by two-foot screen and the demonstration was followed by a meeting in the Board Room afterwards, where, Ashbridge noted, Moseley did most of the talking and 'delivered a long harangue about the development of a great British industry'. He also suggested a potential market of 4 million television sets, and most of what he said was, according to Ashbridge, 'hopelessly exaggerated ... Moseley laid tremendous stress on the question of starting up a new British Industry'.[52]

Following the demonstration, Baird wrote to the Postmaster-General on 12 April reiterating requests for finance (a penny from each licence fee in order that the company might continue its television research work) and the perceived American 'threat' from RCA through EMI. Baird argued that his company had 'done all the pioneer work in this country at immense expense'. He ended by warning that 'there is a very grave danger of the whole television industry falling into American hands unless this Company receives the financial support for which I am asking'.[53] Kingsley Wood rejected the idea of providing Baird with a penny from every ten-shilling licence. He also rejected an idea which had originated from Reith – that Baird Television should receive an annual grant of £10,000 for research on the same lines as the Opera Grant, an arrangement by which the BBC acted as an intermediary agency on behalf of the Treasury for Covent Garden opera. As an intermediary, the BBC ensured that the resources were spent in the best way, and in a letter to the Postmaster-General on 23 May, Reith proposed a similar arrangement for Baird Television.[54]

Baird continued to press the GPO for funding, writing again to the Postmaster-General on 9 June reiterating that the Baird Television Company had developed television 'at very heavy expense' and that the BBC, in installing Baird equipment in Broadcasting House, was 'receiving the fruits of those years of unremunerated labour. Baird suggested an annual grant of £10,000 from the Post Office and an annual sum of £5,000 from the BBC. The letter concluded with Baird stating that his own personal preference would be for the BBC to take over the broadcasting aspect of television, leaving the Baird Company to undertake research and development activity.[55] Writing to Baird on 20 June, Kingsley Wood informed him that he had refused the application from the Post Office's point of view but was leaving the question of payment by the BBC to be settled between him (Baird) and the BBC. The reasons for doing so were financial: 'I fear that it is quite impossible ... to ask the Government to add to the national expenditure on scientific research.'[56] On 12 July a meeting was called in light of the government's decision not to provide a subsidy for the Baird Company. Baird and Moseley contended that the BBC had treated them unfairly from the outset and was now endeavouring to exploit their invention without adequate compensation. Baird also suggested in the meeting that after correspondence and a conversation with Reith, the

BBC might consider supporting Baird Television with a grant of around £15,000 per annum. Ashbridge and Murray (representing the BBC) made it clear that there was no possibility of any financial support from the Corporation, and also made it clear that the BBC would not tie itself to one system of television. Then, according to a note of the meeting, 'a rambling and somewhat acrimonious discussion' took place.[57]

The experimental service comes to an end

Despite the limitations imposed by the nature of low-definition television (including the limited bandwidth available), the programming of the Baird–BBC experimental television period between 1929 and 1932 was remarkably ambitious. In addition to vocal and instrumental musical items, programming included sketches (e.g. 'Coal Comfort', broadcast on 11 December 1930 and featuring T. H. Bridgewater, a key member of the Baird – and later BBC – engineering staff, and Joan Dare), talks on a variety of topics including naval history and how to assemble a Baird televisor junior kit, and a farce by Frank Stayton, 'The Double Cross', broadcast on 14 May 1931.[58]

The final programme from the Baird studio at Long Acre was transmitted on 17 June 1932, and soon afterwards the Baird spotlight mirror drum scanner (camera) and other equipment was installed in Broadcasting House. The BBC's decision to run the television service from August 1932 onwards was taken after a good deal of deliberation and discussion. As John Swift notes:

> The BBC, which rarely leaps before it has had a very prolonged look – and then another to make doubly sure – had at last come to the conclusion that the 30-line television experiments were now of sufficient interest to justify their getting more intimate experience of this new medium.[59]

The credit for persuading Reith and the Corporation to fully embrace television should go to the BBC's Chief Engineer, Noel Ashbridge, and Assistant Controller Information, Murray, as the minutes of the Control Board of 27 October 1931 showed (see earlier in this chapter). Effectively, the Baird Television Company supplied the equipment for the television service, but now the BBC, under the leadership of newly-appointed television producer Eustace Robb, provided the programming and had overall control of programme decision-making.[60] It was the first time the BBC had produced and broadcast programmes of its own, and it did so by transmitting vision on 261.3 metres and sound on 398.9 metres in the medium wave band. As Edward Pawley observed in his history of BBC engineering: 'The date really marks a watershed in television history, because it meant that the BBC became directly interested in producing television itself, rather than relaying programmes produced elsewhere'.[61] John Logie Baird, writing in the *BBC Yearbook* of 1933, remarked that in his opinion, the inauguration of the service 'constitutes the most important step which has yet been taken towards the realising of proper commercialisation and the introduction of television to the public at large'.[62] In the same article, Baird took a shot at EMI and the BBC's interest in its television system, noting that his television system had been rejected by the Federal Radio Commission in the USA on the grounds that it was a British concern. 'It might be advantageous to our "Buy British" policy', he wrote, 'if this country were to adopt a similar attitude towards American-controlled concerns.'[63]

T. H. Bridgewater recalled the reaction to the BBC's decision within the Baird Company:

> To us in the rank and file of the Baird Company, and doubtless even more so to the Management, the attainment of this long-sought milestone in the advancement of television was a welcome relief and satisfaction. We felt that our activities had suddenly become respectable – no longer a target of frustrating doubt and scepticism from various quarters.[64]

The decision to effectively provide a television service after years of scepticism and obfuscation can be explained not only by the technical advances made and witnessed by senior staff at the BBC, but also by the fact that the Corporation had a broadcasting monopoly and wished to keep it. If the BBC had declined the opportunity to operate a service then the field would be open to Baird Television or other commercial ventures to take it on and operate as a rival broadcaster to the BBC.[65] It is also worth noting that if television was to be a service which offered liveness, immediacy, outside broadcasts, then a low-definition, 30-line service was not the way forward. Clearly with one eye on developments in the EMI laboratories in Hayes, the BBC felt that now was the time to engage fully and constructively with television. If the BBC were to provide a television service then the Programme Division wanted to do it properly. A memorandum entitled 'Television' from Assistant Director of Programmes Cecil Graves to Charles Carpendale on 26 July made the case that the Division should be permitted to spend up to £100 per week on television programmes, because if not, the standard of programmes would not be up to what Graves considered to be the general standard of the BBC. Moreover, he did not want to be in a position where the BBC might be attacked by Moseley and others suggesting that the programmes were no better than – or even not as good as – the experimental programmes broadcast by 'the Baird people'.[66]

The service was based in the basement of Broadcasting House, in Studio BB, which had been the home of the Dance Orchestra (led by Henry Hall since March 1932[67]) until it was moved to make way for the new service. The fact that the BBC management gave permission for the removal of the band to make way for television signalled the significance that was being attached to the new service. Yet the arrival of television also created tensions within the BBC. On 9 August 1932, Cecil Graves complained to the Control Board that

> those immediately concerned with television were demanding ideal conditions, which would lead to the exclusive use of one studio and great expense in other ways. This expense and interference with broadcasting proper was held to be unjustified in view of the extremely limited public for television and its present limited powers, and A.D.P. [Assistant Director of Programmes Graves] asked for a mandate to tell those concerned [Robb and Birkinshaw] that they could go so far and no further and must view the matter in its right proportion.[68]

In the build-up to the launch of the new service, *Radio Times* devoted column space to television, providing some background information for its readers. In addition to describing the make-up that performers were required to wear in order to be televised clearly ('we encountered a stately lady with navy blue lips and eyelids and a pale, dull-pink complexion'), readers were also informed that '[b]runettes are generally considered to televise better than blondes'.[69] Within a few days of this information being published, the new service went on the air.

Notes

1. Ronald H. Coase, 'The Development of the British Television Service', *Land Economics* Vol. 30, No. 3 (1954), 208.
2. *Radio Times*, 27 September 1929, 682.
3. Sydney Moseley, *John Baird: The Romance and Tragedy of the Pioneer of Television* (London: Odhams Press, 1952), p. 119; Andrew Martin, *Sound and Vision: Television from Alexandra Palace (and Some Other Places). A Programme Index 1929–1939* (Birmingham: Kaleidoscope, 2021) [pre-published document loaned to author]; Joe Moran, *Armchair Nation: An Intimate History of Britain in Front of the TV* (London: Profile, 2013), p. 17.
4. Moseley, p. 120.
5. Asa Briggs, *The History of Broadcasting in the United Kingdom. Volume II. The Golden Age of Wireless* (Oxford: Oxford University Press, 1995), p. 507.

6. Marconi Archive MS328. The Marconi Wireless Telegraph Company began to research into television in 1930, although the interests of the company were primarily in the commercial applications of the technology rather than developing television as entertainment (Swift, *Adventure in Vision*, pp. 47–8).
7. *BBC Yearbook 1930* (London: BBC, 1930), p. 452.
8. Charles Morgan, 'The Future of Entertainment. Stage: Screen: Wireless: Television', *BBC Yearbook 1930* (London: BBC, 1930), p. 41.
9. <http://www.bairdtelevision.com/crystalpalace.html> (last accessed 17 July 2018).
10. POST 33/2516. Original underlining.
11. Ibid.
12. Ibid.
13. In fact, the Baird Television Development Company had transmitted the farce *Box and Cox* in December 1928, under the terms of an experimental licence, but this was seen by only a handful of people and did not form part of a service as such.
14. Moseley, *John Baird*, p.133. Moseley was also the joint producer. Interestingly, the play was produced by the BBC a number of times during the pre-war period, including a version by Jan Bussell's London Marionettes puppets (see *Television* Vol. 4, No. 39 (1931), 91).
15. Briggs II, p. 509.
16. Unfortunately, despite playing a key part in ensuring that the play was broadcast, Gielgud was ill with influenza when the play was broadcast (see Val Gielgud, *British Radio Drama 1922–1956* (London: Harrap, 1957), p. 75).
17. *The Listener*, 11 June 1930, 1,033.
18. *Evening Herald*, 4 July 1930, 7.
19. *Radio Times*, 11 July 1930, 77.
20. For a detailed analysis of Sieveking's radio work at this time, see David Hendy, 'Painting with Sound: The Kaleidoscopic World of Lance Sieveking, a British Radio Modernist', *Twentieth Century British History* Vol. 24 No. 2 (2013), 169–200.
21. *Television* Vol. 3, No. 30, August 1930, 253. However, this comment contradicts Gielgud's statement that he missed the production due to influenza. The article included a picture of the chequered sliding board used for scene changes, showing it having worn at the bottom, which was caused by friction in the groove.
22. Alexandra Palace Television Society Archive 3839: Lance Sieveking, Recollection of 'The Man with the Flower in His Mouth', 1930.
23. McLean, Donald F., *The Dawn of Television Remembered – the John Logie Baird Years: 1923–1936.* Audio CD.
24. *Sheffield Daily Independent*, 14 July 1930, 2.
25. *The Times*, 15 July 1930, 12.
26. *Belfast News-letter*, 15 July 1930, 11.
27. *Sheffield Daily Telegraph*, 15 July 1930, 5.

28. *Television* Vol. 3, No. 30, August 1930, 247.
29. The Baird Television Development Company and Baird International Television merged in June 1930 to form Baird Television Ltd.
30. BBC WAC T16/42/3: TV Policy (Baird).
31. *The Listener*, 23 July 1930, 130.
32. P. P. Eckerlsey, 'The Drama and Television', *Popular Wireless* 9 August 1930, 588.
33. Eckerlsey, 'The Drama and Television', 588.
34. BBC WAC T16/42/3: TV Policy (Baird).
35. Baird Television Ltd was an amalgamation of Baird Television Development Company Ltd (formed April 1927) and Baird International Television Ltd (formed June 1928).
36. Briggs II, p. 512.
37. BBC WAC T16/42/3: TV Policy (Baird).
38. Ibid.
39. Post 33/3853: Baird Television Ltd. Licensing, development, experiments, Part 2.
40. BBC WAC R3/3/7 – Control Board Minutes 1931. Interestingly, it was noted in minutes of the Control Board meeting on 26 March that this fee would be waived for the time being, but the principle that it was due was maintained.
41. BBC WAC R3/3/7 – Control Board Minutes 1931.
42. See Briggs II, p. 51; Russell Burns, *John Logie Baird, Television Pioneer* (London: IEE, 2000), pp. 217–19.
43. BBC WAC T16/42/3: TV Policy (Baird).
44. POST 33/3853: Baird Television Ltd. Licensing, development, experiments, Part 2. The reference here to 'American hands' refers to the EMI company based in Hayes, which had ties with RCA in the USA. EMI had begun to experiment with television on ultra-short waves.
45. Briggs II, pp. 517–18.
46. Ibid., pp. 519–20.
47. BBC WAC R3/3/7: Control Board Minutes 1931.
48. Briggs II, p. 520.
49. *Television* Vol 5, No 58, December 1932, 361.
50. BBC WAC T16/42/4: TV Policy (Baird).
51. POST 33/3852: Baird Television Ltd. Licensing, development, experiments, Part 1.
52. BBC WAC T16/42/4: TV Policy (Baird).
53. POST 33/3852: Baird Television Ltd. Licensing, development, experiments, Part 1.
54. Ibid.
55. Ibid.
56. BBC WAC T16/42/4: Television Policy: Baird.
57. BBC WAC T16/42/4: Television Policy: Baird. It is not clear whether this happened or not.

58. Andrew Martin, *Sound and Vision: Television from Alexandra Palace (and Some Other Places). A Programme Index 1929–1939* (Birmingham: Kaleidoscope, 2021) [pre-published document loaned to author].
59. John Swift, *Adventure in Vision: The First Twenty-Five Years of Television* (London: John Lehmann, 1950), p. 56.
60. Eustace Robb joined the BBC on 14 July 1932. He was in charge of 30-line television until the service ceased in September 1935. According a note on his staff file: 'There was never any doubt as to his interest in and devotion to his work. He was, however, always rather a difficult person to deal with and it is fair to say that this was largely due to his personality' (BBC WAC L1/365: Eustace Robb).
61. Edward Pawley, *BBC Engineering 1922–1972* (London: BBC, 1972), p. 142. Although Pawley considered it a watershed, it is interesting to note that Briggs does not mark the new service in his history of the BBC.
62. *BBC Yearbook 1933* (London: BBC, 1933), p. 441.
63. Ibid., p. 445.
64. T. H. Bridgewater, 'Just a Few Lines ...', Supplement, *British Vintage Wireless Society Bulletin* Vol. 17, No. 4 (1992), 3.
65. Coase, 'The Development of the British Television Service', 209–10. I am also grateful to Dr Donald F. McLean for his insights on this matter.
66. BBC WAC T16/214/1: TV Policy: TV Development 1928–1936.
67. See Briggs, II, pp. 82–3.
68. BBC WAC R3/3/8: Control Board Minutes 1932.
69. *Radio Times*, 19 August 1932, 414.

CHAPTER 5

A Service and Two Rivals, 1932–1935

At 11.02 p.m. on Monday, 22 August 1932, the first programme of the BBC's 30-line television service went on the air. Lasting for only 35 minutes, the programme began with Roger Eckersley, the BBC's Director of Programmes, who welcomed viewers and introduced John Logie Baird. Baird thanked the BBC and said a few words of welcome (prepared for him by the BBC) before a number of musical acts performed for the audience. These included Betty Astell, Betty Bolton and Fred Douglas, who were to appear regularly on the 30-line television service. The response in the press was positive, with several papers commenting on the clarity of the picture and the artistes being recognisable (the implication being that this had not been the case previously). The BBC permitted a representative of *Television* to attend the first night and a report appeared in the August 1932 edition of the journal. Interestingly, the representative referred to the difficulty he felt the performers had of acting in front of the camera with no immediate audience response, coming as they had from theatre variety backgrounds. He also noted that the songs and sketches were chosen to suit the small screen.

It was noted that a clear image was received on receiving sets in London, and while facial detail was absent in the dancing, 'the interpretation of the dance tune as expressed by the rhythm of the body movement could be followed and appreciated'. Good reception was also noted by the journal correspondents in Newcastle upon Tyne also, and in Crieff, Perthshire, 400 miles from London.[1]

Programmes

There is no doubt that the quality of programmes – in terms of the content but, more importantly, the visual experience of watching – improved between 1929 and 1935. The technical issue of the available bandwidth on the medium wave bedevilled the earlier programmes. As G. V. Dowding, editor of the *Book of Practical Television*, wrote in 1935, the technical issues were 'always the underlying limit to artistic expression'.[2] The early programmes produced by the Baird Television Company had been basic and fairly static (in terms of movement), on the whole, in terms of what appeared on screen. That said, the early producers had been experimenting in form and content to see what might – and might not – work on screen. For example, sketches involving two or more people were produced in December 1930 together with a ballet-dancing demonstration. In April 1931, Victor Bridges' farce *Another Pair of Spectacles* was broadcast and produced by Harold Bradly (who later went on to offer courses on 'Learn to Televise' for budding television performers) and in the same month there was a talk on naval history illustrated with models.[3] However, as the technology improved throughout the early 1930s, so did the quality of the viewing experience. The 30-line system of 1929 was vastly different from the 30-line system of 1932–5. As Donald F. McLean notes, 'We do not fully appreciate that there was a continual progress in quality, right from Baird's experimental days to its demise in 1935 ... Right from the time that television broadcasting began, the camera system improved significantly.'[4]

Between August 1932 and February 1934, programmes were made from Studio BB in Broadcasting House. The studio was larger than that at Long Acre and had its own separate control room on the same level. The lighting consisted of four banks of photoelectric cells on wheels, each controlled separately in the control room in order to get the correct lighting balance. The fixed view of the camera which characterised the programmes emanating from Baird's studios in Long Acre was replaced by a mirror drum camera system in 1932 which allowed for moderate panning and tilting, which meant that the camera operator could follow the movement of the artistes. T. H. Bridgewater, who by this point was employed by the BBC, recalled that there was more flexibility in the BBC's studio. The camera was mounted in the control room and shone through a window into the studio and the beam from the camera could pan and tilt. It also had the benefit of being able to focus in close-up and at a distance. This, noted Bridgewater, allowed for more imaginative productions. Eustace Robb, the first television producer (see below), used the new system in creative ways. For example, a dancer would be introduced in close-up and then gradually and slowly she would move backwards while dancing, allowing the camera to remain focused on her, until she was at the back of the studio, some twenty

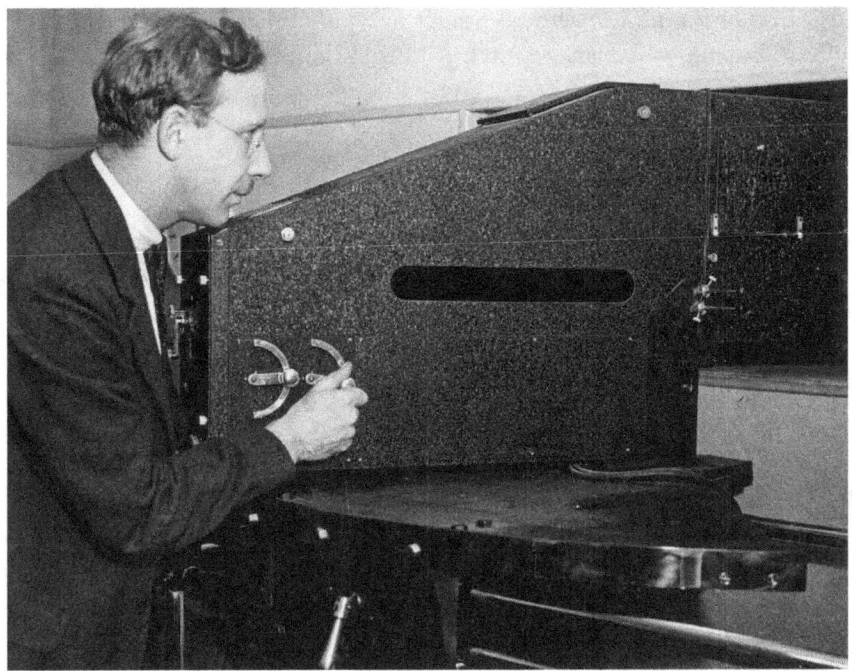

Figure 5.1 The Baird 30-line scanner installed in Studio BB, Broadcasting House in 1932. BBC Copyright.

feet from the camera. By this point, the viewer would be able to see the dancing rather than just the dancer's profile or facial features.[5] Among those who appeared regularly on the television service were the singer and comedian Arthur Askey, the singer Josephine Baker, the actress and performer Betty Bolton and the singer Fred Douglas. One might well ask why these personalities and artistes would subject themselves to being made-up a very extraordinary way for the scanner, perform under intense light and be viewed by only a handful of enthusiasts. The answer lies in the belief that television might eventually becoming 'something', and that it was an adventure, something new and exciting.[6] Reflecting the early days of radio at Savoy Hill, this was a time when mistakes were made and experimentation in form and production took place. Eustace Robb and his team were testing the waters and seeing how far one might take television within the confines of the studio and the 30-line system.

When Val Gielgud recalled 'the engaging antics of a performing sealion and his exceedingly "fish-like smell" at close quarters' during his experience of the experimental television service,[7] he was reflecting the fact that programmes were becoming more ambitious and varied in their entertainment value and content. This was highlighted in the BBC's *Yearbook* for 1933:

> Dancers, acrobats and jugglers have been successfully televised at the time of writing. Animals, too, look like coming into their own: a performing seal recently flip-flopped his way across the entrance hall of Broadcasting House, and successfully projected himself on two wavelengths.[8]

The restoration and discovery of a recording of the first television revue, *Looking In*, from 21 April 1933 by Donald F. McLean finally put paid to the notion that all pre-1936 television was static in the sense of involving only limited movement on the screen. The high-kicking Paramount Astoria Girls, for example, were fast, furious and entertaining.[9]

Television production staff and engineers

The driving force behind the BBC's television service from 1932 was Eustace Robb, a former guardsman with a public school background who was appointed television producer following an interview on 19 May 1932. He joined the television service from the Corporation's Gramophone Department and clearly impressed both Roger Eckersley, the BBC's Director of Programmes, and Val Gielgud, the latter noting on file, 'He seems to have enough technical knowledge without too much, and is a good type for our work. No technical knowledge of television, but the right interested attitude towards any new thing.'[10] The key attributes highlighted by Gielgud were Robb's enthusiasm, vision, and 'right attitude' towards the new method of broadcasting. Likewise, T. H. Bridgewater commented that 'Robb not only saw clearly the various points to heed but, even within the constrictions, soon envisaged and in due course was to realise a potentiality far beyond any we could have dreamed of'.[11] However, it is clear that Robb's tenure as television producer was not without its share of difficulties. The first bone of contention was his salary. On 29 June Robb received a letter from Carpendale offering him the post in television on £300 per annum, but on 3 July Robb responded, disappointed with what he perceived to be the low salary. Two days later Carpendale replied saying that increments might be forthcoming once the BBC had time to judge the output of television once the transmissions had started. On 17 October Robb wrote to the Director of Programmes, Roger Eckersley, to register the fact that he was still unhappy about what he saw as being paid too little given the work involved in producing television.

In addition, Robb was unhappy about the attitude of BBC management regarding his overall working conditions. Due to the television service's programmes being transmitted very late in the evening, Robb took to taking taxis as part of his journey home. This practice had been questioned by Roger Eckersley and others due to the costs involved. There followed a series of memoranda in September and December 1932 during which Gielgud (as Robb's line manager) offered his support for his colleague, noting the 'extraordinarily uncomfortable conditions' under which Robb undertook his work in Studio BB, and suggested that anybody questioning the hiring of taxis should spend three or four hours in the studio and then see 'if after that he would enjoy walking about London in the small hours of the morning in order to get home'.[12] A memo from Gielgud to the Assistant Director of Programmes on 24 September 1932 warned that

> unless the conditions of his employment are reviewed, and to some extent ameliorated, he will either resign, or crack up. If either happens, television would be almost bound to come to a stop, which, considering its most promising start from Broadcasting House, would be lamentable.[13]

A similar memorandum to Eckersley on the same day argued that the improvements that had been seen in programme content since television had moved from Long Acre from Broadcasting House were due solely to Robb.[14]

It is also clear that Robb felt that the television service was not receiving the support that it should within the Corporation. In a long and detailed memorandum to Gielgud on 29 December 1932, he complained that he was given only fourteen days to prepare for the organisation and production of four programmes a week. As the Corporation was not prepared to pay television artistes the same rate as for radio artistes, Robb claimed that he had to rely on 'a personal appeal ... to get artistes other than those of the lowest standard'.[15] Despite his own feeling that the BBC management failed to understand the future importance of television, he nevertheless wanted to invest his efforts in order to stimulate public interest in the new medium for the sake of the country and for the prestige of the BBC. When the BBC announced plans in November 1933 to move the television studio from the basement of Broadcasting House to 16 Portland Place in February 1934, Robb was not consulted directly and apparently learned of the move via a memorandum into which he was copied.[16] In a memorandum to the BBC's Director of Entertainment on 20 November 1933, he warned of his fears of moving to what he considered to be unsuitable accommodation for television and hinted that there should have been closer co-operation between the Programme and Engineering branches in considering the move.[17]

By 1934, it would appear that Robb's relationship with Val Gielgud was strained. In a damning indictment of Robb in a memorandum on 25 June 1934, Gielgud wrote:

> I have watched with admiration his success in making bricks without straw as far as television programmes are concerned. I have observed with considerably less admiration, and with a definite apprehension, the persistence of the one-track angle of his mind, his inability to see other points of view, and his persistence in refusing to recognise the necessity for give and take in such an organisation as this – and, in fact, his general maladjustment of personality to the conditions of our work ... in the event of ... an expansion [of the television service], I would submit that it is most undesirable that the control of television work should be left in the hands of Mr. Robb. I do not think that he possesses the necessary savoir faire or personality.[18]

The final straw came in November 1935. On 20 November Gerald Cock, the recently-appointed Director of Television, wrote to Charles Carpendale to say that he (Cock) had been trying to get Robb to engage with the television re-organisation in preparation for the new regular service, but to no avail.[19] He now wanted confirmation that Robb was no longer a member of the television staff and that a replacement would be appointed soon as there was a considerable amount of work to be done on the new service. 'I am sorry about this unhappy business', he went on, 'and regret my inability to cope further with Robb. He might have been useful, but in my considered opinion any potential usefulness is negatived by a peculiar and impossible mentality.' A week later, Cock wrote to Carpendale again noting that he felt obliged to request Robb's removal from the Television Service. He accused Robb of having done no work since the 30-line television programmes had ended, of being non-cooperative, and of disregarding all instructions. He was, according to Cock, undisciplined and unsuited to the job and would not be a good influence in the 'new organisation'. After what would appear to be a period of no action being taken, on 7 February 1936 a letter sent to Robb from Basil Nicholls (Controller Administration) confirmed the termination of his contract to the BBC, and Robb's television career was at an end.[20]

Eustace Robb only merits a fleeting mention in two separate sentences in Asa Briggs' work on the history of the BBC, and is mentioned only once in Aldridge's work on the birth of British television. He deserves more credit for what he achieved. He was a major advocate of the new service, suggesting more than once in an article in *Radio Times* in November

1932 that television might, one day, usurp radio and prove itself to be the superior medium. Recalling his first experience of a 'crude and unrealistic' 'talkie' film, he then explained that he had seen a silent film of higher artistic merit two days later:

> but I had already heard a talkie, and something seemed to be missing. And that apparently was the opinion of millions of others, for we know the history of the cinema during the last five years. Will it be the same with the listener, and will he miss sight in Broadcasting [sic] once he has seen it, however imperfect it may be?[21]

There is no doubt that Robb was a strong and difficult character who had a clear vision for television and for the potential for the new service. Yet he felt let down by his immediate managers, who, in his opinion, did not appreciate the work he was undertaking in establishing and maintaining the regular television broadcasts on limited resources. A tribute to the contribution made by Robb appeared in the March 1935 edition of *Television and Short-Wave World* following Gerald Cock's appointment as Director of Television:

> For thirty months Eustace Robb has worked enthusiastically to produce programmes of the greatest possible interest within the limitations of a thirty-line picture. That he has succeeded in presenting programmes of distinction and variety, every looker who has followed developments will agree. Imagination, unremitting effort and a catholic taste have combined to produce this result and experience acquired in this pioneering effort should be invaluable in the future direction of television.[22]

Robb was keen for closer collaboration between the Programme and Engineering side of the 30-line television service, and the BBC was fortunate during this period to have the services of three key engineering staff, their surnames incidentally spelling out 'BBC': T. H. Bridgewater, Douglas Birkinshaw and Desmond Campbell. Bridgewater and Campbell were engineers with the Baird Television Company and were tasked with installing the Baird equipment in Studio BB in Broadcasting House. When the BBC's service began in 1932, they both transferred to the BBC, Bridgewater ending his career with the Corporation in 1968 as Chief Engineer (Television). Birkinshaw was engineer-in-charge working alongside Eustace Robb, who later went on to become engineer-in-charge at Alexandra Palace. The three formed a formidable team and played a major role in ensuring the success of the 1932–5 television service and in laying the foundations for the regular public service that began in November 1936 from Alexandra Palace.

A rival for Baird Television

It was at this time that the attacks on the BBC from advocates of Baird Television increased as the Corporation began to show an increasing interest in an electronic television system being developed by Electrical and Musical Industries Ltd (EMI) at its laboratories in Hayes. The company had been formed in 1931 by the merger of the Columbia Graphophone with the rival Gramophone Company (incorporating the His Master's Voice – HMV – record label). EMI employed some of the brightest and best research engineers under the leadership of Isaac Shoenberg, including Alan Blumlein (considered by many to be 'Britain's best electrical and electronic engineer'[23]) and J. D. McGee, and their work on television began in December 1931 when they obtained their first experimental licence from the GPO.[24] The main bone of contention for those who were opposed to the BBC's interest in EMI was that the Radio Corporation of America (RCA) held shares in the company. Baird had already alluded to this when he wrote to the Prime Minister in September 1931 (see above), but two articles in the *Daily Herald* on 20 January and 30 January 1932, written in all likelihood by Sydney Moseley, who had a contract with the newspaper, repeated the fears of American interests trying to get a foothold in the British television market.[25]

By the end of 1932, EMI was in a position to demonstrate its television system and Shoenberg extended an invitation to the BBC to attend a demonstration at the Hayes laboratories of the company. On 30 November, Noel Ashbridge, the Corporation's Chief Engineer, and H. W. L. Kirke, a BBC engineer, saw for the first time EMI's television in operation. In a confidential report for the BBC, Ashbridge noted the main features, including less flicker and higher image quality than was the case with the Baird system. The system relied on the use of ultra-short waves (which allowed for the heightened quality) and could not, therefore, be transmitted on the ordinary medium-wave wavelength as used by the 30-line system. Interestingly, the demonstration consisted of transmitting silent films over a distance of around two miles, which led Ashbridge to conclude that film would be 'the only way in which we can develop the televising of actualities'.[26] He also made a number of assiduous comments on television from the BBC's point of view. Firstly, he did not consider that television had reached the same level in technical terms as radio had when the British Broadcasting Company had been formed in 1922. Neither did he see any point in televising a newsreader, an orchestra or a dance band, although he could see some merit in broadcasting drama or vaudeville. Television was, he concluded, going to be a 'luxury service' and would not enjoy the immediate growth and support that radio had in the early days, on the basis of the high costs involved but also the fact that it had to be viewed in a darkened room. Ashbridge's report ended on a more positive note and, despite his serious reservations, stated that the BBC should not 'hold back in developing a new invention of this type to its greatest extent', albeit with careful attention paid to the financial and technical implications.[27]

By the beginning of December 1932, the Baird Television Company was collaborating with the BBC in transmitting experimental programmes between 3.00 and 5.00 p.m. on ultra-short waves (mainly artistes rehearsing in the television studio in preparation for the regular 30-line service).[28] When Baird got wind of Ashbridge's visit to Hayes, he wrote to Reith pointing out that his company had been developing a television system in the laboratory on ultra-short waves using 240-lines scanning. The results, he argued, were far superior to the experimental transmissions being transmitted through the BBC, but the success and further development of the transmissions were dependent on the Corporation's engineers giving 'all available support and encouragement to the pioneer television company, that is, the Baird Company!' and not, by implication, EMI.[29]

The rivalry between Baird Television and EMI intensified during 1933 while at the same time relations between the BBC and the GPO were being tested with the Corporation facing growing accusations from a number of quarters of supporting an American company at the expense of a British one. At the meeting of the Control Board on 3 January 1933, it was reported that EMI was keen to produce television sets for the autumn, a move deemed 'out of the question' from BBC's point of view.[30] The Control Board also discussed reports that the Baird Company was likely to go into mass production of television sets shortly while the BBC was considering reducing transmissions. A report by Ashbridge on current television developments on 4 January underlined the fact that the BBC would be reducing the number of transmission hours for the 30-line system, with a view to ending the service in March 1934 as had been agreed with Baird when the service began. Ashbridge also stated clearly that EMI should not be rushing the BBC into establishing a television service quickly 'so that they can get well ahead in the receiver market for television sets'. Ashbridge's preferred way forward was to experiment further with ultra-short waves on a higher definition (120 lines or more).[31] By the time of the meeting of the Board on 31 January, a letter had been sent to Baird warning against mass-producing the 30-line sets as the company was expected to be demonstrating a higher-definition television system to the BBC in a few months' time.[32]

In the meantime Ashbridge and Kirke had been to Hayes to see another demonstration at EMI. The company was keen for the BBC to carry out experiments with its system and the request was now under consideration at the BBC. Baird Television got to hear of the meetings between EMI and the BBC and got wind of the possibility of EMI installing apparatus in Broadcasting House for experimental trials. Sydney Moseley wrote to the Postmaster-General on 28 January accusing RCA (a shareholder in EMI) of '"muscling in" through the back doors of the B.B.C.'. He questioned the BBC's commitment to British industry and threatened to call a public meeting to draw attention to what he called a 'public scandal'.[33] Baird wrote directly to Reith on 31 January noting that his company was almost ready to install apparatus at Broadcasting House which would permit the transmission of higher-quality images than the 30-line system on ultra-short waves. Like Moseley, he also referred to the American connection of EMI:

> it is the duty of the Corporation to encourage British enterprise and in co-operating with H.M.V. [EMI] in this matter to our disadvantage, [Mr Moseley] maintains that you would be encouraging an enterprise virtually controlled by the Radio Trust of America. It is of the utmost importance that broadcasting in this country should not be under foreign influence, directly or indirectly.[34]

The GPO was clearly concerned by the arguments made by Moseley, and wrote to Charles Carpendale on 1 February requesting the Corporation's 'observations'.[35] Reith responded to the GPO on 3 February noting that the BBC did not at any time agree to *not* carry out research on television by methods other than the Baird method, and so any discussions with EMI were in line with this. Reith also stated that the Baird Company had offered a demonstration of a higher-definition television system at the end of January but that this had now been deferred. The BBC's view was that both systems should be compared and then it should be considered 'what, if any, system should be adopted on a more permanent basis for programme purposes, having regard to technical and policy considerations'.[36]

Baird continued to vent his frustration at the BBC's actions. In mid-February he wrote to the Postmaster-General protesting at the proposal to install EMI equipment at Broadcasting House and stated that his company had developed equipment capable of transmitting at the same bandwidth as EMI. F. W. Phillips of the GPO rang Harold Bishop, the BBC's Assistant Chief Engineer, on 18 February suggesting that it would be 'a severe and grossly unfair blow to the Baird Co.' if the EMI equipment were to be installed. Phillips wanted to know if the BBC could delay its arrangements with EMI should the Baird Company produce a transmitter to transmit a 120-line picture. Bishop responded by saying that the BBC had been awaiting a demonstration from Baird but that it had been postponed twice already. Bishop's note of the conversation ended: 'Quite obviously Mr. Phillips was afraid to face the issue and wanted to temporise by getting us to delay our negotiations with E.M.I.'[37]

On 21 February, Sir Godfrey Thomas, Private Secretary to the Prince of Wales, wrote to Roger Eckersley. The Prince had received a letter from Baird suggesting that the BBC was 'crushing a pioneer British industry' and giving 'secret encouragement to alien interests'. The Prince thought that Eckersley and Reith should have sight of the letter.[38] Eckersley responded immediately and gave some background information which underlined the tensions between the Baird Television Company and the BBC. He also stated that the development which had given rise to Baird's letter was the discussion being held with EMI. and went on to say that it was not true to say that the EMI system was American – it was being wholly developed and manufactured in England and giving considerable employment to workers in Britain.[39]

At the beginning of March 1933 the GPO, in the light of mounting pressure from the Baird Company, managed to persuade the BBC to delay the installation of the EMI equipment by a month in order to allow demonstrations of both EMI and Baird systems to the BBC and GPO (much to the annoyance of Ashbridge and Reith). After that point, a decision would be made on the installation of apparatus at Broadcasting House.[40] Demonstrations were held on 18 April (Baird Television) and 19 April (EMI) and were seen by BBC representatives (Carpendale, Ashbridge and Bishop) and by staff of the GPO (including Phillips and Colonel A. S. Angwin, the Assistant Engineer-in-Chief). The minutes of the meeting record that the results obtained from the EMI system were 'immeasurably superior' to those obtained by the Baird system. Ashbridge reiterated the BBC's view that the Corporation wished to install the EMI apparatus for experimental purposes because the results were 'vastly better' than those of the Baird Company. Even so, the GPO still asked whether or not the BBC would consider installing both systems to give fair and equal access to the ultra-short-wave transmitter. After being told by Ashbridge that space was at a premium and that such an arrangement would be impractical, Phillips noted that

> the Postmaster-General would not be willing to exclude Baird's entirely since they existed solely for television, whereas E.M.I had other interests, and if it became known that the B.B.C. had allowed the E.M.I system to be installed it would be very damaging to the Baird Co.[41]

The chairman of the demonstration, L. Simon of the GPO, even admitted that were it not for the competing interest of EMI, the GPO would not press the BBC to provide facilities for the Baird Company on the basis of the demonstration alone. The GPO's predicament was summarised by Phillips at the end of the discussion:

> The Post Office were afraid that if the Baird Co. were prevented from installing high definition equipment, questions would be asked in Parliament and in the Press which would be difficult to answer, and the Post Office mainly, and the B.B.C. to a lesser extent, would be blamed for the inevitable bankruptcy of the Baird Co.[42]

After a flurry of correspondence between the BBC and GPO, the Postmaster-General wrote to Reith on 22 May insisting that it would be in the best interests of the BBC and the Post Office 'to treat the two competing systems on a footing of absolute equality'.[43] Reith responded two days later outlining the concerns of the Board of Governors, who had discussed the matter the previous day. The Board were 'really anxious' about the co-operation with Baird Television, for two reasons. Firstly, it was felt that the present collaboration was 'leading nowhere' and was expected to be discontinued in March 1934 in relation to 30-line television at least. And yet, the Board had heard of a hundred sets being sold at £70 each, a 'propaganda dinner', and a further public demonstration scheduled for the following week. Secondly, the Governors felt it would be unfair to delay EMI any further as six months had passed since the first application to install equipment 'and there is no difference of opinion between us as to the state of the Baird apparatus'. The Board called for the go-ahead to proceed immediately with EMI on the understanding that, if Baird were able to demonstrate quality comparable with that of EMI, then experiments with Baird's apparatus would also be installed.[44] At the meeting of the Board of Governors on 28 June, it was reported that EMI apparatus would be installed before long and that the Baird Company had been informed that it would have similar facilities after a satisfactory demonstration had been provided.[45]

In the meantime there were developments at Baird Television. On 13 July, A. G. D. West, newly-appointed Technical Director at the Baird Company, met with Noel Ashbridge. He had been appointed by the Ostrer Brothers, owners of the film company Gaumont-British, which was now the virtual owner of Baird Television having rescued the company from financial difficulties in 1932. According to Ashbridge's note of the meeting, West agreed that there was no future for 30-line television and that the company would be ready to install apparatus for 120-line television 'within a month'. The company had also moved from its Long Acre studios to Crystal Palace in London and had a research licence for various short-wave experiments.[46]

However, tensions still existed between the BBC and Baird Television. On 4 August West wrote to the Postmaster-General reminding him of Baird's achievements in producing the first televised image.[47] Sir Harry Greer, who had been appointed Chairman of Baird Television in place of Lord Ampthill, wrote to Reith on 27 September. In his letter he complained that stories in the press and technical journals regarding the proposed ultra-short-wave experiments assumed that a new company had been given preference over the Baird Company and that no mention had been made of the 120-line apparatus being installed by the company at Broadcasting House. According to Greer, this, in turn, had damaged the company's reputation and had led to a great deal of concern among the company's shareholders.[48] In response, the BBC issued a statement on 12 October which stated its intention to carry out experiments on high-definition television through an ultra-short-wave transmitter at Broadcasting House. The first set of tests would be carried out on Baird Television apparatus and the second set of tests on EMI apparatus. The statement also confirmed that 30-line transmissions would continue until 31 March 1934, although it also noted that no decision had been made as to a further series of transmissions after that date.[49]

Towards the end of 1933, the BBC was becoming acutely aware that a move to higher-definition television would leave the 30-line system in a precarious state. In an aide-memoire on 'Television' on 27 October, the Corporation stated that it was anxious to prevent losses on the part of television set manufacturers and the public. Developments pointed clearly to a higher-definition system with more lines per picture, which necessitated the use of ultra-short wavelengths.[50] The BBC would be prepared, however, to allow the Baird Company to continue with the experimental transmission of television (at 30 lines or more) on the medium wavelength for research purposes only, on the clear understanding that people should not buy sets for this 'obsolete system'.[51] The formal announcement of the end of the 30-line transmissions came on 4 December, noting that experimental work would continue on ultra-short waves in order to provide an improved service in the future. However, the announcement also stated that should high-definition television not be 'stable' by 31 March 1934 then low-definition programmes would continue twice a week for 'experimenters', although there would be no guaranteed duration.[52]

In January 1934, Ashbridge and Kirke attended another demonstration of television (film transmitted on 150 lines) at the EMI laboratories in

Hayes. The report for Reith was a ringing endorsement of the electronic system being developed by EMI:

> The results were extremely good, and there was no question in my own mind that programme value was considerable ... The important point about this demonstration is ... that it was far and away a greater achievement than anything I have seen in connection with television ... Supposing, therefore, the B.B.C. wished immediately to establish a television system it would be almost unnecessary to consider the rival merits of the two firms from the point of view of who supplied the transmitter. This, of course, excludes political considerations.[53]

This final point is a key one and one which is discussed in the concluding section of this chapter.

The 30-line television studio was moved from Studio BB in Broadcasting House to 16 Portland Place in February 1934 and was fitted with the Baird mirror drum transmitter (camera), which had been used since 1929. A month later, on 12 March, Ashbridge, Cecil Graves and others attended a demonstration of 180-line television using a cathode ray tube on an ultra-short wavelength by Baird Television at the studios of Gaumont-British in London. Also attending were GPO engineering staff, Baird Television

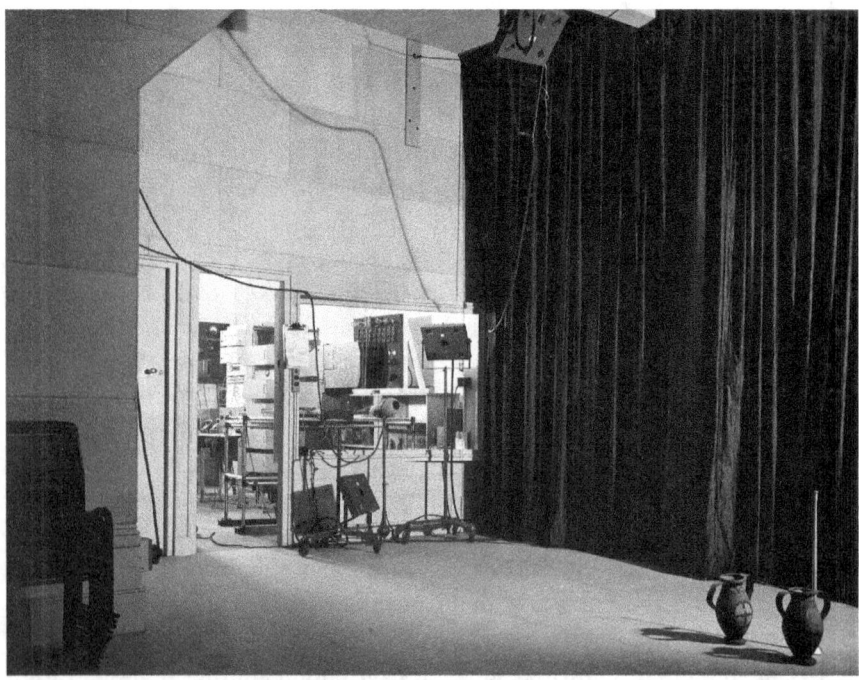

Figure 5.2 The television studio at 16 Portland Place, March 1934. BBC Copyright.

Figure 5.3 The television control room, 16 Portland Place, April 1935. BBC Copyright.

directors and the Prime Minister. In a report to Reith, Ashbridge noted his disappointment at the quality of the living objects (an announcer, a woman playing a violin and a man giving a lecture on architecture), and was rather non-committal about the film transmission also.[54]

The Television Committee (Selsdon Committee) 1934

Following a meeting of GPO and BBC representatives on 5 April 1934, it was decided that the best way forward in terms of dealing with a myriad of issues relating to television (for example, the best way of providing a public service, the use of the service for the transmitting of news and plays, consideration of other television systems such as those being developed by Cossor and Scophony Ltd, and the use of film television in cinemas) would be for the government to establish a committee to advise the Postmaster-General on all television matters.[55] The meeting also discussed the merits of the two competing systems.[56] The BBC, in particular, was keen for the committee to begin as soon as possible given that the Baird Company was pressing for licence to broadcast and EMI was pressing the BBC for a transmitting station in London.

Figure 5.4 Josephine Baker in Studio BB, Broadcasting House, October 1933. BBC Copyright.

On 25 April, Kingsley Wood, the Postmaster-General, wrote to Ramsay MacDonald, the Prime Minister, informing him of his intention to establish the committee and asked for recommendations for a chair and deputy chair.[57] A number of names were suggested by MacDonald, including Lord Reading and Sir William Jowitt. The Postmaster-General contacted the Earl of Crawford, chair of the 1925 Broadcasting Committee, asking him to consider chairing the Television Committee, but Crawford declined. Finally, following a recommendation by the GPO, the former Postmaster-General, William Mitchell-Thompson (now Lord Selsdon), was appointed chairman. Writing to Selsdon on 28 May, the Postmaster-General apologised for not being able to make the first meeting of the committee the following day, but also underlined the importance of the committee:

> I am convinced that having regard to the developments that have already taken place in the science of television and to its future potentialities, it is imperative in the public interest that in coming to decisions upon the matters which I have asked your Committee to consider, I should have before me the best possible advice obtainable,

and I am confident that by appointing your Committee I have ensured that this condition shall be fulfilled.[58]

In addition to Lord Selsdon, other committee members were Sir John Cadman (Vice-Chairman), Colonel A. S. Angwin and F. W. Phillips (both of the GPO), Sir Noel Ashbridge and Vice-Admiral Charles Carpendale (both of the BBC), O. F. Brown (from the government's Department of Scientific and Industrial Research (DSIR)) and J. Varley Roberts from the GPO as Secretary of the Committee.

The Committee took evidence from a wide range of sources and interested parties, including, on 7 June, representatives from Baird Television and on 8 and 27 June representatives from Marconi-EMI.[59] The Committee also viewed demonstrations of both television systems during the course of its deliberations. Having gathered evidence from both major companies with a vested interest in television developments, the GPO compiled a file on the salient points arising from the written evidence submitted and oral evidence provided. One of the key points noted relating to the Baird Company was that it was British and had, through its laboratories and studios at Crystal Palace, a base from which to provide a television service to London.[60] Yet as Donald F. McLean has argued:

> In the UK, during the competition with Marconi-EMI, BTL made much of the fact that they were fielding a fully British development. However the system they supplied included an enhanced British implementation of the Fernseh system providing the German television service. BTL had been an active partner of Fernseh AG (Aktiengesellschaft) since its foundation.[61]

Marconi-EMI had emphasised its British credentials by highlighting that all the television development work of the company had been undertaken at its laboratories at Hayes in Middlesex. Unlike the Baird Company, Marconi-EMI was not interested in providing a *service* itself, focusing instead on the transmitting and receiving apparatus. Again, unlike the Baird Television Company, Marconi-EMI saw no future in large-screen or cinema television, arguing that it was not a profitable enterprise, and that television in the domestic setting was the only way forward.[62]

On 30 November 1934, the Committee met with Reith, the only representative from the BBC to speak to the Committee. Lord Selsdon suggested that 'as the relation between sight and sound broadcasting is so close as to be absolutely indissoluble, it is impossible to conceive of any other authority being entrusted with visual broadcasting than ... the B.B.C.', and asked Reith whether or not he had any 'insuperable objection' to undertaking the work. 'No, Sir', Reith responded, 'we are quite prepared to do it.'[63] Selsdon then went on to suggest the establishment of an Advisory Council for television which could act as a 'buffer' for the BBC, a suggestion to which Reith agreed. The Director-General was then asked for his views on 30-line transmissions. His response underlined Reith's objection to the low-definition programmes and heralded the demise of the experimental service: 'Unless your committee were very anxious, and for good reasons, for their continuance, we should be glad to stop them. We do not appreciate the benefit to be derived from the continuance.'[64] Nevertheless, the committee was aware of the strong feelings of television enthusiasts, many of whom had written in protest to the committee on hearing of the BBC's plans to end the service. Reith, however, was fully aware that technical developments would soon lead to a higher-definition service and was concerned that should the 30-line service be allowed to continue, the public would be 'duped' into purchasing sets which would soon be obsolete.

In a written statement to the Selsdon Committee on 6 December 1934, Reith's deputy, Charles Carpendale, revealed that the Corporation had developed a keen awareness of television as a distinctive medium. No longer was it sufficient to merely transpose sound programmes to television, and the material broadcast needed to be considered carefully:

> the television service should primarily be considered as running in parallel, and in acute liaison, with [sound] broadcasting, borrowing and adapting material frequently, but fundamentally relying upon such material for its own purpose. It cannot be run as a subsidiary fifth wheel to the Broadcasting coach.[65]

He also noted that a film intended for cinema viewing which appeared on the small television screen could not offer the same experience for the viewer. There was a need to think of films made for television projection, not cinema projection – productions that were simpler, shorter and cheaper. Carpendale also provided estimated costs for television per annum of £217,340. No allowance was made for Sunday programmes, and estimates were based on an evening 'programme' of 2¾ hours. Television studio variety was estimated at £78,000 p.a.[66]

In its oral evidence to the committee, the Television Society recommended the continuance of the 30-line transmissions: 'The present transmissions have a definite entertainment value and are easily received on inexpensive apparatus. They serve to maintain public interest and afford some facilities for amateur experimental work.'[67] The Society also called for an extension to the television service as 92 per cent of respondents to its survey noted this.[68] It is interesting also to note that 45 per cent of the

Television Society members who responded to the survey expressed an interest in television from an entertainment point of view, while 80 per cent were interested in television from the point of view of experimental science. The Society also argued that television should be accessible to the public in an inexpensive form, and yet it also recommended that the low-definition service be supplemented by high-definition transmissions on short and ultra-short wavelengths (not medium wavelengths) with a view to allowing these to supersede the low-definition service when sufficiently developed. In its submission, the Society also called for a longer-term national television policy. It argued that there was potential to develop a new industry like the radio broadcasting industry, but recognised that the public would need to be assured of a longer-term service in order to justify the purchase of a receiver. As members of the committee were questioning them, the Society's representatives noted that 57 per cent of respondents to the Society's survey noted that they thought the BBC should not be solely responsible for television – only 38 per cent said that the BBC should be wholly responsible. There were also concerns among 57 per cent of respondents that sound (and the sound service) would suffer a drain of resources as a consequence of the BBC taking responsibility for television programmes.

The Committee came to a clear consensus on matters relating to the potential of television in programming terms and in terms of who should be responsible for developing a television service in the future. In notes prepared for the preliminary draft report, the Committee listed some of the programming areas in which they felt television would excel. These included news (if it had 'spectacular quality'),[69] sport, public ceremonies, theatrical plays, variety shows, music (including orchestras and vocal concerts) and lectures.

Turning to the future development of television, the Committee stated that while the cinema had started with the visual and then added sound, broadcasting had begun with sound and was now moving into the visual. It noted that 'Television ... will probably be ancillary to sound. Immediate future development should be based in this probability.'[70] For this reason, the Committee agreed, television should be developed by the BBC on condition that it produce popular programmes to 'tempt' the public to buy receivers, and that the Corporation saw as one of its primary functions the stimulation of the technical development of television in order to make it popular among the public.[71]

On the eve of the publication of the Television Committee's report, the editorial of *Practical Television* reassured its readers regarding the future of 30-line television and heralded a new age in communication:

> It is certain that, whatever form television ultimately takes, it is unlikely that the 30-line system will suddenly be discontinued. It is still capable of yielding excellent results and will undoubtedly form a useful medium for further experiments as well as an interesting first step for the experimenter and the amateur ... The year 1935 will ... be that in which the listening public has the scales removed from its eyes and is cured of radio blindness.[72]

The Report was published on 14 January 1935. The Committee had interviewed 38 witnesses, received written submissions from organisations and individuals, and consulted with various government departments. Visits had also been undertaken to Germany and the USA in order to examine the current state of experimental television research and practice in these countries. While the Committee acknowledged that low-definition 30-line television had 'been the path along which the infant steps of the art' had gone, and that 'Television doubtless still affords scientific interest to wireless experimenters', the overall conclusion was that low-definition television 'would fail to secure the sustained interest of the public generally'. As a result, the Committee recommended that the 30-line television should not be adopted as the system for the regular public television service.[73] Given that the Committee wanted to see television 'increasing its utility and entertainment value' and providing viewers with a positive viewing experience, the Committee came to the conclusion that a service of not fewer than 240 lines per picture and 25 or 50 frames per second should be the minimum standard.[74] The Committee was also clear on the relationship between television and radio, and noted that 'the promotion of Television must not be allowed to prevent the continued development of sound broadcasting'.[75] One of the key recommendations of the Committee was that the operation of the television service should be entrusted to the BBC, primarily as this would be in the public interest and on the grounds of the 'close relationship which must exist between sound and television broadcasting'.[76]

Another key recommendation made by the Committee was that the television service should be offered in London initially on 'an extended trial of two systems' (i.e. the Baird and Marconi–EMI systems), in comparable conditions and alternately, not simultaneously.[77] There were also recommendations as to the types of programming that might be transmitted (although the Committee acknowledged that this was beyond its remit). Sport and public events were noted as distinct possibilities.[78] Finally, the Committee recommended that an Advisory Committee be established to 'plan and guide' the development of the service in its early days.[79]

Writing to the Postmaster-General on the same day as the report was published, Selsdon informed Kingsley Wood that he was submitting the

Report but drew attention to a legal matter. Having taken legal advice, the Committee was not sure whether television was covered by the Wireless Telegraphy Acts 1904–26. Selsdon requested that Parliament expand on the definition of 'Wireless Telegraphy' in the 1904 Act to include television specifically. He also noted that he had not included this point in the Report itself lest the Postmaster-General be embarrassed, and so he was putting it in a confidential note. If something should come up in the future, however, he hoped that the Committee would be absolved of all blame.[80]

The report elicited a generally positive response among television enthusiasts and the specialist press. *Practical Television* stated that the report would create a new industry in Britain. 'The Report', it added, 'is an historic document, and worthy of the extended space we have accorded to it.'[81] Likewise, *Television and Short-Wave World* welcomed the development of a high-definition public service.[82] A broadcast by the Postmaster-General on 31 January, reprinted in *The Listener* in February 1935, reassured listeners and potential viewers that the licence fee would not increase from ten shillings. He also offered a reassurance that, despite concerns that had been raised by some members of the public during the Television Committee's deliberations, television could not 'make it possible for the outside world surreptitiously to witness what was going on inside the house ... wonderful as television may be, it cannot, fortunately, be used in this way.'[83]

The first meeting of the Television Advisory Committee, which had been established to enact the recommendations of the Selsdon Committee, took place on 5 February 1935 with Lord Selsdon (in the chair), Colonel A. S. Angwin (GPO), Noel Ashbridge (BBC), O. F. Brown (Department of Scientific and Industrial Research), F. W. Phillips (GPO), Sir Frank Smith and J. Varley Roberts (Secretary). It met on a regular basis during the year, considering, *inter alia*, the location of the proposed London Television Station, finance and, crucially, the end of the 30-line television service.[84] On 1 April 1935, the Committee recommended that a site in Alexandra Palace near Wood Green in north London should house the new television service. The report noted that the Hampstead Heath area would have been better from a television point of view but that there would have been opposition from the neighbourhood to the erection of a large mast. Highgate, Sydenham and Shooters Hill sites were also considered, but the height of Alexandra Palace (330 feet above sea level) meant that the signal emitted from the aerial erected could reach a larger area. The site was also in close proximity to the BBC's Maida Vale studios, acquired in the early 1930s for music (particularly orchestral) purposes. The Palace had first opened in 1873 as a grand entertainment and exhibition venue, but by the early 1930s its glory days had passed and when Desmond Campbell, one of the BBC's lead engineers, arrived to assess the building in 1935 he found it to be in 'the most dreadful mess'.[85] In a letter dated 6 June 1935, F. W. Phillips (of the GPO) confirmed with Reith that the Postmaster-General had accepted the Television Advisory Committee's report and recommendation that Alexandra Palace be chosen as the home for the television station. The Air Ministry had also agreed to a mast of no more than 300 feet above ground level.

By the middle of June, the BBC was pushing to close the 30-line service. On 14 June, Charles Carpendale spoke to Frank Phillips of the GPO. From the note of the conversation made by Carpendale, where he describes Phillips as being 'as difficult as ever', it is clear that the GPO was concerned about the criticism the Postmaster-General would attract should there be a hiatus between the closure of the low-definition service and the launch of the high-definition service. Carpendale's frustration is evident from his response regarding the GPO's concern for television enthusiasts in Glasgow:

> Their case is not worth thinking about, as when 30-line shuts down they will get no television at all, and what he calls the hiatus may be three or four years – so why should he bother about a month or two now?[86]

At the Committee's meeting four days later on 18 June, it was noted that the BBC was keen to discontinue broadcasts in order to allow staff to focus on preparing for the high-definition service and to free the studio space in Broadcasting House (Portland Place) for other purposes. The Committee acknowledged that the number of people availing themselves of the 30-line service was probably relatively small (although no precise figures were available); they were nevertheless 'enthusiastic experimenters who may be expected to protest vigorously ... if the transmissions are discontinued some six months or so before a high definition service is available'. There had been suggestions that the low-definition apparatus be moved from London – the site of the high-definition service – to a broadcasting station 'in the provinces' to allow experimenters to continue to receive a service until the point when a high-definition service was available to them. The idea, however, was rejected by the Committee.[87]

On 20 August 1935 Charles Carpendale wrote to F. W. Phillips at the GPO, sending him a copy of a proposed press release noting that the BBC would like to release it as soon as possible: 'Authority having been given for the placing of orders for high-definition Television equipment for the London Station, the B.B.C. have decided to discontinue the present 30-line service.' Phillips replied on 21 August saying that releasing the statement caused no issue for the GPO, and the final 30-line television programme was broadcast on Wednesday, 11 September 1935.[88]

Conclusions

Referring to the decision of the Postmaster-General to allow Baird Television to transmit programmes on the BBC's transmitter in September 1929, Baird wrote: 'The B.B.C. bowed to the decision with a very bad grace and did what they could to give us as small facilities as possible and make conditions as difficult as possible.'[89] Just as there were several factors at play impacting on the BBC's initial response to television (as discussed in Chapters 2 and 3), so there were a number of issues which shaped the Corporation's initial engagement with experimental television during the 1929–35 period.

The economic context and overall financial situation in the early 1930s was a cause for concern for the BBC, and as a result of the depression of 1930–1 the Corporation adopted a cautious approach to spending.[90] A new method of broadcasting with an uncertain future and a handful of

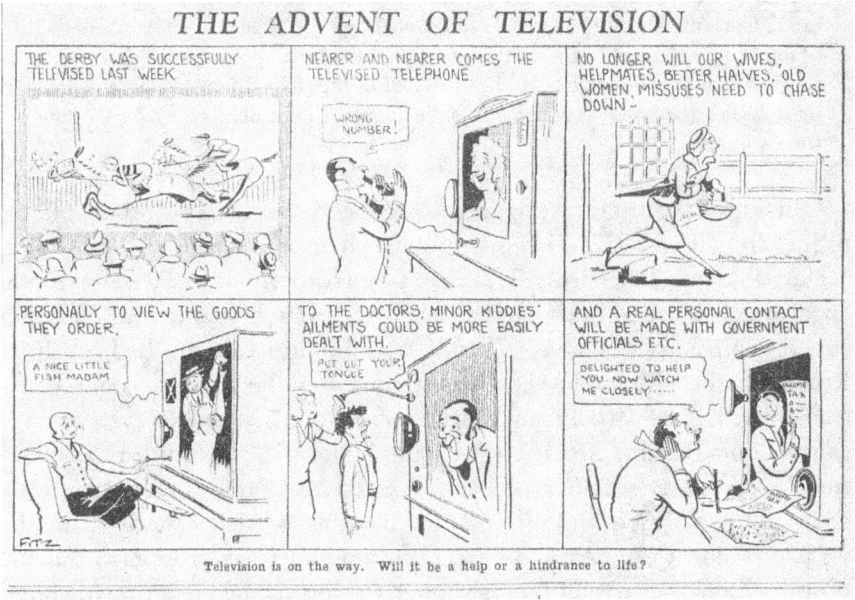

Figure 5.5 Cartoon that appeared in the *Daily Mirror* on 6 June 1932 (p. 9). Reproduced by kind permission of Mirrorpix/Reach Licensing.

enthusiastic viewers was not a sound basis for a major investment of time and finance. The BBC was concerned that the public appetite for television beyond the press interest and amateur enthusiast was not great. It is also fair to say that the precise purpose of television was not clear from the point of view of the public or, indeed, the broadcasters. On 6 June 1932, a cartoon was published in the *Daily Mirror* depicting a series of situations where television might be utilised, including a diagnosis from a doctor and a shopping order.

What is significant about this is that although television broadcasts – albeit it in experimental form – had been transmitted since September 1929, and the format of the programming was becoming clearer, there was still a prevailing sense of uncertainty as to the precise function and future of television.[91] A report that the *Birmingham Evening Dispatch* in the same month suggested that women would soon be shopping by television and that crime might also be solved via television via a picture of a criminal being put up on television screens in police stations.[92] In August 1932, on the eve of the opening of the BBC's 30-line television service, *Television* published an article on the future possibilities of television:

> Images of statesmen and their friendly gestures will mingle among the nations. Television will usher in a new era of friendly intercourse between the nations of the earth. Current conceptions of foreign countries will be changed ... Television will enable the inhabitants of the earth, who do not have the opportunities of travel, to see how their fellow-men live on the other side of the globe. They will learn to enjoy their music, drama and national scenes. Suspicions will be obliterated. New friendships will result.[93]

Outside of the broadcasting arena, television was invading other spheres of life. In March 1932, *Television* published an article under the heading 'Television on an Express Train: A novel experiment'. It reported an experiment that had been carried out by 'a party of radio and television experts' on a train between Sandy and Huntingdon in Bedfordshire. Receiving the BBC television programme on the Baird system being transmitted from Brookmans Park transmitter, a portable receiver was coupled to a Baird televisor on the train: 'This is the first time that television broadcast by wireless has been received on a rapidly-moving railway train; no experiments of this nature have been tried elsewhere in the world.' There was apparently a certain amount of interference, but the programme was enjoyed by all (although the journal failed to provide more details). The purpose was to test to see if 'radio vision' could be received on trains as well as radio sound programmes.[94] And so, if the BBC were unclear on the exact nature and form of a proposed service then it would inevitably proceed with care and caution.[95]

Radio was still the dominant service and, indeed, the priority for the Corporation during the late 1920s and early 1930s, and the BBC Chairman Lord Gainford's statements to both Reith and the Baird Television Company noted earlier in the chapter testify to this. The Corporation was torn between maintaining the provision of the now well-established sound broadcasting service for its valued audience and developing the new medium, the future of which was uncertain at this time and the audience for which was relatively tiny. And yet, there was undoubtedly political and commercial pressure on the BBC to pick up the television baton and run with it. As John Swift wrote in 1950:

> The BBC ... were torn between loyalty to their listeners on the one hand – they could not be expected to give up valuable air space for the minority – and on the other their now open support for television and an anxiety to keep Britain well ahead in the race for the coveted honour of being the first country to establish a public service.[96]

There were concerns within the BBC and the radio industry that television posed a threat to radio both in terms of its programming (e.g. the predicted demise of radio drama) and in terms of trade and manufacturing as evidenced by the so-called 'television scare' of 1935. A *Practical Television* editorial in early 1935 warned that a drop in radio sales might be a sign that television would ultimately displace radio as a medium of entertainment. On 6 March 1935 Ashbridge received a letter from the Bristol and West of England Radio Traders Association voicing its concern that television would render radio obsolete and noting its plans to take out a full-page advertisement in two local papers in an attempt to reassure listeners that this was not the case.[97] It is clear from files in the BBC Archives that the radio industry (in particular the Radio Manufacturers Association, the RMA) was concerned over the burst of television publicity at the beginning of 1935 as a result of the publication of the Selsdon Report. There were real fears about the impact on radio sales and concerns that radio would come to an end. A memorandum from the Acting Controller (Publicity), W. Gladstone Murray, to Reith and others on 22 January 1935 noted:

> They [the RMA] say there are signs that sales have already been arrested and that their business is threatened with paralysis, listeners generally being under the impression that they will be able before long to buy receivers which will give them visual as well as audible programmes.[98]

The RMA demanded counter-statements from the BBC to reassure the public, and so Murray prepared a statement for release:

> There is evidence of the spread of an impression amongst listeners that Television is about to be introduced suddenly, rendering obsolete the ordinary broadcast receiving apparatus. I have no knowledge of the contents of the report of the P.M.G.'s Committee on Television, presided over by Lord Selsdon, but I think that it is inconceivable that there is anything in the report that would lead to a revolutionary change in the nature of the main broadcasting service, or of methods of its reception. Whatever may be done either by the B.B.C. or elsewhere to develop Television, it is clear that the B.B.C. must continue to provide a full service of non-visual programmes for may [sic] years to come. Listeners, therefore, can continue to rely on the provision of a service which will enable them to obtain full value from their receivers.[99]

Yet the concerns of the RMA continued. On 25 March 1935, D. Grant Strachan (the Director of the RMA) wrote to J. Varley Roberts (Secretary of the Television Advisory Committee). Although, Strachan noted, it was clear that a regular high-definition television service was not imminent, there had been a slump in the sale of radio receiving sets, not only in London but 'throughout the provinces, owing to what is termed the "television scare"'. The RMA Council was reassuring the public that they could safely continue to buy present-day sets, but if it were announced that the London television service was to be started during what Strachan called 'radio season' (August–December or early in New Year) then the season's trade could be affected, with 'a consequent large increase in unemployment'.[100]

One of the overarching themes of the period covered by this chapter is that of national pride, or the 'Britishness' of television as an industry and medium. The discourse of the period highlights the ways in which the BBC was accused of not supporting British industry by not fully engaging with its development. There was also a clear sense among advocates of television that the fledgling industry in both Germany and the USA was receiving more support from both government and broadcasters in these respective countries than in Britain (this issue will be considered at the beginning of the next chapter). In a letter to the Television Committee Secretary, J. Varley Roberts, on 27 December 1934, Isaac Shoenberg mentioned a *Daily Express* statement referring to Marconi-EMI as being 'Anglo-American' and Baird as 'All-British', insinuating that somebody from Baird Television had been talking with the newspaper. He also added that, in fact, Baird was not 'All-British' and that it was 'known to everyone that the greater part of the apparatus for that system has been obtained from Germany, and that they are closely associated with British Gaumont [sic] of which the American Fox Films own 50 per cent'.[101] A related theme was the interaction, competition and debate between the BBC, the GPO, the Baird Television Company and EMI (later Marconi-EMI). There was a degree of inevitability about the government, at a time of economic depression and uncertainty, wanting to promote a fledgling British industry and 'invention' such as television. There were sound commercial reasons for doing so beyond the realm of national pride. During his interview with the Selsdon Committee, Reith was being pressured to agree that a 'British' television system (i.e. the Baird Television system) would give a 'considerable advantage' to manufacturers in Britain.[102] Yet there were also sound commercial reasons for EMI venturing into television at this time. Sales of radios and gramophones had declined during times of economic hardship, and so the company needed to invest in what had the potential to become a major player in the communications industry. This investment put EMI ahead of the game in many ways. As Briggs argues:

> The real reason why Baird was outstripped by EMI was not because EMI was a powerful Anglo-American financial combination, the kind of 'sinister' grouping that he and Moseley had painted in deep black for the benefit of the Postmaster-General, but because EMI had at its disposal the laboratory facilities for developing television which Baird lacked.[103]

One final word about programmes. In an interview with the Royal Television Society, Douglas Birkinshaw was adamant that far more mistakes would have been made – both in terms of technical issues and programme content – in the subsequent 405-line service at Alexandra Palace had the BBC not had the experience of running the 30-line service from Broadcasting House and Portland Place.[104]

As in the early days of radio at Savoy Hill, there was a good deal of excitement and energy surrounding the years of the BBC's first, experimental television service. Indeed, John Swift suggests that 'these were carefree days in that responsibility was taken lightly upon the shoulders. Mistakes mattered little. They were "experiments" … it was all rip-roaring, adventurous, pioneering fun for the programme staff.'[105] When the regular public high-definition service was launched in 1936 the pioneering spirit continued, and this is the focus of the next chapter.

Notes

1. *Television* Vol. 5, No. 55, September 1932, 243–6.
2. G. V. Dowding (ed.), *Book of Practical Television* (London: Amalgamated Press, 1935), p. 36.
3. Martin, *Sound and Vision*.
4. McLean, *Restoring Baird's Image*, pp. 183, 185.
5. BBC Oral History Collection: Mr Tony Bridgewater (filmed 26 April 1983).
6. Cyril Fletcher makes this point in relation to his experiences at Alexandra Palace in an interview with the Royal Television Society which appears on Donald F. McLean's ground-breaking CD, *The Dawn of Television Remembered – the John Logie Baird Years: 1923–1936*.
7. Gielgud, *British Radio Drama*, p. 75.
8. *BBC Yearbook 1933* (London: BBC, 1933), p. 153.
9. McLean, *Restoring Baird's Image*, pp. 205–13. A copy of the restoration can be found on McLean's *The Dawn of Television Remembered*. McLean also restored images from 1934 or 1935 of the singer Betty Bolton, which can also be seen on the disc.
10. BBC WAC L1/365: Eustace Robb.
11. Bridgewater, 'Just a Few Lines', 10.
12. BBC WAC L1/365: Eustace Robb.
13. Ibid.
14. Ibid.
15. In an interview with the Royal Television Society in 1975, John Bliss, who was seconded from radio to work on the television service in 1932, recalled that many artistes, including comedian Arthur Askey and dancer Marie Rambert, performed on the 30-line service or helped arrange performances 'for next to nothing' as a result of their friendship with Robb (RTS Archive 6/6).
16. Although he was aware, in December 1932, of rumours that the television studio would be moved in order to improve the accommodation of the service.
17. BBC WAC L1/365: Eustace Robb. That said, it would appear that Robb enjoyed a positive working relationship with the engineers on the 30-line service.
18. BBC WAC L1/365: Eustace Robb.
19. This included a memorandum on 21 June 1935 from Cock to Robb, asking him (again) whether or not he would like to join the staff of the new television service 'in a spirit of complete co-operation'.
20. BBC WAC L1/365.
21. *Radio Times*, 11 November 1932, 416.
22. *Television and Short-Wave World* Vol. 8, No. 85, March 1935, 139.
23. McLean, *Restoring Baird's Image*, p. 131.
24. BBC WAC T16/65. The licence cost £3.00 and noted that 'no public service of any kind must be afforded'.

25. Cuttings in the Marconi Archive MS1503. The company had already been experimenting with television by early 1931. In a letter to Television editor W. G. W. Mitchell on 28 January 1931, Alfred Dinsdale (who had been a keen supporter of Baird when the Television Society was launched in 1927) wrote that he was expecting a rival concern to take an interest in television and was sure that Baird was 'furious'. However, in a surprising attack on Baird, he went on: 'Baird can't expect everybody to stand around in awed silence while he fritters away time and money doing nothing' (RTS Archive Box 3 File 5. There were further attacks on the Baird Television Company in letters from Dinsdale to Mitchell on 5 July 1931).
26. BBC WAC T16/65.
27. Ibid.
28. BBC WAC T16/42/4.
29. Ibid.
30. BBC WAC R3/3/9. This view was reiterated in a meeting on 4 January between Reith and Alfred Clark, the Chairman of EMI (BBC WAC T16/65).
31. BBC WAC T16/65.
32. BBC WAC R3/3/9.
33. POST 33/3852.
34. BBC WAC T16/42/5. Baird underlined his argument in a further letter to Reith on 14 February, stating (a) that RCA had a 27 per cent share in EMI and (b) that he expected the BBC to 'explore fully the possibilities of British television before it gives any encouragement to a Company which is not entirely free of foreign domination' (POST33/3852).
35. BBC WAC T16/42/5.
36. POST 33/3852.
37. BBC WAC T16/65.
38. BBC WAC T16/42/5. The theme of Reith and the BBC not supporting British industry and a (perceived) British invention was a common one from 1926 onwards.
39. BBC WAC T16/42/5.
40. POST 33/3852.
41. BBC WAC T16/42/5.
42. Ibid.
43. Ibid.
44. BBC WAC R1/69/2.
45. BBC WAC R1/3/1.
46. BBC WAC T16/42/6.
47. POST 33/3852.
48. BBC WAC T16/42/6.
49. BBC WAC T16/42/7.
50. POST 33/5271. A further internal memorandum on 'Television' by Noel Ashbridge on 28 October stated that the BBC 'is of the opinion that

whatever programme is produced the technical limitations are such as to prevent it having true entertainment value from the point of view of a member of the general public who has little interest in the technical side' (BBC WAC T16/42/7).
51. POST 33/5271. F. W. Phillips responded to the aide-memoire noting that this was a matter for the BBC and Baird, and not the GPO.
52. POST 33/5271. On 21 March 1934, the BBC announced that the 30-line transmissions would be scaled back to twice a week, to Tuesdays 11.00–11.30 p.m. and Fridays 11.00–11.30 a.m.
53. BBC WAC T16/65.
54. BBC WAC T16/42/8. A note on the demonstration in the GPO archive notes that the Prime Minister 'congratulated Mr. Baird on the success he had attained and the very great improvement on his earlier attempts' (POST 33/3852).
55. Baird, II, pp. 537–8. Roy Hattersley argued that television development in other countries was a factor in the decision to establish a Committee of Inquiry: 'Broadcasting in Britain has always progressed by way of public inquiries stimulated by the success of foreign competition. And so it was with television' (Roy Hattersley, *Borrowed Time: The Story of Britain between the Wars* (London: Abacus, 2009), p. 248). Given developments in the USA and Germany, this may be the case. Indeed, during the evidence-gathering process, members of the Committee visited these two countries.
56. BBC WAC T16/42/8.
57. POST 33/4713 (Part 1).
58. Ibid.
59. On 22 May 1934, a new company was registered following a merger between Marconi Ltd and EMI Ltd, Marconi-EMI Television Company Ltd. Lord Inverforth was chairman of the new Board (Marconi Archive MS 325).
60. Baird Television had pressed the Committee to be permitted to offer a television service independent of the BBC.
61. Donald F. McLean, 'The Great British Broadcasting Competition: A Multi-Disciplinary Analysis of the Emergence of BBC television', *Media History* Vol. 24, No. 1 (2018), 51.
62. POST 33/4682 (Part 3). The Committee also took evidence from representatives from other companies developing television, including Scophony Ltd, Cosssor Ltd and Plew Television Ltd.
63. POST 33/4682 (Part 2).
64. Ibid.
65. BBC WAC R4/62/2.
66. BBC WAC R4/62/2. There is an interesting use of the word 'programme'. The meaning here refers to the schedule for the evening, the package of programmes which would be broadcast. However, the use also betrays a theatrical link with the way in which television was viewed.
67. RTS Archive Box 6 File 44.

68. POST 33/4713 (Part 1). Around half of the 350 members of the Society responded.
69. I suggest that by 'spectacular' the Committee was referring to stories which had a clear visual impact, given that nature of the medium. A regular BBC Television news programme did not begin until 5 July 1954, and even then there were concerns among senior BBC staff that stories for television news had to have a strong visual element for them to be deemed 'newsworthy'.
70. POST 33/4713 (Part 1).
71. Ibid.
72. *Practical Television* Vol.1, No.6 (1935), 125.
73. *Report of the Television Committee. Cmd. 4793* (London: HMSO, 1935), p. 9.
74. *Report of the Television Committee*, pp. 9–10.
75. *Ibid.*, p. 11.
76. Ibid., pp. 12–13.
77. Ibid., p. 17.
78. Ibid., p. 19.
79. Ibid., p. 25. The recommendations of the Committee were adopted by the Postmaster-General at a meeting of the Cabinet on 24 January 1935 (National Archives CAB/24/253).
80. BBC WAC R4/56/1. The Postmaster-General agreed to this last request in a letter to Selsdon on 16 January 1935.
81. *Practical Television* Vol.1, No. 7 (1935), 149.
82. *Television and Short-Wave World* Vol. 8, No. 84, February 1935, 51.
83. *The Listener*, Issue 317, 6 February 1935, 248.
84. POST 33/5489.
85. Bruce Norman, *Here's Looking at You* (London: BBC/RTS, 1984), p. 118.
86. BBC WAC T16/42/8: Television Policy (Baird).
87. POST 33/5489.
88. POST 33/5489. In a memorandum from Ashbridge to Cecil Graves, it was noted that the BBC had received only four letters complaining about the end of the 30-line service (BBC WAC T16/214/1).
89. Malcolm Baird (ed.), *Television and Me: The Memoirs of John Logie Baird* (Edinburgh: Mercat Press, 2004), p. 96.
90. Briggs II, p. 514.
91. *Daily Mirror* 6 June 1932, 9. The cartoon appeared a year after the televising of the Derby horse race in June 1931, and in the same month as Baird broadcast the 1932 Derby into the Metropole Cinema in Victoria, London.
92. *Television* Vol. 5, No. 53, July 1932, 168.
93. *Television* Vol. 5, No. 54, August 1932, 217.
94. *Television* Vol. 5, No. 49, March 1932, 26. The LNER train company had already equipped one of regular express trains 'with a wireless set, and sterilised headphone, which are hired out at a nominal fee'.
95. A series of memoranda in November 1934 (BBC WAC T16/78) underline this point. Even at this juncture, when the likelihood of a television service

being given to the BBC was becoming apparent, there was no agreement among the Corporation's executives as to what the service might comprise. One notion, for example, was that television would merely be a cinema for the home.
96. Swift, *Adventure in Vision*, p. 54.
97. BBC WAC T16/214/1.
98. BBC WAC T16/168/1.
99. Ibid.
100. POST 33/5531.
101. POST 33/5271.
102. POST 33/4682 (Part 2).
103. Briggs, II, p. 526.
104. RTS Archive Box 19 File 2.
105. Swift. *Adventure in Vision*, p. 58.

CHAPTER 6

Preparing for the High-Definition Service

This focus of this chapter is on the period leading up to the launch of the regular high-definition television public television service provided by the BBC from the studios at Alexandra Palace in north London between the beginning of November 1936 and the beginning of September 1939. The next chapter will then examine the programme output and the audience engagement with television before concluding with an assessment of some of the critical issues of the period. This chapter begins with a brief section on the state of television in other leading countries at this point, notably Germany and the USA, before considering the preparations which were being undertaken at Alexandra Palace. This included appointing staff and producing programmes for the annual Radiolympia exhibition at the end of the summer. The chapter ends with the services opening ceremony.

Developments in Germany and the USA

By the mid-1930s, television was being developed in a number of countries, including Germany, the USA and France. Just as experimental broadcasting using the Baird mechanical system had been ongoing in Britain since 1929, so in Germany and the USA experimental programmes were broadcast during the first years of the 1930s to test image quality and transmission.[1] On 22 March 1935, partly as a response to the announcement of the Selsdon Committee that a regular British television service would be authorised in the near future, the German Post Office opened a public television service in Berlin, with programmes scheduled for around two hours each weekday. The service operated on a 180-line mechanical system and programmes were broadcast not directly into people's homes but in viewing theatres or parlours (which held between 40 and 400 people) around Berlin. The reason for this was that only between 200 and 1,000 television sets were manufactured, and so this precluded any widespread individual or household ownership.² Uricchio also notes that the German authorities had decided that the 180-line service was a temporary measure while a higher-definition service was being developed. With domestic sets not being rolled out, the public would not be affected when a change came.³ A limited number of sets were made available for domestic use to party officials and ministerial appointments, but for the majority of Berlin viewers the experience of television was a communal one. Programmes consisted of the transmitting of film as well as programmes using the Intermediate Film System (IFS). Although the television transmitters were destroyed in a fire during the 1935 Radio Exhibition, by 1936 new ones had been erected.

The desire to be the first to offer a television service needs to be understood in the context of notions of national pride and international standing. Both Britain and Germany were developing television and, indeed, were discussing progress at regular intervals (as exemplified in the Selsdon Committee visits in 1934, as noted in Chapter 5, and the interest in the research work of large German companies such as Fernseh AG and Loewe). In his study of culture and modernity in Britain and Germany, Bernhard Rieger highlights the importance of technology in terms of national pride and leadership:

> Technological innovations not only underpinned the competitiveness of national economies as well as both countries' military might; a large range of artifacts [sic] also became national symbols and prestige objects that signalled international leadership in a variety of engineering disciplines.[4]

Likewise, Anne-Katrin Weber argues, in her excellent work on radio and television exhibitions in the inter-war period, that these events in Europe and the USA 'ritualized performances of national identity and the fostering of patriotic sentiments'.[5] Thus, becoming the first country to provide a public television was seen to be an essential thing at a time of international instability. Although Hickethier suggests that Germany rushed ahead with its television service, and William Uricchio argues that the regular service was indistinguishable from what other countries were describing as 'experimental' broadcasts,[6] by the summer of 1936 the German Television Service had televised the Olympic Games held in Berlin. The journal *Television and Short-Wave World* reported briefly on the televising of the Games, noting that the quality of the picture had been 'very good'.[7] In addition to the IFS, three larger iconoscope cameras were used (one of which was used as the cover photograph for *Television and Short-Wave World*), together with a Farnsworth Image Dissector Camera.

Although pre-war television in Germany never extended beyond Berlin, interest in the medium had been aroused. In August 1938, colour television in 180 lines was demonstrated at the Berlin Radio Exhibition and a new 441-line transmitter in Berlin was opened, but it was forced to close after two days due to a technical problem. By August 1939, a new television set was on show in the exhibition that would allow ordinary members of the public to see television in their homes.[8] The outbreak of war in September 1939 halted further progress.

Meanwhile, in the USA, experiments had been undertaken for a number of years by this time, primarily, but not exclusively, by the Radio Corporation of America (RCA). In a speech to the shareholders of RCA at their annual meeting on 7 May 1935, David Sarnoff, the company's president, announced confidently:

> The results attained by RCA in laboratory experiments go beyond the standards accepted for the inauguration of experimental television services in Europe. We believe that we are further advanced scientifically in this field than any other country in the world.[9]

The key word to note in Sarnoff's statement is 'laboratory'. By this point, the BBC was providing regular television programmes, albeit on low-definition 30 lines and often at unsocial hours – but they were produced in a studio and not in a laboratory. The journal *World-Radio* announced in December 1936 that progress in television on both sides of the Atlantic was, in fact, evenly matched, although the correspondent also suggested that Britain was slightly ahead because of the publicly available service. Television in the USA, of course, was being developed along the same lines at radio – that is, on a commercial basis and not within an established public service framework. To this end, *World-Radio* noted that television in the USA

> will definitely be held back until it is perfected in practically every degree before the great commercial plunge is made – this rather than it should reach the public in an uncertainly developed state that might retard its popularity and standing at the start.[10]

Sarnoff had persuaded the Russian scientist Vladimir Zworykin to establish his research laboratory within RCA by the end of 1927. During his early years at RCA, Zworykin developed his 'iconoscope' – an electronic television camera. It is no coincidence that the iconoscope formed the basis of the 'Emitron' camera that was being developed by EMI at its Hayes laboratories at this time, given the connection between the two companies (as noted in Chapter 5). RCA was experimenting with 343-line television by the mid-1930s,[11] and in the shareholders meeting in April 1936, Sarnoff announced that a new television transmitter was being erected on the Empire State Building in New York and that an experimental television station would start on 29 June 1936. At the same time he struck a conservative note, characteristic of much US rhetoric around television:

> This corporation is second to none in the scientific and technical development of television. We have gone much beyond the standards fixed elsewhere for experimental equipment. But this is a far cry from the expectations of such a service aroused by pure speculation on the subject. There is a long and difficult road ahead for those who would pioneer in the development and establishment of a public television service.[12]

The following year, Arthur Van Dyck, the Manager of the RCA License Laboratory, responded to a question about when the public would have television in a similarly conservative vein:

> We have television right *now*, under the definition of technical possibility. We will probably have it in a year or two if we limit the definition to include only those people who live within a few miles of a station, with only two or three stations in the country. However, if we mean when will a television service be available to most of the people of the country, it seems safe to say that the years between then and now will be goodly in number.[13]

Alexandra Palace

Meanwhile, in Britain, the Television Advisory Committee had decided upon a north London site for the London Television Station (see Chapter 5). Alexandra Palace, or at least the part leased by the BBC, covered a total floor space of 55,000 square feet in the south-east corner of the Palace. As John Swift stated, 'To convert that part of the Palace to something for which it was never intended was a structural undertaking of some magnitude'.[14] The halls on the lower floor would be converted into transmitter rooms, a film-viewing room, a restaurant and kitchen. The next floor up would house the studios with control rooms and rooms for the equipment. Dressing rooms and make-up rooms were also constructed, as were spaces for scenery. As a result of a decision of the Television Committee to allow both the Baird and Marconi-EMI systems to be used in providing the service, two separate studios were required, one for each system. The studio spaces were 70 feet by 30 feet and 25 feet high.[15] Studio A was the Marconi-EMI studio, soundproofed by sheets of asbestos and containing two sets of curtains for interchangeable backgrounds. Lighting was provided via a lighting bridge across the studio ceiling which could house lights similar to those used in film studios. More lights and microphones were on the studio floor, and high above the studio was the control room where the producer and sound and vision mixers worked. The Marconi-EMI telecine room for televising films was next door. Next along the corridor came the Baird Company-equipped spaces: the telecine room, the spotlight studio and scanner and then the control room, which faced the Baird studio, or Studio B. While both studios were the same size, the layout of Studio B had a large stage facing a glass-fronted room which housed the Intermediate Film Scanner.[16] There was a good deal of interest in the specialist journals, with *Television and Short-Wave World*, for example, devoting several pages to describing the studio apparatus complete with pictures and diagrams.[17]

Staff

One of the main tasks of the BBC in the period after the Selsdon Committee's report was to appoint staff to the new television service. The first in post was Gerald Cock, who was appointed Director of Television in February 1935. As discussed in Chapter 5, despite the fact that Eustace Robb led and produced the 1932–5 television service, and took the 30-line service to its limits, he was overlooked for the new role and subsequently left the BBC in 1936, despite Cock's attempts to engage him in the forthcoming new service. Cock had been a very successful Director of Outside Broadcasts and had overseen many of King George V's broadcasts. More importantly, he was an enthusiast for television and saw the potential that the new medium had to offer the BBC. However, his enthusiasm and tendency not to involve Broadcasting House-based senior staff in problems or issues when they arose often raised eyebrows and led to some tension. Reith, in particular, was concerned that Cock would act in an autonomous manner, leading a service which was geographically (and perhaps culturally) distanced from the Corporation's headquarters in central London. Following a series of interviews which Cock did with the press about television which alarmed some within the radio industry (relating to the so-called 'television scare' discussed in Chapter 5), Reith wrote to Basil Nicholls, the Controller (Administration), on 14 March 1935. He was clearly concerned about keeping the new appointee in line and asked Nicholls and Noel Ashbridge to 'pull him up periodically and see that mistaken or extravagant ideas are corrected and that he is kept on the rails and at the proper speed from the beginning'. Reith also underlined the importance of making sure that Cock was keeping everybody informed of his plans, and that he was controlled properly – otherwise Reith said he foresaw 'a lot of bother'.[18]

Matters came to a head in December 1936 when Cecil Graves met with Cock as his line manager to have a 'full and frank discussion' about his responsibilities as Director of Television. While acknowledging the difficulties in establishing a new service, Graves told Cock that he felt as though there was a 'hands off television' approach in his dealings with management at Broadcasting House. The record of the meeting also suggests that Graves was keen for Cock not to try to deal with all the problems arising in the new service on his own, but that he should call on Graves when necessary.[19] Despite a sometime difficult relationship with senior managers at the BBC, Cock was the ideal person to get television off the ground. He was ambitious, far-sighted, and driven by a desire to make television a success. Dallas Bower, a television producer appointed during the pre-war era, thought that the BBC was 'lucky' to have Cock at the helm. 'He didn't think the be-all and end-all of broadcasting was parlour games. He felt that broadcasting should do rather more than that.'[20] Cock was aware that in launching a regular high-definition service, television had stepped up a gear. While the experimental service of 1929–32 and the 30-line BBC service of 1932–5 had started to engage an audience and ignite an interest in television, the new service would require a change in emphasis and take on a clearer public service mantle.[21] Writing in *Radio Times* in October 1936, Cock stated that '[t]he medium has been created by physicists and research workers. To adapt it for the greater good of the community is a heavy responsibility.'[22]

In addition to Gerald Cock, other key appointments were made to the television staff in 1936. Cecil Madden joined the television service as Programme Organiser, having previously worked in the Talks Department and the Empire Service. In addition to having overall responsibility for the schedule, his background in the theatre and as a playwright meant that he was extremely well-connected with London's theatres. He took on the role of Variety producer and was successful in attracting a huge number of West End celebrities to Alexandra Palace during the first three years of the television service. Madden was a creative man, full of ideas about the potential of television. A handwritten A4 sheet headed 'Television Ideas' sits in his file in the BBC's Written Archives, and includes cookery lessons, boxing matches, characters from the London markets, famous detective writers, physical jerks, the Indian rope trick, goldfish and fish series and – in capital letters – chess.[23] Also in the file is a memorandum from Madden to D. H. Munro and Gerald Cock headed 'Classification of

Emitron Shots'. In a pioneering fashion, he had compiled a list of terms to use in the studio:

> Close shot/Close-up: object/part of object photographed so covers whole of screen.
> Medium shot: Scene in middle distance, photographing character so half or two-thirds of figure is shown
> Long shot: Shooting from a distance
> Full shot: complete group of people or crowded scene filling screen
> Detail shot: Photograph of some detail – a clock, telephone etc.
> Tracking/tracking shot: Movement of camera forwards or backwards to follow object in motion
> Pan/Panning: Swinging camera horizontally or vertically.[24]

Michael Barry, who joined the BBC as a drama producer in 1938, described Madden as follows: 'bird-like and with an ingenious persistence, he possessed a flair for the world of entertainment that was able to bridge the gap between all that was functional in the BBC ... and what came to be called "Show Business".'[25] Like Cock, Madden was ambitious and wanted to aim high. He deliberately placed an emphasis on entertainment and said in an interview with the Royal Television Society that he wanted to make Saturday night Variety night, thus laying down the pattern and setting the tone for a later period in television's development.[26] Throughout his time in the pre-war television service, Madden proved himself to be a tireless worker. His annual staff appraisals with Gerald Cock testify to his commitment and passion for television. Despite there being some aesthetic differences between Cock and Madden over television content (with the latter liking the variety/theatrical format more than the former), in his first report on Madden in January 1937, Cock wrote: '[Madden] has worked harder than anyone on the Television staff. While I personally do not always see eye to eye with him in matters of taste and quality, his work has been most efficient, loyal and effective.' The following year saw the same praise, together with some evidence of creative tensions between the two: 'Astonishingly avid and tireless worker and enthusiastic. Taste at times a little "New York Variety". Stubborn as a mule. Excellent with ideas. Work is his whole life. He is probably irreplaceable in these pioneer conditions, but is apt to make one scream with rage at moments!' In the final appraisal prior to the suspension of the television service, Cock wrote of Madden: 'Untiring worker, unceasing energy, some bright ideas, and a stubbornness that can drive one to drink. Unique in his way.' This stubbornness and creative tension clearly worked, however, and Madden's contribution to the success of pre-war television cannot be over-estimated.[27]

Other producers appointed in 1936 were: George More O'Ferrall (Drama; a highly-rated producer and well-liked by Gerald Cock, who admired his producing abilities and who noted that 'he is invaluable in other ways, such as dealing with artists, temperamental or otherwise, most of whom he knows well'[28]); Stephen Thomas (Music); Dallas Bower (a film sound technician, editor and director who specialised in opera and film and a person to whom Cock once referred as 'incorrigibly highbrow' in a positive way[29]); Cecil Lewis (Talks, who later developed television outside broadcasts); and D. H. Munro (who, like Cecil Lewis, transferred from Radio). Peter Bax, who had theatre design experience, was appointed as Studio Manager, and was the person in charge of television design and was assisted by Harry Pringle. Mary Allen was in charge of make-up and wardrobe and Mary Adams, the first female television producer, who went on become Head of Television Talks, was appointed in 1937 with a view to developing programmes for women. Others such as Ian Orr-Ewing (Outside Broadcasts) and Fred O'Donovan (Drama) joined in 1938 and 1939 respectively. Michael Barry also joined the television staff as Drama producer in 1938, coming from a theatre background. What is interesting about the production staff is the fact that they came from a variety of backgrounds (theatre, film, design, radio), emphasising the relationship that this new medium had with existing areas of work. This undoubtedly influenced the developing 'language' of television. Each one brought their experience with them to bear on their television work, thus making television a dynamic and exciting place to work. Engineering staff included Douglas Birkinshaw, who was Alexandra Palace's Engineer-in-charge, T. H. Bridgewater, who had previous experience of the 30-line television service, and Desmond Campbell, who became responsible for lighting in the television studios.

In addition to production and engineering staff, the BBC appointed three announcers who would appear on-screen and act as 'hosts'. Leslie Mitchell became the first male announcer at Alexandra Palace and the Corporation appointed Elizabeth Cowell and Jasmine Bligh from over one thousand applicants for the female announcer posts. It is clear that both Cowell and Bligh settled into their roles. On 10 September 1937, D. H. Munro wrote to Cowell and Bligh thanking them for their hard work in Radiolympia that year. 'In the present state of television it is extremely difficult to judge audience re-action but I have heard from many friends who are viewers excellent accounts of how attractively the announcements were put over.'[30] However, despite all three having to undertake roles which were completely new and without precedent, and all effectively being in the same boat, Mitchell appears to have been

PREPARING FOR THE HIGH-DEFINITION SERVICE   117

treated more favourably, having had experience on the stage, on film, and within the BBC's Variety Department as compère. His experience and background led him to negotiate the terms of his contract, and in the summer of 1936 to write:

> The job is a highly specialised one which can only be filled by a picked man of some considerable experience. It would be quite impossible, on my present salary, to keep up an appearance compatible with the position I will occupy. I am definitely senior, both in years and in experience of every kind, to the two ladies who will be sharing the announcing responsibilities; which presumably will mean that they will rely to a certain extent on my help in any difficulty ... it would appear that the job of Television Announcer will entail a tremendous amount of nerve strain under somewhat arduous conditions and it is essential that I should be able to live in a certain degree of comfort in my off-time.[31]

In addition to a dress allowance of £50, Mitchell was awarded an extra £50, thus giving him a salary of £450 per annum, £100 more than the salaries of Elizabeth Cowell and Jasmine Bligh, his co-announcers. After

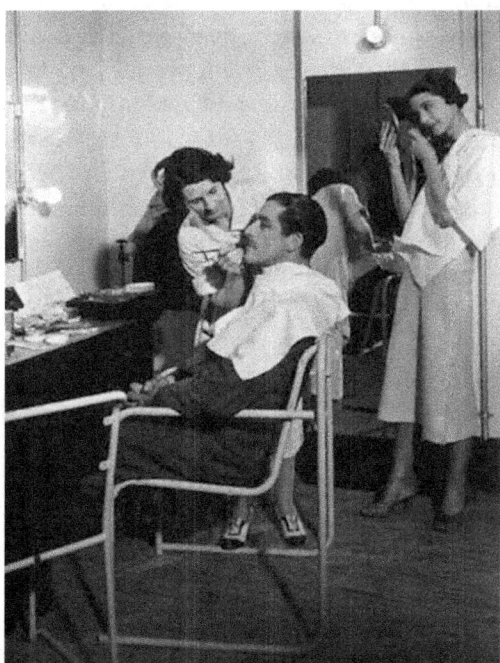

Figure 6.1 Leslie Mitchell and Elizabeth Cowell in the Alexandra Palace make-up room with Mary Allen. Reproduced by kind permission of the Alexandra Palace Television Society. Copyright unknown.

much discussion between Mitchell and Cock, Mitchell's salary was raised to £600 in April 1937.[32]

Reflecting on his experiences at Alexandra Palace, Michael Barry wrote: 'All about were men and women, intently busy and absorbed by a common purpose. They were of different ages and from a variety of social, cultural and regional backgrounds.'[33] That spirit and sense of working to make television a success – that common purpose – among the staff of the pre-war service was a key factor in ensuring that by 1939 television was ingrained in the minds of the public.

Preparing for the service

Once key staff had been appointed, a weekly meeting was established to begin to formulate the parameters of the television service, to consider how the television programmes might work, and to consider the basic grammar of television programmes. The first meeting was held on 11 November 1935 and included Gerald Cock, Leonard Schuster (responsible for television administration), Douglas Birkinshaw, D. H. Munro and the engineer Terence Macnamara. Over the months the committee met, issues of policy and guidelines were discussed. In the first meeting, for example, Birkinshaw warned that 'certain precautions in dress would have to be taken, as some dresses were considerably more revealing under television than in the ordinary way'.[34] This would inevitably have an impact on the type of clothing that could be worn in studio. Decisions on nomenclature were made at the third meeting of the committee on 25 November, and so the scanning apparatus would be known as 'the camera' and to view an artist through the apparatus would be known as 'scanning'. The final meeting of 1935 discussed vision mixing, whereby the gallery would be able to see which picture was being transmitted and which would follow it. The developing grammar of television is clear from the suggestion that it would be 'possible to fade artistically from one to the other', and by the April 1936 meeting, Munro was keen to prepare a glossary of terms to be used in television.[35]

Radiolympia 1936

The 1936 Radio Exhibition at Olympia in west London was held between 26 August and 5 September. This was an annual opportunity for the radio industry to engage the public and boost support for the wireless industry. Given the timing, there were a number of television set manufacturers who were keen to sell their sets and seven companies attended: Baird,

Cossor, Marconi-EMI, GEC, Ferranti, Ediswan and Phillips. One of the features of all sets was the extortionate pricing – between 95 guineas and 150 guineas, which put the sets way out of reach of the ordinary family at a time when the average male weekly wage was £3.00.[36] The cost of sets was a barrier to the early take-up of television and will be discussed further at the end of Chapter 7.

In mid-August, Gerald Cock gathered the television staff in the Council Chamber at Broadcasting House and allotted jobs to those assembled. After the meeting everybody made their way to Alexandra Palace in Wood Green, north London, to settle in and to use the remaining months prior to the launch familiarising themselves with their new surroundings. By the time Cecil Madden reached his office in the south-east tower at the Palace, Gerald Cock had rung and had informed him that the BBC wished to use the opportunity to demonstrate television, and so the staff had ten days in which to prepare material for the exhibition.

Radiolympia provided the BBC with an important opportunity to promote the television service. This meant that both the Baird system and the Marconi-EMI system had to be ready to broadcast programmes by 26 August. As it happened, both systems were ready in time, Marconi-EMI with two days in hand, Baird just in time for the spotlight transmitter, although the Intermediate Film System had not been tested prior to the press view at the exhibition.[37] For Baird Television, this was a huge test. Up until around 1933, the company had had no real competition in the field of television, but now the system would be on trial in a very public way, facing competition from Marconi-EMI.[38] There was, therefore, an element of risk for all involved, the BBC included. A memo from Gerald Cock to Stephen Tallents on 6 July 1936 underlined Cock's concerns about the transmissions to Radiolympia. He foresaw a number of technical and programme problems and therefore wanted to keep things relatively simple:

> I think the whole project is dangerous, and on the whole undesirable, but if it is decided to take such a serious risk, we shall of course do our utmost to make a simple but fairly attractive programme and are prepared to work night and day to do so.[39]

Noel Ashbridge, likewise, speaking on the eve of the show on the National Programme, struck a note of caution. While the purpose of the transmissions to Olympia was to test the programmes and technical apparatus, he said:

> you all know enough of scientific invention to appreciate that its development is seldom free of difficulties ... If I have seemed rather cautious in what I have said, it is because I am most anxious not to raise any false hopes. As I see it, this is an adventure

upon which the B.B.C. and the public are entering together, and for this reason we should be frank.[40]

Even Leslie Mitchell's announcements during the programmes transmitted from Alexandra Palace were clear that these were experimental demonstrations, lest potential television set buyers be put off by the rudimentary material they saw: 'We want to emphasize this, because the programme is the first of its kind, and we have not had the opportunity to attempt anything more ambitious – as yet.'[41] There was great anticipation among television enthusiasts. Test transmissions had begun on 12 August, sometimes in sound only, sometimes sound and vision, but they were sporadic and did not allow enough time for any viewers who might be watching to judge the quality. *Television and Short-Wave World* readers were told that 'zero hours' had been reached and that there was a real possibility of seeing 'real television' at the exhibition.[42]

The day before Olympia opened its doors to the public, the press were invited for a demonstration. However, the demonstration faced technical problems which were the result of an attempt to sabotage the presentation. An engineer had attempted to connect eight viewing booths with a central amplifier and in doing so caused a 7,000-volt short-circuit. On investigation, it was found that a large amount of tin foil had been placed in the plug points, thus causing the short-circuit, but the culprit was never found, although many suspected a saboteur from the radio industry.[43]

Despite the concern over the potential sabotage, the first high-definition programme went on the air from Alexandra Palace on 26 August 1936. Cecil Madden was the producer, assisted by George More O'Ferrall, and the Stage Manager was Harry Pringle. The Baird system was used on that first day, the company having won the toss of a coin to decide who should go first – but things did not get off to an illustrious start. Technical issues meant that Leslie Mitchell had to broadcast several apologies during the afternoon programme. A good deal of the afternoon session's output consisted of films and film excerpts, including Paul Rotha's documentary film *Cover to Cover*, and other British films. One item that was broadcast successfully was Helen McKay singing Ronald Hill's *Here's Looking at You*, composed especially for the exhibition. The chorus reflects some of the wonder of being able to see at a distance:

Here's looking at you
From out of the blue.
Don't make a fuss
But settle down and look at us.
Here's looking at you

It hardly seems true
That radio can let you sit and watch the show.
This wonderful age goes to show that all the world's a stage.
First you heard, now you see
And you wonder what the next thing on the list will be.
What hullabaloo!
We're peering through
To say 'How Do'
Here's looking at you![44]

The following day, 27 August, the Marconi-EMI system was used to broadcast programmes to Radiolympia. Once again a number of film excerpts were broadcast, but in addition, and thanks to the flexibility of the electronic system, the programme also included the first outside broadcast when Cecil Lewis provided commentary on the outside of Alexandra Palace with a camera on the balcony of the Palace. Cecil Madden also produced a 30-minute variety show – the world's first such television show – with The Three Admirals singing *Here's Looking at You*, the television orchestra under the baton of Hyam Greenbaum, Helen McKay, Miss Lutie and her performing horse, Pogo, and a dancing act from Chilton and Thomas. The show closed with the whole cast singing *Here's Looking at You*.[45]

The 1936 exhibition provided the BBC with a useful experience in producing attractive programming for a potential audience. As no check was made on exactly how many people saw the television demonstrations, estimated figures vary between 123,000 and 160,000 people. At least 7,000 people queued to see television on the opening day of the exhibition.[46] The total attending Radiolympia 1936 was up by 10,000 on the previous year, possibly due the added attraction of television demonstrations. There were even some viewers who saw the programmes from a converted waiting room at Waterloo Station – travellers being entertained while they waited to depart.[47]

If, on the whole, the audience reaction was positive (and the BBC's research at the event suggested that was the case), there were some areas of criticism.[48] In his review in *Television and Short-Wave World*, K. P. Hunt, strongly criticised the number and type of films broadcast. He pointed out that visitors to Radiolympia were hustled along, and so many people would have had an opportunity to look at a television screen only for a short time. 'If it so happened that they got in while that tedious book-making film was in progress, I am afraid they did not go away with a pleasant or true impression of the new television. What a pity.'[49] Grace Wyndham Goldie, the radio (and later television) columnist for *The Listener*, shared these sentiments, writing that direct (live) television was much more appealing than film. The reason she gave was that the framing of the screen was produced *for* the small television screen, whereas 'talkies' were produced for the large cinema screen and therefore looked cramped and crowded on a television set. The other impression that she took from Radiolympia was that television was directed *at* the audience – there was a degree of intimacy which made those appearing on the screen 'real'. She concluded by arguing that television would not signal the death of radio drama but the birth of something new and exciting.[50]

Following the Radiolympia broadcasts, the BBC took stock and addressed some of the technical issues that had arisen. Writing to J. Varley Roberts, Secretary of the Television Advisory Committee, on 27 August, Noel Ashbridge conceded that the transmissions had been a success, 'but it is noteworthy', he added, 'that the apparatus is hardly in a state fit for permanent transmissions'.[51] A. P. Ryan, the BBC's Assistant Controller of Public Relations, was more convinced of the attraction of television, noting a memorandum on 15 September that the main impression left on him by Radiolympia was that the public would prefer television to sound broadcasting just as they had taken to talkies rather than silent films. At the same time he recognised that there would be some time before affordable sets became available to the public on a national level and programme quality improved, and so he advised being honest with the public in all publicity surrounding television.[52] A report on the exhibition by Noel Ashbridge, Controller (Engineering), on 7 September 1936 began by stating that the demonstrations to Radiolympia had generated more valuable information than he had anticipated. In terms of the 'rival' systems used, both worked well, and both faced technical issues and breakdowns, and while the report had them reasonably evenly matched, Ashbridge did add that he had doubts about the future of the Baird Intermediate Film System. One of the main conclusions of the report was that it became clear during the exhibition that the public were not interested in film transmissions. They were not considered to be television. More interest was shown in the announcers and in conversations with Cecil Lewis, and Ashbridge concluded that 'there is no doubt that general opinion is that a good variety turn is better than an interesting film from the point of view of television'.[53] Interestingly, Ashbridge also commented on what he considered to be unfair comments about the announcers – their appearance, dress and make-up. These two observations were important ones in that they provided a base on which to develop television – from the point of view of content, but also in terms of a consideration of the exposed nature of television announcers who were at the mercy of the comments of many overly critical viewers.

On the same day, Gerald Cock sent Charles Carpendale and Cecil Graves a report on his views of Radiolympia. Many points were similar to those covered by Ashbridge. He noted that urgent attention was required to improve both systems, including the reduction of the flicker, the replacement of the Intermediate Film process in the Baird system, the speeding up of the dissolving from one camera to another (then taking 8 seconds), and the development of a satisfactory viewfinder for the Emitron camera in the Marconi-EMI system. Cock also commented on programmes on the basis of feedback from the exhibition. Programmes (apart from variety shows) should be no longer than ten minutes with an interval of five minutes between each one. One of the most important conclusions Cock drew from Radiolympia was that the notion that 'anything' would do in the early days of television, just because of the curiosity about the medium as a scientific achievement, was mistaken. This is the shift that took place, as noted by Briggs earlier. It is the shift that took television away from T. H. Bridgewater's idea that people would watch television rather than watch what was *on* television just because seeing at a distance was a scientific miracle. Cock then demonstrated his foresight and keen awareness of the future direction of television as an intimate medium:

> It is almost certain that Television will be judged entirely on its programme value in competition with other available entertainment ... it seems likely that the success of Television programmes will depend largely upon outside broadcasts, 'actuality' probably counterbalancing any deficiencies in entertainment. Pleasant informality in announcements is obviously required. Stilted, formal and impersonally delivered announcements should be avoided.[54]

Further trial transmissions for the television service took place for one hour in the morning (12.00 noon–1.00 p.m.) and one hour in the afternoon (3.00 p.m.–4.00 p.m.) from 1 October onwards.[55] This period, according to Asa Briggs, marked a shift of emphasis in the history of pre-war television. 'Hitherto almost everything had depended on techniques', he wrote. 'After Radiolympia 1936 it depended on programmes also.'[56] On 8 October, the first edition of the magazine programme *Picture Page* was broadcast for test purposes and for the trade. Edited by Cecil Madden, produced by George More O'Ferrall and hosted by the Canadian actress Joan Miller, the programme became one of the most popular and enduring of the BBC pre-war television output, and continued when the service resumed after the war. Miller would sit at a switchboard and put viewers through to various celebrity acts and artistes who would do a 'turn'. The first programme included sixteen-year-old actress Dinah Sheridan, Flora Drummond the suffragette,

124   THE EARLY YEARS OF TELEVISION AND THE BBC

Figure 6.2 Musings from *Punch*, 9 September 1936 (p. 289) after Radiolympia. Reproduced by kind permission of the Punch Cartoon Library/TopFoto.

and a busker, John Snuggs. All were interviewed by Leslie Mitchell.[57] Described by some as a television version of the popular radio series *In Town Tonight* (which began on the BBC's National Programme in 1933), it was an exciting and pioneering programme in many ways. In an interview, Miller described her experiences of working on the programme as adventurous and likened the experience to homesteading as the production team went along as everybody was trying to work out how best to make television programmes – everybody was finding their way.[58] The following day, 9 October, Cecil Lewis presented a programme of new models of British cars in conjunction with the Society of Motor Manufacturers and Traders. There was some concern in the press that this might be construed as a 'sponsored programme', contrary to the BBC's Charter, but the Corporation's Public Relations Department was relaxed about the affair. A. P. Ryan compared the programme to a book review or motoring notes in newspapers, and it passed without comment apart from a comment in the *World's Press News* the previous day.[59] Other programmes shown during the period included those on fashion and on model aeroplanes, Henry Hall and the BBC Dance Orchestra, a boxing demonstration and dancing lessons. There were also a number of documentary films shown, many produced by John Grierson. The final test transmission day was 28 October, at which point the Television Service prepared itself to launch its regular transmissions.

The opening ceremony

The BBC's regular, high-definition Television Service was launched officially on 2 November 1936. The Television Advisory Committee had been discussing who should perform the opening ceremony and the possibility of inviting the King (George VI) was mooted although the idea seems to have been dropped subsequently. Internally, the BBC's senior management had differing views on who should be invited to open the service, as this internal memorandum from 5 December 1935 to the Deputy Director-General, Charles Carpendale, demonstrates:

> D.Tel. [Director of Television] suggested obtaining Princess Elizabeth to open the official Service. C.(E) [Controller (Engineering)], C.(A) [Controller (Administration)], and C.(P) [Controller (Programmes)] joined in regarding the proposal with horror: as one person put it, it was exactly the sort of thing that you would expect Baird's to try to do if they were running Television. The feeling was that it was to some extent a prostitution of the Royal Family. D.Tel. urged the proposal on the grounds of sentimental appeal (a sob in the throat of every woman looker): from the point of view of the others, this statement was a very effective crystallisation of their objections. They felt that the Royal Family should not be dragged into it and that in any case, as things are constituted, the proposal bore an atmosphere of stunt and was undignified. C.(PR) [Controller (Public Relations)]'s feelings on the subject were not as strong as those of the other three Controllers.[60]

The Selsdon Committee had decided to require the BBC to operate both Baird (240-line) and Marconi-EMI (405-line) systems for a trial period, although it remains a mystery as to why this trial was played out in public rather than in a controlled environment prior to the launch of the service itself. As Donald F. McLean argues:

> The service that started on 2 November 1936 initially alternated between two, unproven, technically and operationally incompatible television systems, using two completely different methods of making television programmes, in an on-air competition that would have been more appropriate as an internal commercial trial.[61]

It could be that in Britain, Baird was synonymous with television. He had introduced the whole notion of television to the country and had demonstrated true television for the first time in 1926. To establish a television service without a Baird presence would have been inconceivable. The Television Advisory Committee (TAC) had decided to toss a coin to determine which system would be used for the opening week of the regular public television service. The Baird Television Company won the toss. At a meeting of TAC on 15 October, there was concern among members that Baird Television had won. Noel Ashbridge said that the spotlight system would not be appropriate for the opening ceremony and that the Intermediate Film System (IFS) had not yet proved reliable. As a result, J. Varley Roberts wrote to the Secretary of Baird Television on 16 October. He noted that TAC had received a report from the BBC on television test transmissions from Alexandra Palace, and that on the basis of the report TAC had unanimously decided that the spotlight system of transmission was 'inadequate and undesirable' for use on the opening night on 2 November. The Intermediate Film process was also considered unreliable at the time and there were doubts as to whether or not it was safe to use it for the opening ceremony. Roberts then stated that TAC wished to have demonstration of the IFS on a Baird receiver from Alexandra Palace on 26 October. After that, the committee would decide on the suitability of using Baird equipment for the opening ceremony.[62] According to Russell Burns, the tests – which included the new Baird electronic camera as well as the IFS – confirmed Ashbridge's suspicions. However, Baird Television was against the idea that its equipment would be used in a public service at a later date and therefore TAC decided to televise the opening ceremony twice, firstly on the Baird system and then on the Marconi-EMI system, in case the Baird system should fail. In a letter to Alfred Clark, the Chairman of EMI, J. Varley Roberts, the TAC Secretary, noted that Lord Selsdon, on a visit to the EMI site at

Hayes in October 1936, had received representations (possibly from EMI, although the letter is unclear) and TAC had now reconsidered the arrangements for the first week.[63] The opening ceremony, therefore, would be broadcast twice, first from the Baird studio (Studio B) and then, following a short sound-only musical interlude, from the adjacent Marconi–EMI studio (Studio A). Not having explained the full reason for the repeat performance to Marconi–EMI, Alfred Clark responded to Varley Roberts' letter, very happy with the decision.[64] At 3.00 p.m., Leslie Mitchell, sitting in the small Baird Spotlight Studio, announced the speakers, the guest entertainment and the fact that viewers who had dual receiving sets which could receive both television systems would need to switch their sets from the Baird system to the Marconi–EMI system during the interlude.[65]

As one might expect on a historic occasion such as this, a number of speeches were televised, the first by the Chairman of the BBC, R. C. Norman. In a reference to Baird and others, Norman paid tribute 'to those whose brilliant and devoted research, whose gifts of design and craftsmanship have made television possible'. A patriotic note was sounded by the Corporation's Chairman:

> The foresight which secured to this country a national system of broadcasting promises to secure for it also a flying start in the practice of television. At this moment the British Television Service is undoubtedly ahead of the rest of the world. Long may that lead be held.[66]

The Postmaster-General, Major George Tryon, opened the service officially, noting that the government was 'confident that the Corporation will devote themselves with equal energy, wisdom and zeal to developing television broadcasting in the best interest of the nation and that the future of the new service is safe in their hands'. Tryon ended, as had Norman, with a message which celebrated this British endeavour: 'I welcome the assurance that Great Britain is leading the world in the matter of television broadcasting, and, in inaugurating this new service, I confidently predict a great and successful future for it.'[67] The final speaker was Lord Selsdon, who continued the patriotic thread: 'Technically, Britain leads to-day, and we shall try ... to "keep our light so shining a little in front of the rest".'[68] Following the official opening, the audience was treated to a variety show which included the singer Adele Dixon, Buck and Bubbles (the black vaudeville act) and the BBC Television orchestra under its conductor, Hyam Greenbaum. The latest British Movietonews was also shown to a relatively small audience – figures from the Radio Manufacturers Association suggest that around four hundred television sets had been sold prior to the launch of the service.[69] Dixon's song was especially composed for the opening of the service and reflected the wonder and the magic of television, but also nodded to the domestic setting of television:

> A mighty maze of mystic, magic rays
> Is all about us in the blue,
> And in sight and sound they trace
> Living pictures out of space
> To bring a new wonder to you.
>
> The busy world before you is unfurled –
> Its songs, its tears and laughter, too.
> One by one they play their parts
> In this, the latest of the Arts
> To bring new enchantment to you.
>
> As by your fireside you sit,
> The news will flit,
> As on the silver screen.
> And just for entertaining you
> With something new
> The stars will then be seen. So …
>
> There's joy in store
> The world is at your door –
> It's here for everyone to view
> Conjured up in sound and sight
> By the magic rays of light
> That bring Television to you.[70]

Writing in the December 1936 edition of *Television and Short-Wave World*, K. P. Hunt gave an insight into how the opening ceremony had to be timed perfectly when transmitted on the Baird system. While Leslie Mitchell was finishing his announcement in the spotlight studio, the BBC Chairman, R. C. Norman, had begun his speech some thirty seconds earlier. This was due to the slight lag in the Intermediate Film System where the film was processed and developed before being broadcast. The Baird engineers did, however, have an electronic camera on stand-by should the need arise.[71]

Sir John Reith, the BBC's Director-General, had been invited to attend the ceremony, and there has been some contention as to whether or not he attended. In their biography of John Logie Baird, Antony Kamm and Malcolm Baird note that Reith was on holiday in Scotland at the time of the opening ceremony.[72] However, a report on the opening ceremony in the December 1936 edition of *Television and Short-Wave World* opens by stating that '[e]veryone at Alexandra Palace was genuinely pleased to see Sir John Reith, the B.B.C.'s Director-General at the opening ceremony'. The report goes on to say that many staff were disappointed that he had not taken an active part in the ceremony, deciding instead to sit in the audience. Interestingly, the report also argues that 'Sir John has shown a great personal interest in television since its very beginning'. There is even a suggestion that Reith mingled with staff in the Alexandra Palace canteen during the day.[73] A study of Reith's personal diary confirms that he was present at the ceremony and that, although he had been invited to take part, he had declined the offer. 'To Alexandra Palace for the television opening. I had declined to be televised or to take any part. It was a ridiculous affair ... and I was infuriated by the nigger stuff they put out. Left early ...'[74]

John Logie Baird had also been invited to attend the ceremony but had not been invited to sit with the dignitaries who were being televised. As he wrote in his memoirs:

> All the notabilities in any way connected with television appeared on the platform and were televised, all except Mr. Baird, who was not invited but sat in considerable anger and disgust in the body of the hall amongst the rank and file. Thus is pioneer work recognized ... I sat snubbed and humiliated among the audience.[75]

Although the lack of invitation may have caused consternation to Baird, he was no longer managing director of the Baird Television company. The Baird Television Company was represented by Sir Harry Greer, the company's chairman, just as Marconi-EMI were represented by the chairman, Alfred Clark, during the second ceremony from Studio A.

Surprisingly, perhaps, the Control Board meeting on 3 November, the day following the launch, made only a passing reference to television: 'The programmes of the opening day ... were discussed.'[76] The meetings of the BBC Board of Governors before and after the launch, on 28 October 1936 and 11 November respectively, failed to mention television at all. Although this might appear to be a deliberate snub to television, the fact remains that although the event is seen to be momentous from our perspective today, in a time where television has become ubiquitous and pervasive, in 1936 television was a luxury only a handful of people could afford and a minor part of the overall BBC operation. Members of the Television Advisory Committee, however, were provided with sets especially for the occasion as a cost of between £500 and £600.[77] Cecil Graves, the Controller of Programmes, met with Gerald Cock on 12 November, stating that senior staff (including Reith and the Deputy Director-General Charles Carpendale) were 'all very disappointed' with the opening ceremony, although no specific reasons were given in the note of the meeting. Graves then took some of the blame, as Cock himself was away due to illness and not present in Alexandra Palace for the ceremony.[78] He then had a word of encouragement for the Director of Television, suggesting that as this was a completely new service and that it was not bound by any former methods of presentation or formats, he could 'literally do anything he liked with it'. However, in the next breath, Graves went on to highlight five areas which he considered needed addressing in taking the television service forward in a way which could be interpreted as Broadcasting House stamping its authority on the fledgling service: a move away from film technique; avoidance of 'stupid familiarity' such as the use of Christian names by the announcers; 'the undesirability of negroid performances' when the hours of transmission were so short; the avoidance of any Americanisation in programmes; and dance music to be the very best of its kind, 'and no close-ups of crooners'. Having laid out these ground rules, Graves concluded his meeting by informing Cock that his job 'was primarily the control and training of his staff to work along the right lines and to understand B.B.C. policy', and he was to do this 'in such a way that he did not curb initiative'.[79] The zarebas to which Cock referred in his letter to Reith in August 1935 were being erected.

On 1 December 1936, some four weeks after the launch of the regular television service, the Control Board met to discuss television at length and a small but significant change of attitude can be detected from the minutes. Reith remarked that he was more impressed by television than he had expected and that it had developed more quickly than had been imagined. In true Reithian form, however, he commented that 'the service had at any rate high informative and educational potentialities even if the purely entertainment possibilities were more limited'.[80] The Corporation's Controller of Public Relations, Sir Stephen Tallents, had no doubts about the *popular* appeal of the new service:

> This appeal ... would be strongest among the less educated, who derived special advantage from the double support of sight and sound impressions. On that supposition development would be controlled by factors of cost and technique, and not by lack of public demand.[81]

Over the next three years cost, technique and public demand would all play in the development of the television service, and that is the subject of the next chapter.

Notes

1. Knut Hickethier, 'Early TV: Imagining and Realising Television' in Jonathan Bignell and Andreas Fickers (eds), *A European Television History* (Oxford: Blackwell, 2008), p. 69.
2. William Uricchio, 'Introduction to the History of German Television, 1935–1944', *Historical Journal of Film, Radio and Television* Vol.10, No. 2 (1990), 115. Nevertheless, Briggs notes that Joseph Goebbels, the German Minister of Propaganda, suggested to one of the directors of the Baird Television Company that the prospect of Hitler and himself being broadcast into every home in Germany interested him (Briggs, II, p. 540).
3. Uricchio, 'Introduction to the History of German Television, 1935–1944', 116.
4. Bernhard Rieger, *Technology and the Culture of Modernity in Britain and Germany 1890–1945* (Cambridge: Cambridge University Press, 2005), p. 224.
5. Anne-Katrin Weber, *Interwar Television Display: New Media and Exhibition Culture in Europe and the USA, 1928–1939* (Amsterdam: Amsterdam University Press, forthcoming), p. 159 (draft manuscript).
6. Uricchio, 'Introduction to the History of German Television, 1935–1944', 115.
7. *Television and Short-Wave World* Vol. 103, No. 9 (4 September 1936), 493.
8. John Swift, *Adventure in Vision*, pp. 94–5.
9. POST 33/5143.
10. *World-Radio*, 11 December 1936, 7.
11. *Television: Collected Addresses and Papers on the Future of the New Art and Its Recent Technical Developments. Volume I July 1936* (New York: RCA, 1936), p. 3.
12. *Television: Collected Addresses and Papers I*, p. 7.
13. *Television: Collected Addresses and Papers on the Future of the New Art and Its Recent Technical Developments. Volume II October 1937* (New York: RCA, 1937), p. 75. For more on the early development of American television, see Abramson, Albert, *The History of Television, 1880 to 1941* (Jefferson and London: McFarland, 1987) and Garth Jowett, 'Dangling the Dream? The Presentation of Television to the America Public, 1928–1952', *Historical Journal of Film, Radio and Television* Vol.14, No. 2 (1994), 121–45.
14. Swift, *Adventure in Vision*, p. 73.
15. MS Marconi 326: BBC Press Release, 23 August 1936.
16. Bruce Norman, *Here's Looking at You: The Story of British Television 1908–1939* (London, 1984), p. 119.
17. *Television and Short-Wave World*, October 1936, 574–82, 599.
18. BBC WAC: T16/78.
19. BBC WAC L2/40/1.
20. RTS Archive 19/4: Interview with Dallas Bower.
21. Briggs, II, p. 553.
22. *Radio Times*, 23 October 1936, 7.

23. BBC WAC S24/9: Special Collections. Cecil Madden.
24. BBC WAC S24/9.
25. Michael Barry, *From the Palace to the Grove* (London: Royal Television Society, 1992), p. 4.
26. RTS Archive T17: Interview with Cecil Madden.
27. BBC WAC L1/1, 773/1: Cecil Madden.
28. BBC WAC L1/308/1: George A. More-O'Ferrall.
29. BBC WAC L1/46/1: Dallas Bower. For more on Bower, see Wyver, John, 'Dallas Bower: A Producer for Television's Early Years, 1936–9', *Journal of British Cinema and Television* 9.1 (2012), 26–39.
30. BBC WAC L1/103/2: Elizabeth Cowell.
31. BBC WAC L1/307: Leslie Mitchell.
32. BBC WAC L1/307. Cowell and Bligh were on a salary of £350 per annum when appointed in May 1936 (BBC WAC L1/103/2).
33. Barry, *From the Palace to the Grove*, p. 37.
34. BBC WAC T16/112: Television Weekly Meeting Minutes 1935–9.
35. BBC WAC T16/112.
36. Burns, *British Television: The Formative Years*, p. 415.
37. POST 33/5536.
38. Burns, *British Television: The Formative Years*, p. 410.
39. BBC WAC T23/77/1.
40. Ibid.
41. Ibid.
42. *Television and Short-Wave World*, September 1936, 491.
43. *Television and Short-Wave World*, October 1936, 555.
44. BBC WAC S24/19/1: Special Collections. Cecil Madden.
45. BBC WAC R5/5/1: Here's Looking at You; Martin, Andrew (ed.), *Sound and Vision: Television from Alexandra Palace*.
46. Juliet Gardiner, *The Thirties: An Intimate History* (London: Harper Press, 2010), p. 431.
47. Swift, *Adventure in Vision*, p. 76; *Television and Short-Wave World*, 555.
48. See Noel Ashbridge's report in BBC WAC T23/77/2: TV Publicity.
49. *Television and Short-Wave World*, October 1936, 567.
50. *The Listener*, 9 September 1936, 470.
51. BBC WAC T23/77/2: TV Publicity.
52. BBC WAC T23/77/2.
53. Ibid.
54. Ibid.
55. BBC WAC R1/72/4: DG's report for Board Meeting (14 October 1936).
56. Briggs II, p. 533.
57. Jennifer Lewis (ed.), *Starlight Days: The Memoirs of Cecil Madden* (London: Trevor Square Publications, 2007), pp. 71–2.
58. Alexandra Palace Television Society Archive 3843: Joan Miller, Recollection of performing in Picture Page.

PREPARING FOR THE HIGH-DEFINITION SERVICE

59. BBC WAC T16/195: TV Policy. Sponsored Programmes.
60. BBC WAC T16/195.
61. McLean, 'The Great British Broadcasting Competition: A Multi-disciplinary Analysis of the Emergence of BBC Television', 60.
62. POST 33/5474: TAC correspondence with Baird Television Ltd.
63. POST 33/5533.
64. POST 33/5561: TAC Correspondence with Marconi-EMI. After the opening ceremony, the Baird and Marconi-EMI systems were used on alternate weeks until February 1937 when the Marconi-EMI system was adopted (see Chapter 7 under 'Programmes').
65. As the Baird system operated on 240 lines and the Marconi-EMI operated at a higher definition on 405 lines, some television sets had a switch which would allow viewers to move from one system to another, although these were relatively expensive and at the higher end of the market. During the trial period, which lasted from November 1936 until February 1937, viewers were reminded in *Radio Times* about which system was operating on a particular week.
66. BBC WAC T16/193: TV Policy: Opening Ceremony.
67. BBC WAC T16/193.
68. Ibid.
69. POST 33/5531.
70. <http://www.screenonline.org.uk/tv/technology/technology5.html> (last accessed 31 July 2021).
71. *Television and Short-Wave World*, December 1936, 705. The Baird Television Company had been developing an electronic camera based on American Philo T. Farnsworth's electronic camera system, but its arrival came too late in the day and it was still not in its final state at the beginning of the television service.
72. Kamm and Baird, *John Logie Baird: A life*, p. 285.
73. *Television and Short-Wave World*, December 1936, 705.
74. BBC WAC S60/5/4/4. Reith Diary, 2 November 1936. The 'nigger stuff' to which Reith disparagingly referred was Buck and Bubbles, a vaudeville act who were the first black performers on British television.
75. Malcolm Baird (ed.), *Television and Me: The Memoirs of John Logie Baird* (Edinburgh: Mercat Press, 2004), p. 124.
76. BBC WAC R3/3/11: Control Board Minutes 1936.
77. POST 33/5489: TAC Reports.
78. BBC WAC L2/40/1. Referring back to Kamm and Baird's statement that Reith was not at the opening ceremony – might this be the reason for the error?
79. BBC WAC L2/40/1.
80. BBC WAC R3/3/11.
81. Ibid.

CHAPTER 7

The BBC Television Service, 1936–1939

The trial period

Television programmes were broadcast between 3.00 p.m. and 4.00 p.m. in the afternoon and between 9.00 and 10.00 p.m. every weekday and Saturday and could be seen within a 25-mile radius of the Alexandra Palace transmitter.[1] Following the recommendation of the Selsdon Committee, the BBC was obliged to use both the Baird Television system and the Marconi-EMI system to broadcast programmes for a trial period. Edward Pawley's detailed account of BBC engineering history provides useful descriptions of both studios and systems:

> In [the Baird] studio one camera was placed near the side wall, bolted to the floor and quite immobile. This took a picture of the scene on film, which was immediately developed, fixed and very briefly washed. While still wet, the film was put into the disc scanning device ... in which the television signals were generated. The most rapid processing methods were used, and the operation took 64 seconds; this intermediate film system was the only way of transmitting a large studio scene on the Baird system. The camera was a 17.5mm Vinten film camera using 35mm film installed in a glazed enclosure so as to prevent pick-up of camera noise by the studio microphone. The fact that the camera could not follow the artists was a serious limitation, because the movement of artists had to be subservient to the camera rather than vice versa.[2]

In addition, the Baird Spotlight studio was used to broadcast 'live' (without the 64-second delay). This depended on a moving spot of light much like in the old 30-line system and could be used for announcements and smaller-scale scenes. The studio was kept in complete darkness and those using it had to wear blue-green make-up to counter the sensitivity of the photo-electric cells.[3] One area in which the Baird system excelled was in telecine, the televising of films which, although transmitted on 240-lines (as opposed to Marconi-EMI's higher definition 405-lines), were considered better-quality.[4]

Figure 7.1 Studio B – the Baird Studio – in Alexandra Palace, showing the intermediate film scanner (left), August 1936. BBC Copyright.

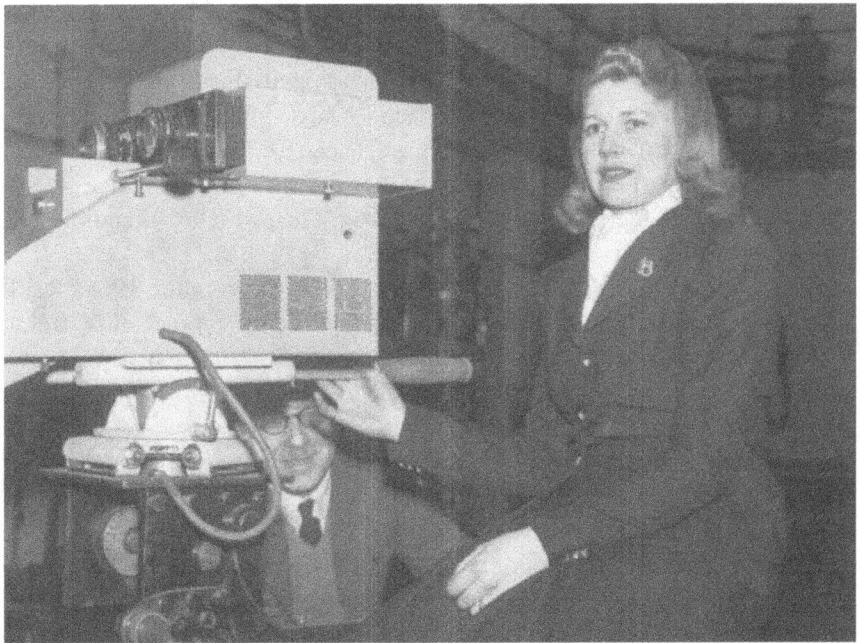

Figure 7.2 Jasmine Bligh with an Emitron camera at Alexandra Palace. Reproduced by kind permission of the Alexandra Palace Television Society. Copyright unknown.

The Marconi-EMI studio 'conformed much more closely to operational needs', according to Pawley. 'There were three all-electronic cameras ... which could easily be moved around the studio.' However, one disadvantage was that the camera operator could not tell whether or not the picture was in focus, the only way to tell being to open the side of the camera and use a port-hole. This was not conducive to studio work and therefore it was not long before an optical viewfinder linked to the main lens was added. 'The three cameras were moved in accordance with the plan of the production, close-ups and long shots could be taken and fading between the various cameras could be done ...' Pawley concluded his assessment of the studios thus: 'The EMI studio thus provided much greater scope for studio productions than the Baird studio, and the EMI system could be applied to outside broadcasts.'[5] It was clear from the outset, therefore, that the Marconi-EMI studio offered producers and artists a great deal more flexibility. From the announcers' and performers' point of view, the Baird studio presented a number of problems. Elizabeth Cowell recalled the bright light of the spotlight studio 'boring into your brain' in the otherwise darkened room, and having her ribs poked by a studio attendant out of shot: once for a smile, and twice to speak.[6] Leslie Mitchell likewise had to suffer being poked in the ribs while sitting on a high stool in front of a bright flickering light in the spotlight studio with no idea whether what he was saying was being broadcast.[7] Cecil Madden would have difficulty getting artists to appear in front of the Baird system due to its inflexibility, and Alan Bray, one of the engineering staff, whose job it was to ensure that the equipment ran smoothly, was just as frustrated: 'I was absolutely staggered when I saw the Baird system, because it didn't have a chance – not a single solitary chance against these other cameras, which you could move about, and the quality wasn't very good.'[8]

In his report to the Board of Governors in November 1936, Reith noted that the Marconi-EMI system was producing good results, which included some outside broadcast programmes. The Baird system results were 'very variable', on the other hand, and while transmissions of films had yielded positive results, live televising was 'most unsatisfactory'. He did add, however, that the Baird studio was now getting some good results with the electronic camera that Baird Television had been developing.[9] The nail in the coffin for the Baird system came on 9 December 1936. The Director of Television, Gerald Cock, published a report on the experience of transmitting on both systems between 2 November and 9 December. In summarising the Marconi-EMI system, Cock highlighted the convenience and reliability of the studio set-up, which had 'established a large measure of confidence in producers, artists and technicians'. In addition, outside broadcasts and multi-camera productions had added to the attraction of the programmes. Concluding his summary of the system Cock reported that 'with improved lighting, additional staff and studio accommodation, single system working by Marconi-EMI would make a service of general and entertainment interest immediately possible'.[10] The summary of the Baird system was in complete contrast:

> Alterations in apparatus are constantly taking place. Breakdowns, with little or no warning, and, even more serious, sudden, unexpected, and abnormal distortions are a frequent experience. In such cases, it is difficult and embarrassing to make a decision to close down, since there is always the possibility that faults may be corrected within a short time.[11]

Given that the Baird system used what Cock called 'four sub-systems' – the spotlight scanner, the intermediate film system (IFS), the electron camera, and the telecine scanner for film transmission – there were additional problems as the first three had different lighting and make-up requirements. Referring specifically to the IFS, Cock noted that the transmission delay created problems for presentation and production, and the fact that the film reels lasted only sixteen minutes created further problems for programme production. The electron camera being developed by Baird Television was, Cock added, showing more promise, but he posited that the fire at the Crystal Palace research laboratories of the company would set any further developments back considerably.

In coming to a recommendation for the Television Advisory Committee as he was required to do, Cock had to weigh up a number of technical issues. At the end of his report, he added a further consideration: 'It is logical to anticipate from present indications', he suggested, 'that artists and celebrities may quite likely refuse to appear in Baird programmes, thus making still more difficult the problem of programme building.' He finished by arguing that the future of television now 'depends on a decision in favour of single system working, in conditions that permit of picture quality, production facilities, flexibility and reliability, such as are available by the Marconi-EMI system'.[12]

Reith's report to the meeting of the Board of Governors on 9 December also helped to seal the fate of the Baird system:

> It can be fairly said that the Marconi-E. M. I. apparatus gives a degree of reliability and performance which is satisfactory for a programme performance ... [T]he same cannot be said of the Baird system. Its reliability is poor, and the average result obtained very indifferent, with the exception of the film apparatus. On certain occasions, the Intermediate Film Apparatus has given good results, but this is the

exception rather than the rule, while the flicker – which as far as one can see must always be present until the frame frequency is changed – becomes more and more irritating as time goes on.[13]

On 12 January 1937, the Television Advisory Committee, on the basis of Cock's report, agreed unanimously that the future of television lay with the Marconi-EMI system. A note on 13 January to the Postmaster-General, who had the authority to make the final decision on behalf of the government, underlined the very serious nature of the decision. It also noted that the Baird Television Company acquiesced in the proposal decision 'without serious protest and seem to take a practical interest only in the questions of the manufacture of receiving apparatus'.[14] A notice to the press on 4 February announced the Postmaster-General's decision. There was also a statement noting that the standards adopted (i.e. 405-line television) would not be altered for at least two years, presumably to reassure potential viewers and to encourage the purchase of television sets.

The decision to continue with the one television standard elicited a mixed reaction among staff. Producer D. H. Munro referred to the Baird system as 'the biggest headache' and 'heaved a great sigh of relief when it was finally decided that Baird would go',[15] although Jasmine Bligh felt some sadness when Studio A eventually closed.[16] Although the BBC ceased using the Baird system in February 1937, it was not until the summer that year that it had the opportunity to carry out reconstruction work on the studios. In order to do this, studio-based programmes were suspended for three weeks from 26 July and staff given a 'much needed holiday'.[17] In fact, Studio B was not in full use as a second Marconi-EMI studio until autumn 1938.

A number of communications historians, such as John Bray, have argued that Baird was 'doomed to ultimate failure' due to his reliance on, and adherence to, mechanical methods of scanning the picture.[18] Referring to the decision in 1937 to drop the Baird system in favour of the Marconi-EMI system, Bray argues that

> it is natural to have every sympathy with John Logie Baird who laboured unceasingly for many years, often in poverty and ill health – but it became clear that the mechanical scanning system had reached a peak of development and had no future.[19]

Yet, it was Baird, in Britain at least, who raised public awareness of the *possibilities* of television and – through the conduit of the GPO – managed to persuade the BBC to take television seriously. Realising that his own advances to the BBC were falling on deaf ears, he played the patriotic card with the Postmaster-General, and secured a measure of co-operation with the BBC. He was a consummate experimenter and entrepreneur, but possibly lacking in a keen business sense.

Programmes

In an article published in 2004 exploring the pre-war television service, Neil Robson argued that 'the short-lived experiment, lasting less than three years up to 1939, completely failed to achieve its potential ... the broadcast fare stayed solidly middle-brow and numbingly worthy.'[20] I hope to show over the following pages that this was not the case and that the range of programming during the 1936–9 period was extensive, both within the confines of the studio and in terms of outside broadcasts. Although none of the pre-war programmes exist – all were broadcast live with no technology to record them at the time – there is some evidence of the type and form of programming. Desmond Campbell, of the engineering staff at Alexandra Palace, recorded behind-the-scenes footage in 1938, which gives an insight into programmes and programme-making in the early years.[21] Although Robson acknowledged the contribution of the early television producers in establishing production techniques that provided a foundation for the post-war television service, he contended that by mid-1939 the service was 'virtually dead in the water ... and cold shouldered by an indifferent public with its mind on other matters. Its sudden closure turned what should have been the success of the age into a passing curiosity.'[22] Again, I aim to show that this was not the case and that there were calls from the public and politicians during this period for the television service to be extended beyond London and that the plans that were in place to do this would have been realised had war not broken out in September 1939.

The defining characteristics of the 1936–9 television service were the emergence of a variety of programme formats or genres, the development and adoption of a television 'language', the establishment of television as a domestic and therefore intimate medium, and a pioneering spirit that allowed producers and artists the creative freedom to experiment and test the boundaries of the medium. Early critical reactions to television can be found in *The Listener*, the BBC's weekly magazine. In November 1936, the psychologist Professor T. H. Pear considered what television might offer the public and came to the conclusion that immediacy and actuality were two its strengths, as were friendliness and intimacy.[23] The following month, Ernest H. Robinson wrote about television's past and present and suggested that television's greatest potential was in programmes which combined both entertainment and education, citing programmes on zoo animals and ballet as examples.[24] In June 1937, the broadcasting critic of the magazine, Grace Wyndham Goldie, welcomed television not only as a medium for 'day-to-day entertainment', but as a medium which provided a direct relationship with the person in front of the camera – an intimacy not felt in the cinema.[25] Television during this period also developed a clearer sense of purpose. By August 1937, *The Listener* pointed to one of the key strengths of television, 'its ability to present viewers with a picture of current events while they actually take place', pointing to the Coronation, the Wimbledon Tennis Championships and the Davis Cup as recent examples.[26]

Television staff were also becoming more aware of what (or who) would, and would not, work on the small screen in visual terms particularly. A series of memoranda in September 1936 prior to the official launch highlight this. Cecil Lewis, the producer responsible for talks on television, had asked colleagues for recommendations for potential speakers on the new service. Lewis was looking for speakers who were already radio personalities, who could be trusted in front of the microphone, and would talk fluently. He also stressed that while he would welcome suggestions for those who could talk on 'serious' topics, he wanted to keep them 'on the more popular human side' at the outset.[27] Among the suggestions received were: a social psychologist who looked 'about as black and sinister as the devil himself'; a Romanian-born man with a bushy red beard and lots of personality; an attractive speaker who was 'pleasant to look at'; an excellent speaker on economics, although the memo noted that 'his appearance is against him'; and an ex-miner who, despite having 'a very slight Welsh intonation', had 'a satisfying "British workman" appearance'.[28] Janet Quigley, the radio producer with responsibility for talks for women, had two suggestions: Mrs Daisy Pain, the laundress, whom Quigley considered would be ideal for television. Being 'buxom and comely she would look so entirely convincing and attractive if televised', and laundry work, in particular ironing, was 'obviously one of the subjects calling for illustration'. The second suggestion was Mrs Rama Rau, who 'would look extremely effective sitting telling one of the Indian legends that she says Indian mothers tell their children'.[29] What is clear from these articles and from these internal memoranda is that television in the 1936–9 period was creating for itself a clear sense of identity and was laying a firm foundation for the future.

Drama

Drama in the pre-war television service was a mainstay of the schedules, be that excerpts, original plays, adaptations for the studio, or full-length plays direct from the West End of London. Programme Organiser Cecil

Madden had a clear vision for the new service: 'Planning the television schedule there was never any doubt in my mind that the emphasis should be on drama.'[30] This might appear strange for a medium that was beginning to form itself around the notions of immediacy and actuality (see above), but I believe that the other defining characteristic of television that was now emerging – intimacy – played into what Jason Jacobs termed the 'aesthetic and stylistic thinking' around television drama at this time.[31] In all, 326 plays (excluding repeats) or parts thereof were televised between 1936 and 1939, fourteen of which were original plays for television.[32] During the three years of the service, the team of drama producers increased to eleven, including Madden, George More O'Ferrall, Jan Bussell, Dallas Bower, Royston Morley, Denis Johnston and Michael Barry. Actors who appeared on screen during the pre-war service included Greer Garson, Trevor Howard, Sybil Thorndike, Laurence Olivier, Michael Redgrave, Peggy Ashcroft, Ralph Richardson and Anthony Quayle. According to John Wyver, the first television drama on the high-definition service was broadcast on 19 October 1936 during the test transmission period which preceded the launch of the service on 2 November. Scenes from T. S. Eliot's *Murder in the Cathedral* were broadcast and the production returned to Alexandra Palace before the end of the year.[33] It was during the December production of Eliot's play that symbolic effects were first put to use in the studio, having the temptations appear as ghosts and whispering into Becket's ear by means of positioning and 'double takes'.[34] The first television drama which was broadcast after the opening of the service was the Scottish comedy *Marigold*, and extracts from the play were performed in the Baird studio on the evening of Friday, 6 November.

On 8 July 1937, George More O'Ferrall produced George Bernard Shaw's *How He Lied to Her Husband*. Shaw himself visited Alexandra Palace to watch the play go out live at just after 3.30 p.m. He then agreed to be televised and gave a commentary on his play (not one of his best, he admitted) before meeting the cast (Greer Garson, Derek Williams and D. A. Clarke-Smith) and staying for tea. As was the norm, the play was repeated that evening, without the playwright being present. Drama was also a suitable vehicle for undertaking the BBC's public service remit. Within the eclectic mix of drama production in the pre-war period, there was opportunity for producers such as George More O'Ferrall and Dallas Bower to experiment. More O'Ferrall wrote a lengthy article on televising drama in the 'Television Supplement' of *Radio Times* on 19 March 1937. He argued that film techniques should not dominate television drama and that although the television producer's work was closely aligned to that of a film director, the producer also required a knowledge of theatre.[35]

John Caughie has argued: 'Within the BBC's mission of cultural improvement drama lent prestige. In the pre-war years, its limited audience gave television drama the freedom to experiment with some of the cutting-edge modernist dramas of the interwar years.'[36] More O'Ferrall was responsible for producing the November 1937 production of R. C. Sheriff's *Journey's End*. Grace Wyndham Goldie was bowled over by the production. Writing in her column in *The Listener*, she extolled the virtues of the play and the producer: 'Let me say first that technically this was amazing, a colossal success. It is far the most ambitious dramatic production television has so far attempted ... Mr More O'Ferrall, the producer, deserves every kind of congratulation.' One of the major developments was the combining of live studio with pre-filmed excerpts, a technique which had not been attempted up until then. Interestingly, however, while praising the production on the one hand, Goldie did suggest that the play veered towards the cinematic at the expense of the intimate, a characteristic of television of which she was so fond.[37] *Journey's End* was also mentioned in Reith's report to the Board of Governors in December 1937. It was the first play to be televised anywhere close to full length, a full hour and twenty minutes despite the script being cut. The cast were mostly actors who had played the parts in stage productions and viewers' comments suggested that an hour and twenty minutes was not too long for sustained viewing.[38] Dallas Bower was a producer who embraced the contemporary European modernist tradition, being a regular at Film Society screenings in London.[39] Those filmic influences also impacted on the way he approached television studio production – he wanted to operate as a film studio rather than as a theatre.[40] One of his most daring productions was that of *Julius Caesar*, which was broadcast on the evening of 24 July 1938. Adapted by Bower, the drama was performed by actors in modern dress.

J. B. Priestley's *When We Are Married* was the first play to be televised from a theatre during an actual performance. According to the producer, Basil Dean, 'there was quite a fuss over the preparations that had to be made beforehand'.[41] A large television van was 'anchored' in front of St Martin's Theatre, 'from which an assortment of cables emerged to festoon the passages and gangways' and a number of seats in the stalls were removed and 'runways' for the cameras were built in their place.[42] Interestingly, the play's dialogue had to be cut to fit the BBC programme and the grouping of the characters had to be altered to allow for the restricted movement of the cameras. In addition, as Dean noted in his autobiography, the powerful studio lights completely destroyed the stage lighting. As the televising would cause inconvenience to theatre-goers, special ticket prices of 5s and 2s 6d were released as a concession. At the same time, television's capacity for publicising the event was utilised by the theatre and Dean: 'Following the brief appearance on the screen at Alexandra Palace of one or two of the artistes as a useful "trailer", we managed to secure a full house.'[43] It was clearly a nervous time for Basil Dean and the production team, as he noted that a special screen was put up at the back of the dress circle where J. B. Priestley and Dean 'spent [our] time hovering between drinks and audience to "double watch" the proceedings'.[44] Dean did not think that the televising of the play necessarily helped the theatre run as performances were selling out anyway. 'Moreover, at that early stage of development television aroused only limited curiosity, and gave small sign of the world-wide influence it was destined to become.'[45] However, a number of BBC staff wrote to him to offer congratulations and it was clear to Dean that this 'first' was a big success.[46]

As in many other aspects of television production in this period, Cecil Madden was the driving force behind television drama. Madden's connections with the West End certainly proved useful in the early days when television was finding its feet, not only for dramatic productions but for variety and cabaret also. However, by 1938, it was becoming costly and almost untenable for the television service, not least because of the rehearsal time needed for plays, or extracts of plays, being transferred to the television studio.[47] One of Madden's major contributions was the establishment of the Sunday Night Play. The BBC had introduced an extra hour to the evening viewing on Sundays in April 1938,[48] and according to Madden, Broadcasting House would have liked television to have followed the radio pattern on a Sunday evening of 'bits and pieces', or a mixed programme. 'I was sure a solid wedge of dramatic material was needed', wrote Madden, and with the support of Gerald Cock, he began the strand. In an interesting move, Madden invited the Birmingham Repertory Theatre to come to London on the third Sunday in every month to be televised that evening:

> Our television producer studied the play in the theatre, went to Birmingham for some time in advance, rehearsing his new moves for the cameras with the artists on their own stage, then on a Sunday at crack of dawn a coach started for London from Birmingham's Station Street. The scenery had been reconstructed in advance in our workshops. The actors rehearsed all day in the studio, performed the play about 9.30pm and then, late at night, the coach rolled back to Birmingham.[49]

Outside broadcasts

Once the BBC was operating on a single standard, it began to take the cameras out of the studio. One of the first major outside broadcasts for the

BBC – and one of its biggest tests to date – was the Coronation of King George VI and Queen Elizabeth on 12 May 1937. It is clear from files in the BBC Written Archives that television producer Cecil Lewis had some ambitious plans for the Coronation. In a memo to Gerald Cock on 5 November 1936 he noted: 'It is too big a chance to miss and we can do an immense range of things which sound broadcasting cannot touch.' Lewis wanted the go-ahead from Cock to proceed with his plans (the locations of cameras, commentators, etc. – although the files do not give details). Cock replied in pencil on memo, 'OK', and added 'With restraint, not <u>too</u> much' [original underline]. Cecil Madden passed Cock's reply on, adding that Lewis might like to collaborate with Dallas Bower – as a ceremony such as this was 'up his street' and more than one person could tackle. He also added in the side-lines: 'Some great ideas here.'[50] In a separate memorandum, again dated 5 November 1936, Lewis suggested a series of programmes in the period leading up to the Coronation Day itself, 'to give some idea of the enormous tradition and background of the British Empire'. These plans included a programme of ship models (to represent the Navy, the Army and the Air Force); models and travelogue-type films of the Overseas Dominions; models of the Crown Jewels; and the uniforms which would be worn on the day. Lewis also wanted to get in touch with various government departments for assistance.[51]

Prior to the ceremony, the television service contacted the Radio news editor to request a news item in the evening news bulletin on the eve of the Coronation. 'This will be the first occasion in any country on which members of the public, sitting in their own homes, will be able to watch part of a great national ceremony', read the statement.[52] The television service produced a number of special programmes on the week of the Coronation, including a talk from Gerald Cock in the afternoon and evening of 11 May, explaining to viewers what the BBC's plans were for televising the event the following day. *Music Hall Cavalcade* was broadcast on the evening of 12 May and the Poet Laureate, John Masefield, ended the day with his Coronation Ode. On Coronation Day itself, three Emitron cameras were in action, two on a special platform at Apsley gate fitted with telephoto lenses, and one on the pavement to the north of the gate to give close-up shots of the Royal coach. Freddie Grisewood, who had joined the BBC as an announcer in 1929, had been chosen to be television's first outside broadcast commentator. The procession was televised between 2.00 and 3.00 p.m., but as the Royal carriage came into sight of the television camera at Hyde Park Corner, the television equipment failed. It is said that one of the engineers in the mobile television unit (which had only been received by the BBC two days previously)

Figure 7.3 An Emitron camera being set up by the mobile television unit at Apsley Gate, Hyde Park Corner, in preparation for the Coronation procession in May 1937. BBC Copyright.

kicked the equipment and it sprang back to life just in time. One of the highlights was when the King turned to look at the television camera as the carriage passed, giving the appearance to those watching that the King had looked directly at them.[53] The quality of the pictures on the day was excellent in London and beyond, with letters of congratulations being received by the BBC from Ipswich, Bedford and Cambridge.[54] L. Marsland Gander, the Radio Correspondent of the *Daily Telegraph*, estimated that 30,000 people had watched the Coronation from homes, in shops and in cinemas. Although the bad weather had marred the picture from time to time, Gander enthused that 'the Coronation procession marched into London homes on the television screen yesterday' and called the day 'the supreme triumph of television to date'.[55]

Another major outside broadcast took place in November 1937 when the BBC televised the Lord Mayor's show and the Cenotaph Service the following day. A radio news bulletin on the Sunday summarised the day:

> For the first time this year television widened still further the circle of countless numbers which broadcasting has enabled to share in the Cenotaph ceremony. The weather was perfect for the enterprise – a sky with white clouds sailing past and no

blinding sun to spoil the shots of Big Ben as the hands drew nearer to eleven o'clock. These pictures were interspersed with views of the waiting crowds in Whitehall – until the solemn occasion reached its climax for the new art to broadcast. The Chief Engineer of the B.B.C., Sir Noel Ashbridge, told afterwards how the occasion had been a great landmark in the development of television. The cameras, he said, were extremely well-placed, the production cleverly carried out, and the result 'enormously impressive'.[56]

The review of the coverage in *The Listener* highlighted one of the key strengths of television at the time – the televising of live events as they happen:

> When all is said and done, outside events are what really matter in television. However skilful Alexandra Palace's production of drama, however fascinating those studio programmes ... however lighthearted the interludes of variety and revue, all these things can be done elsewhere ... at the Cenotaph television maintained a smooth and dignified steadiness of vision, turning its gaze only occasionally to Big Ben to watch the passing of the minutes before the eleventh hour ...[57]

The BBC made use of the grounds of Alexandra Palace, televising golf lessons, women's health and beauty programmes, and gardening programmes with the popular C. H. Middleton. The garden was made especially for the television service (the forerunner of the famous *Blue Peter* garden, possibly?) and was a plot of 60 by 52 feet.[58] The addition of a second mobile unit in the summer of 1938 meant that even more outside broadcasts were possible, including a number of sporting events (see below), Trooping the Colour, the Chelsea Flower Show, zoo visits (Regent's Park Zoo in London was a firm favourite), film-making at Pinewood Studios, yacht racing, and the Ideal Home Exhibition at Olympia. Viewers also saw Prime Minister Neville Chamberlain arrive at Heston Airport on 30 September at 5.30 p.m. on his return from visiting Hitler in Munich. Commentary was provided for television by Freddie Grisewood, but viewers also heard Richard Dimbleby's commentary for the National Programme. Interestingly, the event led to Cock issuing a reminder to staff to take care during outside broadcasts. He was concerned that the private remarks of the Prime Minister had been picked up by the microphone and televised; indeed the commentator had stopped commentating specifically for this reason. Cock demanded that the practice stop.[59]

Sport

Richard Haynes, in his detailed study of the formative decades of sport on BBC Television, argued that sport enjoyed a boom period in the 1930s and that spectator sports, in particular, grew in popularity during the 1920s and 1930s (although the economic crisis did result in some sports struggling).[60] Given that horse racing was particularly popular during the inter-war years, Haynes suggests that this might have been the reason for the 1931 Derby having had the honour of being the first televised sporting event. As noted in Chapter 4, Baird Television Ltd televised the Derby that year, and the following year relayed it to the Metropole Theatre in London. These events showed that television, even in its experimental phase, had the capacity to capture live sport.[61] When the BBC's own 30-line television service was operating from Studio BB in Broadcasting House, Eustace Robb arranged for a boxing match to be televised in August 1933.

The first sporting event of the high-definition service took place on the evening of 4 February 1937 – a boxing match between England's F. J. Simpson and L. Bosham from Ireland (replacing T. Bonham, who did not appear) held in the Alexandra Palace Concert Hall, adjacent to the television studios. Purely coincidentally, a programme the following afternoon was entitled *First Aid 3: Accidents in Sports*.[62] The purchase of a mobile outside broadcast unit for the Coronation in May 1937 led to benefits in other areas of television coverage, including sports. In June 1937, BBC Television broadcast from the Wimbledon Tennis Championships for the first time. In a review of coverage in *The Listener*, the television coverage was compared very favourably to the newsreel coverage with which most viewers were familiar. The close-up shots were commended, in particular those of the player serving, the scoreboard, or Queen Mary entering the Royal Box.[63] The review also noted how television commentators spoke less and allowed the images to speak for themselves. The only criticism of coverage was that there was not enough of it! Reith reported back to the Board of Governors on this major step forward in outside broadcasting of sport on 14 July. In general the results were good. Some difficulty had been encountered at the start of Wimbledon, however. There had been a great deal of interference at Alexandra Palace from a hospital in Hornsey, north London, specialising in diathermy, and as a result the Control Board agreed to purchase screening material (as a cost of £200–£300) for the hospital to eliminate interference with the wireless link reception.[64] Two cameras were used at Wimbledon, one from the stand giving a long shot of whole court, and one from the commentators' stand with a telephoto lens giving close-up shots of players in action. Press comment had been positive and had noted the considerable public interest in the programmes from Wimbledon, highlighting how television could bring events directly into viewers' homes 'without time lag' (unlike filmed newsreels).[65]

Other major sporting events covered by the 1936–9 television service included the annual Boat Race between Oxford and Cambridge. A technical issue with television sound marred the 1938 event, but viewers saw the end of the race with commentary from the National Programme.[66] Test Match cricket was also televised although the Programme Board was less than impressed with Captain Wakelam's commentaries for television, which, unlike Howard Marshall's commentary for radio, 'were felt to show a lack of understanding of what was required for viewers'.[67] These were early days and there were no rule books to follow. In many ways, early television sports commentators had to make it up as they went along.

Not all was plain sailing in televising sporting events. In 1938, the directors of the Epsom Grand Stand Association refused to allow the Derby to be televised. On 29 March, Reith wrote to the Chairman of the association using an interesting argument around national identity and pride. No other country, Reith argued, was providing a television service directly to people's homes and there were hopes that a television industry that was of 'great national value' might develop. The BBC was not just providing an entertainment service but was, according to Reith, 'the trustees of a national interest of great potential importance'. In addition, televising the Derby would attract worldwide interest and would draw attention to the British television industry. The Association was concerned that, if the Derby were televised, the numbers attending it would decline. Reith reassured the Chairman that in fact, experience had suggested that televising or broadcasting an event enhanced interest and stimulated attendance.[68] In mid-April, the *World Radio* journal confirmed that televising of the Derby would go ahead and that the FA Cup Final at Wembley would be televised on 30 April for the first time.[69]

Variety and other programmes

By 1938, 30 per cent of studio time at Alexandra Palace was spent on cabaret, Variety and light entertainment programmes.[70] As noted previously, there was a ready supply of material to fill the schedule, primarily from the West End, but from other sources too. *Picture Page* hosted 1,855 items during its three-year run prior to the Second World War and prompted television critic Grace Wyndham Goldie to write: 'It is, in fact, a kind of high speed television circus. It exploits these things of which television is master.'[71] Cookery programmes also found their place in the schedule, with cooks such as Moira Meighn and Marcel Boulestin becoming familiar faces to viewers. There was even an opportunity to watch a programme at 3.00 p.m. on Christmas Day 1936 when B. J. Hulbert demonstrated how to carve a turkey.[72] It was producers of light entertainment, cabaret and variety programmes which received the most memoranda relating to standards. On 16 December 1936, Cock wrote to television producers asking them to avoid satirical verbal references to, or lampoons in cartoon form of, celebrities, particularly foreign heads of state. One political cartoonist had gone too far in lampooning Hitler and the practice was to end.[73] April and May 1937 saw a flurry of memoranda, which highlighted concerns in Broadcasting House that Alexandra Palace did not adhere to the same moral code as central London. On 1 April 1937 a memo was sent from the Director of Administration to the Controller (Administration) on the subject of alcohol at Alexandra Palace:

> there is apparently a tendency on the part of television artists to look upon our dressing rooms there in the same way as they do a theatrical dressing room, i.e., a place where they can with impunity take drinks. Schuster [Television Service administrator] is doing all that he can to stamp out this practice and the producers up there, who have in the past been rather lax and joined in the revelry from time to time, are also being instructed.

The fear was that such behaviour could get out of hand, spread to Maida Vale and Broadcasting House, and become unmanageable.[74] Soon after, on 14 April, the Board of Governors decided that instructions should be given that American influences, especially in variety programmes on television, should be 'resisted and curtailed'.[75] The alcohol issue raised its head again in May when the House Superintendent at Alexandra Palace wrote to the Director of Administration:

> A 'John Haig' bottle containing a small residue of whisky was found in Dressing Room 5 at Alexandra Palace by the charwoman on the morning of Monday, April 26th. It had presumably been left by Messrs. Pritchard and Cunningham, who had taken part in the transmission of the scene from 'Twelfth Night' on April 24th.[76]

Finally, on 12 October 1937, a memorandum was sent from Gerald Cock to television production staff entitled 'Use of undesirable epithets, etc. in television programmes'. Cock noted that he had often asked producers to take particular care to avoid 'unnecessary references to, and pictures of, drinking'. He went on:

> I have also particularly requested producers to avoid such expletives as 'Hell', 'God', 'Damn', and others of the kind (where not strictly necessary, as in dramatic situations, or in classic plays which cannot be bowdlerised). In light entertainment where these expressions are never necessary, and can easily be omitted or bowdlerised, they

must be rigorously excluded. For example, last night in 'Comic Strip', Joan Miller used the expressions 'Oh God' and 'Hell' quite unnecessarily. 'Gosh' and 'Heck' would have done equally well, and do not sound as 'raw' when broadcast. I must ask producers carefully to note this memorandum, as a serious view will have to be taken of future lapses.[77]

Reith may have been some miles away in central London, but his influence was clearly felt in Wood Green.

Other programmes included opera, dance and ballet. At Christmas in 1937, Humperdinck's *Hansel and Gretel* was performed in the studio, a 'considerable step forward' in the televising of opera according to Reith. The orchestra and singers were in one studio (out of sight of viewers) and the opera was performed in another studio in mime by performers. According to Reith, it was the best of both worlds – excellent singing from singers who might not be good actors, and excellent acting by actors who might not be able to sing![78] From the early days, dance was a key part of the BBC's television schedules, with companies such as Ballet Rambert and Vic–Wells Ballet (the company that became today's Royal Ballet) travelling to the studios at Alexandra Palace to perform ballets from their repertoires. There was also experimentation within these forms. On 2 March 1937, Antony Tudor's ballet *Fugue for Four Cameras*, especially written for television, was broadcast. It was an experimental short ballet produced by Dallas Bower, where a single ballet dancer (Maude Lloyd) danced to a fugue in D minor by Bach. As Russell Burns explained: 'By mixing the outputs of the cameras, the images of three of the cameras could be superimposed on that of the fourth.'[79]

Viewers

The BBC's relationship with its audience in the early days of radio was rather one-way, in the sense that no research was undertaken on listeners' views or on their engagement with programmes beyond what was printed in the letters pages of *Radio Times*. John Reith was not one for pandering to audience tastes, preferring instead to provide listeners with what he believed they should have. With the appointment of Stephen Tallents as the BBC's Controller (Public Relations) in 1935, things began to change. Tallents had been secretary to the Empire Marketing Board Film Unit and had then moved to the GPO Film Unit in 1933, working alongside documentary-makers such as John Grierson. With a background in marketing and public relations, Tallents could see the benefit of engaging with audiences and so in 1936 the BBC's Listener Research Unit was established within the Public Relations Division, headed by Robert J. Silvey.[80]

The first attempt to gather information on television viewers took place in January 1937. Notices were placed in the press and announcements made on radio programmes inviting viewers to contact the BBC: 'The B.B.C. is anxious to have the co-operation of viewers during the development of the service. Owners of television sets are therefore asked to help the B.B.C. by expressing ... their opinions about reception conditions and programmes.' This was a break from the past. The BBC was actively encouraging the (albeit small) television audience to help shape the future of the service. As the BBC was unaware of who owned a set, viewers were asked to send their names and addresses to Broadcasting House and the Corporation would contact them asking them questions regarding programme likes and dislikes, and sound or vision reception issues.[81]

The first report, 'Viewers and the Television Service', was published on 5 February 1937. One hundred and eighteen viewers contacted the BBC, and seventy-four of these responded to the request to complete a questionnaire. The BBC estimated that twenty-six of the seventy-four were connected to the radio trade and a number had a professional or scientific interest in television. In terms of programming, 30 per cent of all comments referred to light entertainment programmes and three quarters of these were positive. There was also a unanimous opinion that good variety and cabaret were 'eminently suitable' for television.[82] There were less favourable comments on studio demonstrations and talks: 'Disapproval concentrated largely upon demonstrations of cooking, washing, ironing, etc., which were condemned as of little interest to those who could afford television sets.' This is an important point and one which underlines how the cost of sets was virtually excluding a large section of the potential viewing population. If you could afford a set then you probably had domestic help and would not need Mrs Daisy Pain to demonstrate the art of home washing. Drama was universally praised, as were the outside broadcasts, particularly of sporting events. The survey ended by noting that 109 viewing rooms had been established as a result of the appeal for information, but no information is given as to their locations.[83]

On 23 December 1938, R. A. Rendall, the Assistant Director of Television, sent a memorandum to Television executives noting that there would be more research on television viewers in early 1939 and that he was seeking views on areas for questions. D. H. Munro replied noting that he would like viewers' opinions on (a) explanatory announcements by announcers before plays and other major productions, (b) whether in a programme of several short items they would like slick cueing from one item to another or a short interval between each one, and (c) if summaries of future programmes given by announcers were appreciated by viewers. Outside Broadcasting (OB) producer Philip Dorté also replied and noted that he would like to know whether viewers preferred special television commentary on sporting events or would rather have a full commentary as in radio. He also wanted views on lighting on OB events. A further enquiry was duly held in February 1939, where again viewers would be invited to apply for a questionnaire. The aim, in addition to gathering information on programming and reception again, was to compile a list of names and addresses so that set owners might be consulted from time to time on programming and – interestingly – to find out where their sets were installed. The response was very good, and by the end of February Gerald Cock's secretary had a list of 900 set owners,[84] and by 31 March almost 4,000 questionnaires had been returned completed. Whereas almost a third of responses in 1937 had come from those with a trade connection, this time 91 per cent came from those who owned television sets in the home for entertainment purposes.[85] An interim report published in May 1939 showed that plays and variety programmes direct from theatre, newsreels, *Picture Page* and light entertainment programmes in general were liked by at least 90 per cent of viewers. Outside broadcasts and sporting events came next, followed by full-length plays, cartoons, demonstrations and talks. Most agreed that the length of the evening programme slot (90 minutes to two hours) was just about right, but many would have liked an earlier start. In answer to Dorté's question, 85 per cent of viewers believed that television commentators struck the right balance.[86] A final report was published in June and noted that 91 per cent of those viewing used television for purely entertainment purposes. What also emerged from the survey was that viewers were appreciative of the intimate and friendly nature of television, in particular the friendly and relatively informal tone of the announcers. One or two respondents even stated that they hoped that 'television would not become inhuman like the B.B.C.'.[87] Other issues which emerged in the final report were that a number of viewers – around five hundred – wanted more light entertainment programmes, although some complained that the same artists were appearing all the time. There were calls for a Children's Hour on television, after school at 4.00 or 4.30 p.m. and on Saturdays and Sundays – something which became a feature of the post-war television service. The BBC was encouraged by the overall positive and supportive tone of the responses, particularly in that respondents felt that programming overall was steadily improving. It would have improved further, of course, had hostilities between Britain and Germany not broken out less than three months after the report was published.

Closedown and war

The storm clouds of war had been gathering for some time. On 21 March 1939, the Control Board discussed a paper entitled 'Television in emergency period' in which Harold Bishop noted that television stations in the provinces 'might conceivably be of use in dessimination [sic] of information to the public in war time'.[88] On 24 August 1939, the Control Board discussed what might happen in the eventuality of war breaking out: 'Decided that television should be closed down on receipt of warning message, or executive message if no warning received.' There followed a series of memoranda and calls between the BBC and the GPO over the next few days. It was noted on 30 August that the BBC had approached the GPO with a view to allowing the BBC to take the decision to close down the television service on the outbreak of war. However, F. W. Ogilvie, the Director-General, reported that the GPO had refused this and so the Control Board agreed that 'if circumstances warranted, B.B.C. should nevertheless take action and if necessary argue afterwards'.[89] The following day, the BBC had received information from the GPO that television would be closed down when emergency censorship powers were imposed by authorisation of the Postmaster-General and that the BBC would be informed when that would be enacted. The minute record reflects the mood at the Corporation: 'Noted, but agreed that decision ... concerning independent action should stand.'[90]

On 1 September, the BBC was preparing to broadcast from Radiolympia, with Elizabeth Cowell leading on the presentation. Following an hour of the *Come and Be Televised* programme, the plan was to break before returning for the afternoon programmes, which included Mantovani and his orchestra and a visit to Regent's Park Zoo. There is a common belief that is repeated in many television histories that midway through a Mickey Mouse cartoon – Mickey's Gala Premiere – the screens went black without warning and that this was the end of the television service until June 1946. However, as dramatic as this might seem, the television service did not quite end in that way. Firstly, the BBC's Control Board minutes for 1 September note that 'D.G. [Director-General] to ring Birchall [GPO official] and suggest close-down after morning transmission'. Whether or not this happened is not clear, but it would suggest that the BBC was willing to take the initiative and close the service, as the Control Board discussions above suggest. Secondly, the BBC's 'Programmes as Broadcast' records (or Ps-as-Bs) show that the cartoon did, in fact, run its course, and so viewers would have seen the whole cartoon. A Sound and Image signal was then broadcast – for tuning purposes – and at that point the screen went black without a closing announcement, leaving viewers somewhat perplexed, no doubt.[91] J. D. Percy, an engineer who initially worked for Baird Television Ltd but who then transferred to the BBC staff, recalled the events of 1 September in an interview with the Royal Television Society. His recollection almost matches that of the Ps-as-B record, but differs a little:

> I got on to Pat [Hillyard, Supervisor at Olympia] and said, Look, we've had the bad news, we've finished. Tell Elizabeth to give a summary of the afternoon programmes and what we're going to do tonight. While she's preparing it with you, I'll run a Mickey Mouse film up here [at Alexandra Palace] – and the last thing that went out on sound and vision was Elizabeth Cowell announcing Mantovani and his orchestra for the afternoon programme and the Galsworthy play. Neither went out. We knew it wouldn't.[92]

Whatever the precise details of the closedown, almost three years of pioneering, exciting and experimental work – in the sense of exploring new ways of working, developing new forms and creating a new grammar for television – had come to an end abruptly and the screens at home would be black until 7 June 1946. Cecil Madden's files in the BBC Written Archive Centre contain cuttings of BBC Television programme listings from the

Figure 7.4 One of the last programmes to be broadcast on pre-war television, *The Zoo*, an outside broadcast from Regent's Park Zoo, 31 August 1939. Reproduced by kind permission of the Alexandra Palace Television Society. Copyright unknown.

3–10 September 1939 edition of *Radio Times*. Written on them, in neat handwriting, is 'Never happened'.[93]

Key issues

In this final section, I would like to highlight briefly some of the key issues facing the television service during the 1936–9 period.

Finance

Financing the television service was a constant issue during this period. As Asa Briggs has stated: 'BBC difficulties so often began not in the Post Office but in the Treasury.'[94] The BBC was under pressure from the Television Advisory Committee from early 1937 to increase the hours of television. Given that expenditure on television was estimated at £65,000 capital and £330,000 running costs for 1937, any increase in hours would have implications for the BBC.[95] On 8 June 1937 Reith wrote to the Director-General of the GPO regarding financing the television service. Reith argued that current expenditure on what was essentially a skeleton service was difficult to justify in terms of the immediate public response (which was positive but demanding more). To give a fuller service to the London area or, indeed, to extend to the provinces would involve two or three times the expenditure. If the television service was to continue, stated Reith, then it had to be funded by some sort of subsidy. Reith also stated his reluctance to ask radio listeners to finance television development – diverting finance from radio would be detrimental to that service.[96] The financing of television in 1938 and beyond, he said, must be made dependent on sufficient income from sources outside the present revenue for sound. He requested that the Postmaster-General consider providing finance from the 25 per cent of the net licence revenue retained by the Treasury.[97]

In a meeting of the Television Advisory Committee on 5 October, Charles Carpendale stated that the BBC proposed to give two hours of television on Sundays (separate hours) and also wanted to improve the layout and programmes by using the theatre at Alexandra Palace. The Corporation also wanted an additional mobile unit for £40,000. The total additional costs would be £100,000 capital expenditure and £70,000 running costs. Selsdon also noted that he wanted the BBC to consider extending the evening hours to 2½ hours – 1½ hours from studio and one hour of 'good films'. Frank Smith (Department of Scientific and Industrial Research) agreed that longer hours would induce people to buy television sets, though F. W. Phillips of the GPO argued that the high price was a bar to buying a set, and there would not be a substantial increase in sales until the price came down to around £30 per set.[98]

The financial situation was still an issue in 1938. In a debate in the House of Commons on 9 March, the Postmaster-General, George Tryon, argued for an additional grant of £295,000 for the expansion of the television service, basing his case on the fact that Britain was ahead of other countries in terms of television service at that time. The debate was extensive and heated at times. Many MPs coupled the debate over finance with the question of extending the television service beyond London. Oliver Simmonds, the Conservative MP for Birmingham Duddeston, for example, considered the television programmes to have an 'air of amateurism' about them and hoped that the additional income would not only remedy this but would allow for the development of television in the Midlands.[99]

The following year, in June 1939, the Television Advisory Committee referred to the state of television development as a 'vicious circle'. The television service could only develop if the notion of it as an 'experimental phase' could be dropped and assurances be made that it was on a firmer footing and foundations. Yet, this was difficult to do while the public were still unwilling to purchase sets and accept television as a developed service. The committee called for an announcement (by government and the BBC?) of a long-term plan for the service. At the same time, it is clear that the committee was considering a second station in Birmingham and was even considering the idea of sponsorship or advertising as a means of funding the service.[100]

Increasing the audience

The 'vicious circle' referred to above certainly taxed the BBC Television Service. Gerald Cock was fully aware of the need to broadcast programmes 'which would be likely to sell sets' and the requirement 'to get people to buy the damn things'.[101] In January 1937, the Radio Manufacturers' Association called on the BBC to improve the quality of programming and to increase the amount of hours of transmission, as it had seen a decline in the sale of sets and was laying the blame squarely at the feet of the television service.[102] Yet the programming was only one factor. Having seen the birth and then the death of 30-line television, and having been exposed to 240-line mechanical television and 405-line electronic television, any viewer who was to invest a great deal of money in a set would want to be reassured that the standard now attained – that is, 405-lines – was the one that was going to be around for a while.

The fact that the BBC undertook a number of viewer surveys is testimony to the desire to 'get things right'. Yet, increasing the hours would incur additional expense, as noted above, and so the BBC was in somewhat of a quandary. There were concerted efforts on the part of the BBC to try to increase the numbers of viewers. In July 1937, for example, a 'Television Exhibition' was held at the Science Museum in London. It followed the previous year's successful Radiolympia television debut and featured Baird's mechanical system and electron camera, 30-line transmitting equipment and other features designed to engage the public with television.[103] The following year, the BBC held a 'Television Show' at Selfridges, where thirteen years previously John Logie Baird had demonstrated his experimental television apparatus. There were television talent tests with BBC staff present for some of these sessions (possibly looking for presenters), make-up demonstrations and mannequin parades. In announcing the event to the press on 13 February 1938, the Oxford Street store admitted that the event was a 'dignified stunt' but noted that Selfridges was proud of its association with the new medium.[104] There was hope among the senior staff and Governors that development of outside broadcasts would do much to stimulate interest in, and popularise, television. The Boat Race, the first televised professional boxing match in April (Harvey vs McAvoy from Harringay Stadium with special television commentary by Lionel Seccombe), international rugby (England vs Scotland with commentary from National Programme) were all televised in an attempt to do this. In Olympia, a television studio was set up at the Ideal Home Exhibition with short programmes being broadcast from there in the morning and afternoon for a week. This secured much-needed publicity for television and large numbers of people saw the medium for first time. Several sets were sold there, and several others on approval. Viewing rooms for watching television were also set up, and the television studio had a glass front so that people could watch studio production.[105]

The 1938 Radiolympia Exhibition gave the BBC the opportunity to promote the television service further and highlight the extended hours the service had been granted. Programmes such as *Come and Be Televised* also created interest among an inquisitive public and were aimed at showing the marvel and excitement of television. Television 'personalities' such as Jasmine Bligh and the gardening expert C. H. Middleton were present to talk with members of the public and be televised. The exhibition that year was significant. As the historian Michael Law noted: 'Radiolympia 1938 marked the transition point where television was moving from its own enthusiast origins into a full-fledged consumer

Figure 7.5 The BBC Gardener, C. H. Middleton, broadcasting from Radiolympia in September 1938. Reproduced by kind permission of the Alexandra Palace Television Society. Copyright unknown.

product.'[106] Law goes on to argue that 1938 saw the emergence of a genuinely competitive market for television sets with the appearance of larger-screen, 405-line television.

Television expansion

If increased hours, higher-quality programmes and cheaper sets were incentives for people to purchase television sets, then expanding the service beyond London was another. As early as February 1937, the MP for Cardiff South, Arthur Evans, asked the Postmaster-General when a Welsh regional television station might be established. The answer received stated that once the experience of the London Television Station had been assessed, consideration would be given to extending the service to other parts of the country.[107] The Television Advisory Committee discussed the idea of extending the television service at its meeting in December 1938, noting that any future planning of the television service should bear in mind the original objective laid down by the 1934 Television Committee report – that of establishing a national service by gradually building up a network of television stations across the country. By March the following year, the Radio Manufacturers Association was pressing the GPO for the acceleration of experiments to extend television to other parts of the country with the backing of the BBC.[108] There were also calls from television set dealers to extend the service. In April 1939 a dealer from Norwich wrote to the Chancellor of the Exchequer, Sir John Simon, asking the government to finance the expansion of television to the provinces. This, he argued, would stimulate the home market and the export trade:

> Should the matter be postponed for another year the most feared results would be that America would seize the opportunity of taking the lead, towards which end she is working so hard, thus robbing Britain of an entirely new industry, and the British working men of new employment ... There are thousands wanting television sets![109]

The outbreak of war put a halt to any plans for expansion for the time being and America slipped into the lead.

Cinema and television

The relationship between cinema and television during the 1936–9 period is a subject for a research project on its own. Throughout the years before the outbreak of war, television in cinemas was a topic of discussion for the BBC, the GPO, the Television Advisory Committee and Baird Television Ltd. Reith took an active interest in the idea of showing television in cinemas, an area on which Baird focused following the BBC's decision to adopt Marconi-EMI's 405-line television system in February 1937. In June 1938, Reith and Cecil Graves, the BBC's Deputy Director-General, met with Isidore Ostrer of Gaumont-British. Ostrer had requested the meeting to discuss the installation of large screens in cinemas and the BBC's television programmes to be shown on them. However, it is clear from internal BBC documents that the BBC, having weighed up the advantages and disadvantages, was not satisfied that there was any genuine demand by the public or the trade for rediffusion of television programmes in cinemas. Indeed, in an undated document (published in the summer of 1938), the Corporation noted its concern that such a venture 'is likely seriously to affect the popularisation of home viewing'. There were also concerns over costs, technical standards and suitable programming.[110] Indeed, by November 1938 the BBC was ready to concede that 'the present orientation of the television broadcast service was towards the hearth and home rather than the public hall'.[111] The BBC did, however, broadcast a major boxing match on the cinema screen. On 23 February 1939, the British Lightweight Championship fight between Eric Boon and Arthur Danahar at the Haringey Arena was broadcast to the Marble Arch Pavilion and the Tatlar News Theatre in London where Baird projection equipment had been installed. The Corporation was at pains to highlight that this was not the beginning of cinema television: 'The B.B.C. points out that in connection with the televising of the Boon–Danahar fight ... permission to reproduce the transmission in certain places of public entertainment must not be regarded as a precedent. It must not be taken that any general extension of permission for the rediffusion of B.B.C. television programmes in places of public entertainment is contemplated.'[112]

If the relationship with the cinema industry was strained, as archival documents suggest, there was one exception:

> In view of the distrust with which activities of the Television Service are, for the most part, viewed by the Film Industry, it is pleasant to record that when the London representative of Walt Disney left for America during the recent crisis he deposited with the Television Department for safe keeping all copies of the Mickey Mouse cartoons, leaving it to them to notify his representative here and send him the appropriate fee whenever any of the cartoons were televised.[113]

Radio and television

As has been noted throughout this book, the relationship between the established radio service and the new television service was difficult. In many radio quarters, there was no love lost for television. There were concerns over the diverting of finances from radio to television, together with a sense that television would steal listeners and that its programme formats with their visual appeal would sound the death knell for some radio formats, such as drama. A memorandum sent to Reith from the Director of Features and Drama in December 1936 raised the fear that 'within a very few years the radio play for sound only will be as defunct as the dodo'.[114]

Within the BBC itself, a good deal of what might now be termed cross-promotion is evident in that radio was actively promoting and encouraging television usage. The year 1938 saw an increased number of radio programmes on the subject of television, as the price of sets began to decrease, hours of transmission began to increase, and interest in the medium began to spread. On 1 February, Gerald Cock broadcast on the National Programme outlining the progress of the television service and underlining that television programmes were designed for home viewing. He went on to reassure listeners that the smallness of the screen did not matter if one was in the sitting room (although as noted above, larger screens were on the market by 1938). Once again, Cock drew attention to the immediacy and intimacy of television but also highlighted the financial challenges. Each programme cost 1/500th of a British feature film, he said, and the programme budget for the whole year was less than the budget of an American feature film.[115] In November and December 1938, the BBC's Regional Programme ran a series of six programmes entitled *A Newcomer to Viewing*. The first programme was billed:

> This is the first of the six talks which Howard Marshall is giving from the viewpoint of a lay investigator into the mysteries of television. There are still many potential viewers who hold doubts about buying television receivers. How much, for example, do these things cost? How much room do they take up? Will they be out of date in a year's time? What may the viewer expect from television in return for his money? These are a few of the questions which Howard Marshall will endeavour to answer. In his broadcast today he will describe how he was asked by the BBC to undertake this survey and what his wife thought about it.[116]

Just before the television service was closed down, on 28 August 1939, the BBC produced an innovative – and somewhat experimental – programme which linked the radio and television services. The television programme was entitled *Up from the Country*. It was broadcast at 9.40 p.m., its premise outlined by *Radio Times* in its description of the radio programme *A Modern Pastoral*, which started broadcasting on the (radio) National Programme at 9.45 p.m.:

> Many readers of the *Radio Times* will remember John Pudney's article some weeks ago in which he described the coming of electricity to the remote Essex village in which he lives. Here is a programme recording that event, and it is a programme with a big and interesting difference. Inside the framework of Pudney's own script have been put the voices of the country folk whom the new electricity has affected. The villagers 'played' splendidly, and the programme should provide first-rate comment on a phase of English country life. In the television studios tonight listening to this programme will be some of the villagers who took part in it, so that the effect upon them of hearing their own voices will be seen by viewers.[117]

A shorter billing appeared in the television listings: 'Villagers from a sequestered corner of Essex come to the studio to hear their own voices being broadcast in the National programme.'[118] One can only imagine what the programme looked like from the audience's perspective, although it highlights the fact that the Corporation was not averse to experimenting in its form of programming, although what the viewer is expected to have gained from the reactions of the villagers remains uncertain.

Theatre and television

The relationship between the theatre (including variety and cabaret) and television in the pre-war era was a difficult one on many levels. While

London's West End provided a source of entertainment which was second to none and which producers such as Cecil Madden and Eustace Robb before him knew very well, television, as it began to develop and grow, was seen as a potential threat to the live entertainment industry. In the preparation period leading up to the launch of the regular public television service, William Streeton, who was responsible for all television bookings, met with George Black, a powerful theatre producer and owner of Moss Empires, the largest chain of variety theatres and music halls in the UK. They met on 14 July 1935 to discuss the question of artists under contract to appear at General Theatre Corporation theatres (part of the Moss Empire) who the BBC might like to appear on television. Black stated that he would 'adopt an attitude of extreme caution' with regard to television and that he would not allow any artist under contract with him to appear on television 'until he was able to judge how far television was likely to affect his interests'. Television was, according to Black a 'much greater potential menace to his theatres than sound broadcasting' in that, while people might like to see the actual appearance of radio artists, people would be less inclined to visit the theatre to see personalities made famous by television. He was also concerned that if television were allowed to televise major events from the theatre, for example the Royal Command Variety Performance, then the theatre would be seriously affected in terms of attendance and income. Streeton countered this by suggesting that cinema stars were on screen but that did not stop people from flocking to visit them when they appeared in public in the UK. He also pointed out that the BBC would be most likely to be interested in the 'less important' acts in the Music Hall – dancers, conjurors and novelty acts – and that it might be some time before regular use would be made of people with box-office appeal. With regard to audiences being stolen, Streeton suggested that given the demand for seats at the Royal Variety Performance, he found it difficult to believe that televising it would have an impact on numbers in the theatre. By the end of the conversation, Black agreed to keep an open mind on the matter.[119]

However, throughout 1937 and 1938, tensions ran high between Black and the Television Service. Correspondence in the archives shows that artists were threatened with penalties or dismissal if they appeared on television, or were booked deliberately by Black to be elsewhere at the same time as they were meant to be appearing on television. In an internal document written in May 1938, Streeton noted that 'from the inception of the present television service ... the attitude of G.T.C. has been one of marked and indeed complete opposition'. He then listed a number of case studies where artists had been told that an appearance on television could cost them any further booking by GTV/Moss Empires. These included the ventriloquist Arthur Prince and the comedian Vic Oliver.[120] On another occasion the singer Harry Roy and his band, who had been booked to appear on television on 17 August, cancelled as Val Parnell, acting on behalf of George Black, had threaten to cancel all future engagements with GTC should Roy and the band appear on television. As Roy was dependent on Music Hall and radio appointments through Black, he could scarcely afford to fall out with him.[121]

While one can appreciate the BBC's frustration, particularly Gerald Cock's suggestion that Black was holding back television until the BBC paid a large subsidy to him for his artists, one can also sympathise with the stance taken by Black to a degree. Here was a new and unknown medium which would provide entertainment directly to people's homes, free at the point of delivery, drawing on talent that people would pay to see in the theatre or Music Hall. Although the audience was small, by 1938 there were clear signs that interest in television was increasing and television's hours were extending. From our vantage point we might consider Black's fears unsubstantiated, but at the time, the threat to his theatres was palpable.

Reith and television

> He wrote very little about television in his diary, but the impression remains that he never ceased to regard it as a cuckoo in the nest – in moral terms the lesser medium, and even hostile to those elevated values with which he had sought to imbue radio.[122]

In his perceptive assessment of mass communication in inter-war Britain, LeMahieu argues that 'among the progressives of the inter-war era, Reith was the most influential and he occupies an important place in the social and cultural history of twentieth-century Britain'.[123] There is no doubting the influence and impact of Reith on the shape of British broadcasting, both radio and television. He was, undoubtedly, a very complex character, something which comes to the fore in the books which have been written about him by his family members and others.[124] Reithian Public Service Broadcasting was conceived during the early years of wireless broadcasting and provided the framework within which television was born, nurtured and developed. Reith distrusted the frivolous, and stated in his early 'manifesto', published as *Broadcast Over Britain* in 1924, that broadcasting entertainment only would be a 'prostitution' of the power of the wireless.[125] This, then, was the John Reith who first encountered the notion of television in the mid-1920s and who had to respond to the pressure put upon the BBC by the government, the press, and commercial interests in relation to the new medium.

The most commonly accepted view in television histories is that John Reith disliked television, would have nothing to do with the medium, viewed those involved with establishing and running the BBC's television service with contempt, and refused to watch television programmes. For example, Bruce Norman's book on the early years of British television accused Reith of being 'anti' television,[126] while Mark Aldridge argued that Reith's 'complete lack of interest in (and occasional explicit dislike of)' television reinforced its status as secondary to radio.[127] Malcolm Baird and Antony Kamm, in their detailed biography of John Logie Baird, state that 'Reith avoided attending a television demonstration or indeed any function connected with television',[128] and Emma Sandon, in her work investigating the use of oral history in researching pre-war television, argued that 'Reith ... had nothing to do with television'.[129] The BBC's own website perpetuates this idea:

> He was less interested in the development of television. Anthony Kamm, the biographer of television's inventor, John Logie Baird, says that Reith usually managed to be on holiday when significant events in television took place ... One of his leaving gifts when he left the BBC in 1938 was a television set. He said he would never look at it.[130]

There are *elements* of truth in all these assertions, but the relationship between John Reith and television was far more nuanced. I would argue that Reith's relationship with television was far more complex than has been understood thus far, and that his attitude towards the new technology was shaped by a combination of personal and professional factors. While acknowledging that Reith was wary of television, I would also argue that far from being completely detached from television developments, he played a key role in developing the BBC's position on television, in negotiating with the Baird television interests and with the government, and in tempering the hubris within sections of the press in relation to television.

A study of Reith's diaries provides evidence that he did, in fact, watch television. References to the medium are quite scarce – he may not have recorded every encounter with the small screen and possibly he felt that certain programmes were more worthy of note than others. One of the most revealing references to television in his diary occurs on 11 November 1936, just over a week after the television service had been inaugurated. 'Always to see the children when I get in', he wrote. 'Listened and "viewed" simultaneously tonight. Television is an awful snare.'[131] Even at this early stage of the service, Reith was acutely aware of how television could become a distraction by 'entrapping' the viewer and the fact that television had the power to do this was a factor in his somewhat negative view of the medium.

Further evidence of television viewing is provided in an entry in November 1937, when Reith wrote in his diary: 'We watched ... the television of the Lord Mayor's show and of the Cenotaph ceremony. The latter was excellent & I rang Cock.'[132] Not all television excited him, though. In April 1938 he noted that he had gone to '[Cecil] Graves' flat & watched television of a prize fight from 9.30 to 10.45 – awfully tedious'.[133]

Reith underlined his feelings on television in an interview with Malcolm Muggeridge on BBC 1 on 3 December 1967, when he referred to television as 'a potential social menace of the first magnitude' and accused the mass media (of which television was a part) of contributing to what he felt was a general decline in moral standards in British society.[134] Bill McDowell, in his work on the history of BBC broadcasting in Scotland, suggests that television threatened Reith's public service philosophy as he feared that it would pander to 'popular' taste rather than 'serious' tastes. Moreover, McDowell goes on to argue that due to Reith's natural affinity with sound broadcasting, television posed more of a challenge to the Reithian public service ethos and, therefore, he wished to constrain its authority.[135]

John Reith did, therefore, engage with television in its early years on a number of different levels. However, he did have misgivings and reservations based on a number of factors. Grace Wyndham Goldie, Head of Television Talks and Current Affairs at the BBC in the post-war period, has argued that Reith's dislike, or suspicion, of television stemmed from a belief that 'communication by means of vision would be an evil which would be damaging to the country and to the world'.[136] This is borne out in the televised interview with Malcolm Muggeridge in 1967 where Reith also confessed to having been frightened of television from the start.[137] This was partly due to financial concerns and a fear that a television service would have to be developed from within existing resources (funding therefore having to be diverted from the established sound broadcasting service). Yet the fears also had religious and moral roots. As Kamm and Baird note, 'He was a fervent believer, to whom the Word was God: the broadcast word should be without any ornamentation'.[138] McDowell highlights the concern with the visual and notes: 'Reith had misgivings about the potential impact of television, fearing it would encourage passive viewing among the audience. Others believed that television would make casual listening impossible because of the presence of the visual element.'[139] Writing in 1936, Rudolf Arnheim discussed what he called the 'cult of actuality' – a characteristic of the mental outlook of the day, according to the author:

> to the furtherance of actuality corresponds a retrogression of the spoken and written word, and also of thought. The more convenient our modes of perception become, the more firmly fixed is the dangerous illusion that seeing is knowledge ... If you want to describe, you must abstract the general from the particular, formulate concepts, compare and consider. But where the finger merely points, the mouth is dumb, the pen falls from the word, the mind is stunted ... For the man who can think, draw conclusions and discern, television will be most stimulating. But the man who cannot do these things will be engrossed by the screen without it getting him anywhere ...[140]

Antony Kamm and Malcolm Baird suggest that Reith's 'personal aversion' to television meant that he resisted becoming involved in television policy decision-making, leaving it to his senior staff. They go on to suggest that by the end of 1932, Charles Carpendale (effectively Reith's deputy) and Noel Ashbridge (Controller of Engineering) 'simply did not realise the potential interest that television would generate'.[141] Interestingly, Kamm and Baird refer to television as a 'significant issue'. Although we may view the early days of television as significant from our current perspective, in the early 1930s television was a minor concern within the BBC. While it may have attracted press and enthusiast attention, it was nevertheless a minority interest within the wider broadcasting spectrum. As John Swift, latterly television correspondent for *Radio Times*, notes:

> The BBC ... were torn between loyalty to their listeners on the one hand – they could not be expected to give up valuable air space for the minority – and on the other their now open support for television and an anxiety to keep Britain well ahead in the race for the coveted honour of being the first country to establish a public service.[142]

John Wyver, likewise, has argued that television was not a major priority for BBC management during the 1930s: 'Its audiences, after all, were tiny when compared with radio, with perhaps 60–80,000 "lookers-in" in the London area able to view in 1939.'[143]

It is fair to say that Reith was concerned about the development of a medium which, when fully-fledged, would have the ability to fragment the unified audience for which he strived and which he had succeeded in creating with radio. Television during the pre-war period was the preserve, initially, of the technically-minded and amateur enthusiast (for the 30-line system) and then the affluent who could afford high-definition sets (from 1936 onwards). The cost of sets was initially prohibitive and so, in addition to creating a new and 'separate' broadcasting audience – the viewing audience – where radio had managed to transcend class boundaries by providing a universal service for all, television was now re-enforcing those boundaries.

Reith's Arnoldian vision of providing the 'best of everything' and preserving a high moral tone was paramount. So, as television took on an entertainment role from 1929 onwards, could this explain Reith's unease with the medium? Programming, particularly during the 1936–9 period, was of necessity popular in order to build up an audience to justify the service. It had to appeal to the largest possible potential audience to ensure that sets were sold.

Television was more expensive to produce in the pre-war period, and this was a cause for concern for Reith. In evidence provided to the Selsdon Committee in 1934, he had not been averse to considering some form of commercial funding of television given the high costs of running the service.[144] The government was adamant that the funding for television should come from the ten-shilling licence fee, but this was putting a strain on the Corporation, especially as the television audience was a fraction of the radio audience. On 8 June 1937 Reith wrote to the Director-General of the GPO regarding the financing of the television service. Reith argued that current expenditure on what was essentially a skeleton service was difficult to justify in terms of the immediate public response. To give a fuller service to the London area or to extend to the provinces would involve two or three times the expenditure, Reith stated. If television service was to continue, then it must be funded by some sort of subsidy. Reith was clear that the BBC could not ask radio listeners to finance the television development for fear of detriment to the sound service. The financing of television in 1938 and beyond, argued Reith, must be made dependent on sufficient income from sources outside the present revenue for sound. He requested that the Postmaster-General consider providing finance from the 25 per cent of the net licence revenue retained by the Treasury.[145]

There is no doubt that technical issues played a part in shaping Reith's attitude towards television. As Briggs points out, neither Baird nor EMI could offer technical facilities as highly advanced as the radio engineers offered the BBC in 1922.[146] Reith was also frustrated with the technical debates over standards and felt frustrated at attempts to pressure him into accepting technical standards which clearly did not match his expectations, which explains in part the slow pace at which the BBC engaged with television during the decade between 1926 and 1936 and which also explains the attacks in the British and American press over the slow response to television developments.[147]

There were also other factors at play. According to Goldie, Reith's self-imposed distancing from television developments after the service had been inaugurated can also be explained by the fact that he was preoccupied with personal matters (he offered to resign from the BBC in November 1937 and eventually left in June 1938), but also national matters. By November 1936, the position of King Edward VIII was becoming increasingly untenable due to his affair with the married American Mrs Wallace Simpson. It was Reith himself who travelled to Windsor to oversee the abdication speech over the radio in December 1936.[148] 'In comparison with these personal and national preoccupations', Goldie argues, 'the development of television seemed of negligible importance.'[149]

Writing in the former BBC Director of Television Gerald Beadle's 1963 book on television, Gerald Cock lamented that Reith was 'something less than enthusiastic about television' and that Reith himself had stated that he was 'afraid' of the medium. Rather than taking the comment at face value, Cock interpreted Reith's remark as meaning that he had foreseen 'the calamitous abuse of TV throughout the world' and that this framed his approach. Furthermore, Gerald Beadle argued that 'the BBC accepted television in 1936, but appears not to have embraced it or fully taken it to heart until 1950'.[150] Reith's apparent disdain for television was still evident in a special 'message' printed in the *Sunday Times* special supplement published to commemorate the twenty-fifth anniversary of the BBC Television Service in November 1961. Referring to the 1929–35 period of 30-line television, under the auspices of Baird Television initially and then, from 1932, the BBC, he wrote that 'those in charge of development thought a lot more highly of it than they should have thought'.[151] He then turned his thoughts to the high-definition service:

> There were some respects in which I have nothing to be proud of ... I did not take anything like the personal interest I should have done. Maybe the rather sordid arguments on the technical side were in part responsible ... one was sickened before one had gotten properly on to the job ... Gerald Cock, in charge from 1935, looked to me for support and encouragement which he did not get – anyhow at nothing like the measure he should have. *Mea maxima culpa* ...[152]

Reith's remarks above suggest that Cock did not always have the support of his manager. Indeed on 5 April 1939, Cock wrote to Frederick Ogilvie, Reith's successor as Director-General. Cock had recently received a £200 in bonus pay for exceptional work the previous year. BBC tradition dictated that staff did not usually write to thank management for bonuses, but Cock was breaking with tradition 'because all of us here know quite well that it is your personal encouragement and backing which has made all the difference. It has made a definite (though intangible) difference in atmosphere, and feeling of freedom to do the job, which has spread thro' B.H.'[153] Might this have been a slight directed at Reith?

In a 1938 biography of Reith, the journalist Garry Allighan argued that having to launch a television service

> was not the sweetest pill for the B.B.C. chief to swallow, and when the full history of television is written a large chapter will be devoted to the lack of enthusiasm – to put it politely as possible – on the part of a powerful section of the B.B.C. hierarchy towards the new limb that had been forcibly engrafted.[154]

The perceived 'lack of enthusiasm' on the part of Reith and the BBC stemmed from a host of factors – personal and professional – and rather than being 'forcibly engrafted', television was introduced, nurtured and developed by the BBC in a careful, sometimes guarded, and pragmatic manner.

Conclusion

The BBC's Television Service between 1936 and 1939 was innovative, pioneering and foundation-laying. The puppeteer Jan Bussell, who had performed on the BBC's 30-line television service in the early 1930s, recalled that he had requested a transfer from radio, where he was based, to television – a more suitable medium for puppetry – on more than one occasion. His request having been turned down, he resigned, only to find that a fortnight later, in early 1939, he was dispatched to Alexandra Palace as a television producer. It was, he said, 'one of the happiest jobs of my life, swept away by the enthusiasm of the small band of pioneers'.[155] Val Gielgud wrote in 1957: 'Nothing short of blazing enthusiasm and a consistent refusal to admit that anything was impossible could have achieved the results which by the beginning of the War had given to Great Britain the acknowledged lead in the television field.' For now, that lead was on hold, and when television returned in 1946, unfortunately for Britain, it had slipped a little.

Notes

1. The service did not stick rigidly to these times. See Andrew Martin, *Sound and Vision: Television from Alexandra Palace (and Some Other Places). A Programme Index 1929–1939* for a very detailed breakdown of when programmes were broadcast. There were also occasions when viewers outside of the transmitter could receive a signal.

2. Edward Pawley, *BBC Engineering 1922–1972* (London: BBC, 1972), 147.
3. Pawley, *BBC Engineering 1922–1972*, p. 148.
4. This was caused by a technical issue in the Marconi-EMI film transmission equipment which caused 'tilt and bend' distortion. See Pawley, *BBC Engineering 1922–1972*, p. 148.
5. Pawley, *BBC Engineering 1922–1972*, p. 148.
6. British Library Sound Library. C1248/282: Melvin Harris interview.
7. Royal Television Society Archives. 20/47T: Interview with Leslie Mitchell. Nevertheless, Cowell, Mitchell and others recalled how the delay between filming and transmitting in the Baird system would allow artists to run to the control room and see themselves being broadcast a minute or so after being in front of the camera.
8. Royal Television Society Archives. 19/4: Interview with Alan Bray.
9. BBC WAC R1/72/5: DG's report for Board Meeting.
10. POST 33/5536.
11. Ibid.
12. Ibid.
13. BBC WAC R1/72/5.
14. POST 33/5489. Was this an acceptance of defeat by a superior system? Possibly a relief on the part of those engineers who struggled on a daily basis to ensure that the equipment worked effectively? For Baird Television Ltd it would allow the company to focus on other activities such as television in cinemas.
15. Royal Television Society Archives. 20/17T: Interview with D. H. Munro.
16. Alexandra Palace Television Society Archive. Johnson, Sarah, *Jasmine: A Memoir of Jasmine Bligh, the First Lady of Television*, p. 64.
17. POST 33/5489.
18. John Bray, *Innovation and the Communications Revolution: From the Victorian Pioneers to Broadband Internet* (London: IEE, 2002), p. 100.
19. Bray, *Innovation and the Communications Revolution*, p. 104.
20. Neil Robson, 'Living Pictures out of Space: The Forlorn Hopes for Television in pre-1939 London', *Historical Journal of Film, Radio and Television* Vol. 24, No. 2 (2004), 224, 226.
21. <https://www.bbc.co.uk/programmes/p02cjrwb> (last accessed 1 August 2021).
22. Robson, 'Living Pictures out of Space'. 231.
23. *The Listener*, 11 November 1936, 888.
24. *The Listener*, 9 December 1936, 1,084–5.
25. *The Listener*, 16 June 1937, 1196.
26. *The Listener*, 4 August 1937, 252.
27. BBC WAC R34/888: Policy. Television. Talks 1936–37.
28. BBC WAC R34/888.
29. Ibid.
30. Jennifer Lewis (ed.), *Starlight Days: The Memoirs of Cecil Madden* (London: Trevor Square Publications, 2007), p. 75.

31. Jason Jacobs, *The Intimate Screen: Early British Television Drama* (Oxford: Oxford University Press, 2000), p. 32. Jacobs' study on television drama during the 1936–55 period is a detailed and landmark piece of scholarship.
32. BBC WAC S24/19/1: Special Collections. Cecil Madden.
33. <https://screenplaystv.wordpress.com/2015/12/05/bbc-televisions-first-drama-murder-in-the-cathedral-1936/> (last accessed 1 August 2021). The 'Screenplays: Theatre Plays on British Television' was an AHRC-funded project headed by Wyver and assisted by Amanda Wrigley. The website which was produced as a result of the project is an extremely valuable resource and can be found at http://bufvc.ac.uk/screenplays/.
34. Swift, *Adventure in Vision*, p. 87.
35. *Radio Times*, 19 March 1937, 4–5.
36. John Caughie, *Television Drama: Realism, Modernism and British Culture* (Oxford: Oxford University Press, 2000), p. 37.
37. *The Listener*, 17 November 1937, 1,076.
38. BBC WAC R1/73/9: DG's report for Board Meeting.
39. John Wyver, 'Middlebrow British Culture Being Mediated', Media history seminar series, University of London School of Advanced Study/Institute of Historical Research, 9 November 2016).
40. John Wyver, 'Dallas Bower: A Producer for Television's Early Years, 1936–9', *Journal of British Cinema and Television* Vol. 9, No. 1 (2012), 31.
41. Basil Dean, *Mind's Eye: An Autobiography 1927–1972* (London: Hutchinson, 1973), p. 262.
42. Dean, *Mind's Eye*, p. 262.
43. Ibid.
44. Ibid.
45. Ibid., p. 263.
46. This was not Basil Dean's first encounter with television, as his autobiography notes that he had been invited by John Logie Baird to see 'the shadowy beginnings of television', as Dean put it, in his Soho laboratory in 1928 (Dean, *Mind's Eye*, p. 83). Another successful broadcast from the theatre took place on 2 January 1939 when Michael Redgrave and Peggy Ashcroft were televised performing in *Twelfth Night* at the Phoenix Theatre in London.
47. Jacobs, *The Intimate Screen*, pp. 39–40.
48. BBC WAC R1/74/1: DG's report for Board Meeting.
49. Lewis, *Starlight Days*, p. 108.
50. BBC WAC T16/56: TV Policy: Coronation: George VI 1936–1937.
51. BBC WAC T16/56. There appears to be no response to this on file.
52. BBC WAC T16/189: Sound and Vision – News.
53. T. H, Bridgewater suggests that it was Gerald Cock who had made the request to the King through his Court connections (Royal Television Society Archive 20/T28).

54. Swift, *Adventure in Vision*, p. 91.
55. *Daily Telegraph*, 13 May 1937.
56. BBC WAC T16/189.
57. *The Listener*, 17 November 1937.
58. *The Listener*, 28 July 1937, 179.
59. BBC WAC T16/128/1: Outside Broadcasts.
60. Richard Haynes, *BBC Sport in Black and White* (London: Palgrave Macmillan, 2017), p. 15.
61. Haynes, *BBC Sport in Black and White*, p. 18.
62. Andrew Martin, *Sound and Vision: Television from Alexandra Palace (and Some Other Places). A Programme Index 1929–1939* (Birmingham: Kaleidoscope, 2021) [pre-published document loaned to author].
63. *The Listener*, 30 June 1937, 1297.
64. BBC WAC R3/3/12 – Control Board Minutes 1937.
65. BBC WAC R1/73/7: DG's report for Board Meeting.
66. BBC WAC T16/189: TV Policy: Sound and Vision – News.
67. BBC WAC R34/600/10: Programme Board Minutes.
68. POST 33/5213. Reproduction of BBC television programmes in cinemas (1937–39).
69. POST 33/5213.
70. BBC WAC R1/74/3: DG's report for Board Meeting.
71. Jennifer Lewis (ed.), *Starlight Days*, p. 100.
72. Andrew Martin, *Sound and Vision: Television from Alexandra Palace (and Some Other Places). A Programme Index 1929–1939* (Birmingham: Kaleidoscope, 2021) [pre-published document loaned to author].
73. BBC WAC T16/91/1: Light Entertainment.
74. BBC WAC T25/3: TV Routine. Alcohol.
75. BBC WAC R1/5/1: Board of Governors Minutes.
76. BBC WAC T25/3.
77. BBC WAC T16/151: TV Policy. Programme Policy. Bad Language 1937–1954.
78. BBC WAC R1/74/1: DG's report for Board Meeting.
79. R. W. Burns, *The Life and Times of A D Blumlein* (London: IEEE, 2000), p. 218.
80. See Siân Nicholas's detailed account of early listener research at https://microform.digital/boa/collections/16/bbc-listener-research-department-reports-1937-c1950/detailed-description (last accessed 29 October 2021).
81. *The Listener*, 6 January 1937, 6.
82. BBC WAC R9/9/1.
83. Ibid.
84. BBC WAC T1/6/1: Television Audience Research.
85. BBC WAC T1/6/1.
86. Ibid.
87. Ibid.

88. BBC WAC R3/3/14: Control Board Minutes 1939. It is worth noting that the BBC had clearly been considering expanding the television service outside of London, hence the reference to 'the provinces'.
89. BBC WAC R3/3/14: Control Board Minutes 1939.
90. BBC WAC R3/3/14.
91. Andrew Martin, *Sound and Vision: Television from Alexandra Palace (and Some Other Places). A Programme Index 1929–1939* (Birmingham: Kaleidoscope, 2021) [pre-published document loaned to author].
92. RTS Archive. Box 6. Interview with J. D. Percy. The P-as-B does not show that Cowell made the announcement regarding the afternoon and evening programmes, and there is no record of a Galsworthy play being scheduled.
93. BBC WAC Special Collections S24/19/2: Cecil Madden.
94. Briggs II, p. 443.
95. Burns, *British Television*, p. 457.
96. This was a recurring theme throughout television's development – see Chapters 4 and 5. At the meeting of the Control Board on 1 November 1938, the Director-General, F. W. Ogilvie, noted that 'the Board would be strongly opposed to any financing of television at the cost of sound broadcasting' (BBC WAC R3/3/13 – Control Board Minutes 1938).
97. BBC WAC T16/77/1: Television Policy: Finance.
98. POST 33/5536: Television Advisory Committee Proceedings.
99. <http://hansard.millbanksystems.com/commons/1938/mar/09/broadcasting> (last accessed 1 August 2021).
100. POST 33/5489.
101. C1248/282: Melvin Harris interview.
102. *Television and Short-Wave World*, January 1937, 12.
103. *Television and Short-Wave World*, July 1937, 395–7.
104. History of Advertising Trust: Selfridges Archive SEL1158.
105. BBC WAC R1/74/3: DG's report for Board Meeting.
106. Michael John Law, *1938: Modern Britain. Social Change and Visions of the Future* (London: Bloomsbury, 2018), p. 49.
107. <http://hansard.millbanksystems.com/written_answers/1937/feb/09/television-wales> (last accessed 1 August 2021).
108. BBC WAC R3/10/3: Controllers Meeting minutes.
109. POST 33/5143.
110. BBC WAC T16/176/2: Television Policy: Rediffusion 1b.
111. POST 33/5213: Reproduction of BBC television programmes in cinemas (1937–39).
112. BBC WAC T16/176/3: TV Policy: Rediffusion File 1c 1939.
113. BBC WAC R1/74/7: DG's report for Board Meeting.
114. T16/78: TV Policy.
115. British Library Sound Library: NP10755, Gerald Cock, 'The Television Service', National Programme, 1 February 1938, 9.05 p.m.

116. <https://genome.ch.bbc.co.uk/642708ec0a7f488fbaafbe1561d3355b> (last accessed 1 August 2021).
117. <https://genome.ch.bbc.co.uk/7481ebc12b4d4d02a0b87c7e33119b3c> (last accessed 20 July 2021). The village was Duton Hill, near Dunmore in Essex.
118. <https://genome.ch.bbc.co.uk/8a6e076e63e042f4927ed51b2773bb7d> (last accessed 20 July 2021).
119. BBC WAC T16/23: TV Policy: Artists: General Theatre Corporation 1935–1939.
120. BBC WAC T16/23.
121. Ibid.
122. Ian McIntyre, *The Expense of Glory: A Life of John Reith* (London, 1994), p. 209.
123. D. L. LeMahieu, *A Culture for Democracy: Mass Communication and the Cultivated Mind in the Britain between the Wars* (Oxford, 1998), p. 142.
124. See e.g. Andrew Boyle, *Only the Wind Will Listen: Reith of the BBC* (London, 1972); Charles Stuart (ed.), *The Reith Diaries* (London, 1975); Marista Leishmann, *My Father: Reith of the BBC* (Edinburgh, 2006).
125. J. C. W. Reith, *Broadcast Over Britain* (London, 1924), pp. 17–18.
126. Norman, *Here's Looking at You*, p. 70.
127. Mark Aldridge, *The Birth of British Television: A History* (Basingstoke, 2012), p. 167.
128. Antony Kamm and Malcolm Baird, *John Logie Baird: A Life* (Edinburgh, 2002), p. 115.
129. Emma Sandon, 'Nostalgia as Resistance: The Case of the Alexandra Palace Television Society and the BBC' in Helen Wheatley (ed.), *Re-Viewing Television History: Critical Issues in Television Historiography* (London, 2007), p. 110.
130. <http://www.bbc.co.uk/historyofthebbc/research/culture/reith-6> (last accessed 7 July 2016).
131. BBC WAC S60/5/4/4. Reith Diary, 11 November 1936.
132. BBC WAC S60/5/5/2. Reith Diary, 10 November 1937. Gerald Cock was BBC Director of Television.
133. BBC WAC S60/5/5/2. Reith Diary, 7 April 1938. The fight was between Len Harvey and Jock McAvoy and was broadcast live from Harringay. Commentary was provided by F. H. Grisewood and Lionel Seccombe.
134. 'Lord Reith in Conversation with Malcolm Muggeridge – Part Three', *The Listener*, 14 December 1967, 778. By this time commercial television had been introduced to the UK in the form of Independent Television (ITV), the whole concept of which was anathema to Reith.
135. W. H. McDowell, *The History of BBC Broadcasting in Scotland 1923–1983* (Edinburgh: Edinburgh University Press, 1992), p. 32.
136. Grace Wyndham Goldie, *Facing the Nation: Television and Politics 1936–76* (London, 1977), p. 32.

137. Quoted in Kamm and Baird, p. 110.
138. Kamm and Baird, p. 111.
139. McDowell, p. 41.
140. Rudolf Arnheim, *Radio* (London: Faber & Faber, 1936), pp. 280–1.
141. Kamm and Baird, p. 169.
142. Swift, *Adventure in Vision*, p. 54.
143. John Wyver, 'Dallas Bower: A Producer for Television's Early Years, 1936–9', *Journal of British Cinema and Television*, Vol. 9, No. 1 (2012), 35.
144. James Curran and Jean Seaton, *Power Without Responsibility: Press, Broadcasting and the Internet in Britain*, 7th edn (London, 2010), p. 159.
145. BBC WAC T16/77/1: Television Policy: Finance.
146. Asa Briggs, *The History of Broadcasting in the United Kingdom. Volume II. The Golden Age of Wireless* (Oxford, 1995), p. 528.
147. Briggs, Volume II, p. 537.
148. See Reith, *Into the Wind*, pp. 263–9 for an account of Reith's part in the broadcasting of the speech.
149. Wyndham Goldie, p. 32.
150. Gerald Beadle, *Television: A Critical Review* (London: Allen & Unwin, 1963), p. 42.
151. 'Message from Lord Reith' in *The Times Supplement on Television 1936–1961*, 20 November 1961, ii.
152. Ibid. The often-strained relationship between Reith and Cock was exemplified in an entry in Reith's diary for 1 December 1936: 'Cock is being an infernal nuisance.' No further explanation is provided! Described by Asa Briggs as 'one of the most lively, tough, vigorous – and knowledgeable – persons inside the BBC', Gerald Cock had been Director of Outside Broadcasts at the BBC prior to his appointment as Director of Television in 1935 (Briggs, Volume II, pp. 75–6).
153. BBC WAC L2/40/1.
154. Garry Allighan, *Sir John Reith* (London: Stanley Paul, 1938), p. 266.
155. Jan Bussell, *The Puppets and I* (London: Faber & Faber, 1950), p. 66.
156. Val Gielgud, *British Radio Drama 1933–1956* (London: Harrap, 1957), p. 76.

CHAPTER 8

Conclusions

The aim of this book has been to consider the BBC's engagement with television in the early years as it moved from a primarily laboratory-based experiment to a regular public service. We may consider that television developments today move at a fast pace, and we may find it difficult to keep up with the pace of change. Yet, in reflecting on the 1920s and 1930s, we can observe that for a number of years seeing at distance was a pipe dream. Then, in 1926, it became a reality, albeit in laboratory conditions. Within ten years it had become a publicly-funded service in television studios, with a vast range of televisual output, demonstrating the *potential* to be a game-changer in communication. The pace of change was incredible, and that provides a useful context for thinking about the way in which the BBC perceived television and dealt with television as it evolved over the ten-year period and beyond.

If I had to highlight some of the key issues that stand out for me in the period I have considered, they would be: firstly, that the early years of television show that broadcasting was – and still is – bound up in politics, economics, culture, society. As the historian Asa Briggs once argued, trying to write broadcasting history is like trying to write the history of everything else.[1] Secondly, we need to move away from the narrative that John Reith was the stumbling block in the development of television in Britain. He did have major concerns, but he also took the advice of his senior technical and engineering staff who, in his opinion, were better placed to pass judgement. We now know that Reith *did* engage with television and did watch television. We also know that he felt guilty about not offering more support to Gerald Cock as the first Director of Television. But we know that deep down, he still considered television to be a menace to society. Following on from this, we can perhaps understand the reluctance of the BBC not to fully embrace television at the outset. I have outlined the reasons and so shall not repeat them here, but they were numerous and were both internal and external to the BBC. Fourthly, was it inevitable that the BBC should be given the responsibility to develop a television service? I would say that it was. The BBC had the infrastructure and expertise to deal with television, and given the government's early view that television was an extension of sound broadcasting, it would be reasonable then to entrust television to the nation's sole sound broadcaster. Finally, the BBC was accused, during the 1936 to 1939 period, of not doing enough to promote television. Financially, the service struggled, which meant that additional hours would place a burden on existing scarce resources. Without an increase in programme hours, potential viewers would be unlikely to purchase a television set, which was a considerable investment in pre-war years. Yet set costs would not come down until the numbers purchasing sets increased. It was, as we saw in Chapter 7, a vicious circle. I would argue that, by the summer of 1938, the interest in television was picking up and the television service was maturing and, indeed, flourishing. Things were looking up and the outlook was positive ... until September 1939.

A word about John Logie Baird. I said at the outset that this book was not another history of Baird's pioneering television work. However, as I also said, one cannot write the history of the BBC's engagement with television without reference to him. Some contemporaries of Baird and some historians have been dismissive of his mechanical television system; some of them have been quoted in this book. Others, including those who worked with him such as T. H. Bridgewater take a different view, a view with which I agree. That is, Baird showed that true television was possible. He prepared the way, he kick-started others to research and invent, he proved that seeing at a distance was possible. And although his system was not the one chosen for the BBC Television Service, without him and his pioneering work Britain would not have taken the lead in television when it did and would not have launched the world's first regular public high-definition service, which provided information, education and entertainment in the home.

Future research

I had, at one point, considered covering the period from 1946 to the advent of the rival broadcaster, ITV, in 1955. However, on reflection, and after a good deal of consideration, I decided that post-war television developments, coming as they did in the light of the 1943 Hankey Committee, the roll-out of the television network in the context of initial national austerity and reconstruction, and then a new sense of national confidence and pride, should be the subject of another book – watch this space! There is a lot more work to be done on cinema television, which is something upon which Baird and the Baird Television Company focused after 1937. They had, of course, been experimenting with it long before that. There is also further work to be done on early transnational television history given the international race to launch the first television service. While some work exists on the connections between Britain and the USA, more needs to be done in looking at the connections between what was happening in Britain and in countries such as Germany and France.

And finally ...

The BBC Television Service resumed after the Second World War on 7 June 1946. In welcoming viewers back, and in officially declaring the new service open, the Postmaster-General, The Earl of Listowel, reassured those watching that 'the B.B.C., the Post Office, and the Radio Industry are resolved to build television into a new public service'. He also announced that the first steps in the creation of a national television service were being taken by installing a cable to relay television from London to Birmingham and then to other cities. The Postmaster-General also reflected on how television might become more popular: 'The success of television in the long run will be measured by the number of homes into which it goes. It must become, not a luxury for the few, but a refreshment and recreation for the many.' He ended by looking forward, and predicting the potential impact and benefit of a national television service for viewers:

> They will gain from a nation-wide television service fresh inspiration for the mind, a more vivid awareness of the greatness of their country, as well as pleasure and relaxation after a long day's work. For it will bring before their eyes the colourful pageantry that marks our constitutional and civic life, in addition to thrilling scenes from our national sports, and the finest performances in music, drama, and the ballet.[2]

A new television age was dawning. The 1948 London Olympics and the Coronation of Elizabeth II in 1953 heralded the beginning of the Television Age. By 1955, television was on the way to becoming a truly popular mass medium and the BBC would face a rival public service broadcaster, albeit commercially-funded, that would bring its own challenges.

Television as we know it – and as we have known it since the early days of its development – is changing. The decline of linear television and the growth in streaming have resulted in a change in the ways in which audiences are watching programmes. It is apposite, therefore, that this book has considered in detail the early years of television and the ways in which the BBC engaged with it. At the time of the Radio Exhibition in Olympia in August 1936, the journalist Paul Hobson wrote: 'The dim, flickering outline I once saw in John Baird's tiny Soho workshop at last has become a mighty effulgent beacon lighting the world of men. Whither shall it guide us? What new miracles are at hand?'[3] In just over ten years, the workshop experiments of 1926 had become a regular high-definition public service. Little wonder, then, that Hobson should ask these questions. Now, in the second decade of the twenty-first century coming close to the centenary of the first television experiments, in a multi-platform world of streaming and other changes to the way we engage with television programmes – or perhaps 'content' would be the correct word – we may well ask ourselves the same questions.

Notes

1. Asa Briggs, *The Collected Essays of Asa Briggs. Volume 3. Serious Pursuits – Communication and Education* (Englewood Cliffs, NJ: Prentice Hall, 1991), p. 2.
2. BBC WAC T16/194: TV Policy: TV Reopening Ceremony.
3. *Television and Short-Wave World* Vol. 9, No. 102, August 1936, 443.

Bibliography

Primary sources

Alexandra Palace Television Society archive

3839: Lance Sieveking, Recollection of 'The Man with the Flower in His Mouth', 1930.
3841: Gerald Cock, Recollection of establishing BBC Television in 1936.
3843: Joan Miller, Recollection of performing in *Picture Page*.
Johnson, Sarah, *Jasmine: A memoir of Jasmine Bligh, the first lady of television* [PDF].

BBC Written Archive Centre

L1/1, 759/1: Douglas Birkinshaw.
L1/1, 773/1: Cecil Madden.
L1/44: Jasmine Bligh.
L1/46/1: Dallas Bower.
L103/1–2: Elizabeth Cowell.
L1/307: Leslie Mitchell.
L1/308/1: George A. More-O'Ferrall.
L1/365: Eustace Robb.
L2/5/3: Mary Adams.
L2/40/1: Gerald Cock.
R1/1/1–1/7/1: Board of Governors Minutes.
R1/63/1–R1/65/2; R1/69/1–R1/74/7: DG's report for Board Meeting.
R3/3/7–14: Control Board Minutes.
R3/10/1–3: Controllers Meeting Minutes.
R3/11/1: Director General's Meeting 1933–4.
R4/55/1: Selsdon (Television) Committee 1934. BBC Internal Reports and Memos.
R4/56/1: Selsdon (Television) Committee 1934. Correspondence.
R4/57/1: Selsdon (Television) Committee 1934. Demonstrations and Visits.
R4/60/1: Selsdon (Television) Committee 1934. Report.
R4/61/1: Selsdon (Television) Committee. Evidence from Baird.

R4/62/1: Selsdon (Television) Committee 1934. Written Evidence: Papers 1–25.
R4/62/2: Selsdon (Television) Committee 1934. Written Evidence: Papers 26–45.
R5/5/1: 'Here's Looking at You'.
R9/9/1: Audience Research.
R5/7/1: 'The Man with the Flower in His Mouth'.
R34/600/7: Policy. Programme Board Minutes 1935.
R34/600/8: Programme Board Minutes.
R34/600/8: Programme Board Minutes.
R34/600/10: Programme Board Minutes.
R34/888: Policy. Television. Talks 1936–37.
S2/5: Special Collections. Sydney Moseley. Press Cuttings Baird TV 1928–51.
S24/19/1; S24/9; S24/24/1: Special Collections. Cecil Madden.
S60/5/3/1–2; S60/5/4/4; S60/5/5/2–3: Special Collections. Reith Diaries.
S69: Special Collections. The Gas, Light and Coke Co. 1926.
T1/6/1: Television Audience Research.
T16/23: TV Policy. Artists. General Theatre Corporation 1935–1939.
T16/42/2–5: TV Policy (Baird).
T16/56: TV Policy. Coronation. George VI 1936–1937.
T16/62/1: TV Drama.
T16/77/1–2: TV Policy. Finance.
T16/91/1: Light Entertainment.
T16/112: Television Weekly Meeting Minutes 1935–39.
T16/128/1: TV Policy. Outside Broadcasts 1937–54.
T16/151: TV Policy. Programme Policy. Bad Language 1937–1954.
T16/168/1: TV Policy. Publicity File 1 1934–1954.
T16/176/1: TV Policy. Rediffusion File 1a 1936–1937.
T16/176/2: TV Policy. Rediffusion File 1b 1938.
T16/176/3: TV Policy. Rediffusion File 1c 1939.
T16/189: Sound and Vision – News.
T16/193: TV Policy. Special Programmes. Television opening ceremony 1936.
T16/194: TV Policy. TV Reopening Ceremony.
T16/195: TV Policy. Sponsored Programmes.
T16/214/1: TV Policy. TV Development 1928–1936.
T16/214/2: TV Policy. TV Development 1937–1940.
T16/243/1: TV Policy. Transmission Hours File 1a 1934–1945.
T22/4/1: TV Programme Suggestions.
T23/77/1: TV Publicity. Radio Show, Radiolympia.
T23/77/2: TV Publicity.
T25/3: TV Routine. Alcohol.

BBC Oral History Collection

T.H. Bridgewater.

British Library Sound Library

C1248/282: Melvin Harris interview.

NP10755: Gerald Cock, 'The Television Service', National Programme, 1 February 1938, 9.05 p.m.

British Postal Museum and Archive (GPO Archive)

POST 33/3852: Baird Television Ltd. Licensing, development, experiments, Part 1.

POST 33/3853: Baird Television Ltd. Licensing, development, experiments, Part 2.

POST 33/4588: Television Committee. Visits abroad, arrangements.

POST 33/4682: Television Committee. Evidence, reports, meetings, Part 1–3.

POST 33/4713: Television Committee. Proceedings, terms of reference, meetings, report, Parts 1–4.

POST 33/5213: Reproduction of BBC television programmes in cinemas (1937–39).

POST 33/5474: Television Advisory Committee. Correspondence with Baird Television Ltd.

POST 33/5489: Television Advisory Committee. Reports.

POST 33/5510: Television licence proposals.

POST 33/5531: Television Advisory Committee. Correspondence with Radio Manufacturers Association.

POST 33/5533: Television Advisory Committee. Technical Sub-Committee minutes.

POST 33/5534: Television Advisory Committee. General Papers.

POST 33/5536: Television Advisory Committee. Proceedings.

POST 33/5561: Television Advisory Committee. Correspondence with Marconi-EMI.

POST 33/6050: Television Advisory Committee.

POST 89/10: BBC Cuttings.

POST 89/11 Broadcasting: A study of the case for and against Commercial Broadcasting in the United Kingdom under State Control.

POST 89/13: BBC Capital Requirements.

POST 89/14 Report of the Working Party on Competitive Broadcasting.

POST 89/40–43: Television Advisory Committee.

History of Advertising Trust: Selfridges archive

SEL1157

SEL1158

Marconi archive, University of Oxford

MS325
MS1503

The National Archive

CAB/24/253

Royal Television Society archive

3/5: Letter from Alfred Dinsdale to W. G. W. Mitchell.
6/6: Interview with John Bliss.
6/44: Oral evidence to Selsdon Committee.
19/2: Interview with Douglas Birkinshaw.
19/4: Interview with Alan Bray.
19/4: Interview with Dallas Bower.
20/T47: Interview with Leslie Mitchell.
20/T28: Interview with Tony Bridgewater.
25/22: Letter from Tony Bridgewater to Donald Flamm.
25/23: Letter from Gerhart Goebel to *Radio Times*.
25/25: Notes from Cecil Madden.
25/27: Notes on Marconi Co. demonstrations.

Journals

Cardiff Times
The Listener
Merthyr Express
Practical Television
Radio Times
Television
Television and Short-Wave World

Secondary sources

Abramson, Albert (1987), *The History of Television, 1880 to 1941* (Jefferson and London: McFarland).
Adam, Kenneth (1955), *The Listener*, 7 July, 19.
Aldridge, Mark (2012), *The Birth of British Television: A History* (Palgrave Macmillan).
Allighan, Gary (1938), *Sir John Reith* (London: Stanley Paul).
Arnheim, Rudolf (1936), *Radio* (London: Faber & Faber).

Baird, John Logie (1924), 'An Account of Some Experiments in Television', *The Wireless World and Radio Review*, 7 May, 153–5.
Baird, John Logie (1925), 'Television: A Description of the Baird System by Its Inventor', *The Wireless World and Radio Review*, 21 January, 533–5.
Baird, Malcolm (ed.) (2004), *Television and Me: The Memoirs of John Logie Baird* (Edinburgh: Mercat Press).
Balbi, Gabriele (2009), 'Studying the Social History of Telecommunications', *Media History* 15: 1, 85–101.
Barry, Michael (1992), *From the Palace to the Grove* (London: Royal Television Society).
BBC Yearbook 1930 (London: BBC, 1930).
BBC Yearbook 1933 (London: BBC, 1933).
Beadle, Gerald (1963), *Television: A Critical Review* (London: Allen & Unwin).
Beveridge, William (1953), 'Monopoly and Broadcasting', *Political Quarterly* 24: 4, 345–8.
Beveridge, William (1953), *Power and Influence: An Autobiography* (London: Hodder & Stoughton).
Boyle, Andrew (1972), *Only the Wind Will Listen: Reith of the BBC* (London: Hutchinson).
Branston, Gill (1998), 'Histories of British Television' in Christine Geraghty and David Lusted (eds), *The Television Studies Book* (London: Arnold), pp. 51–62.
Bray, John (2002), *Innovation and the Communications Revolution: From the Victorian Pioneers to Broadband Internet* (London: IEE).
Bridgewater, T. H. (1967), 'Baird and Television', *Journal of the British Kinematography, Sound and Television Society* 49, 60–8.
Bridgewater, T. H. (1992), 'Just a Few Lines ...', Supplement, *British Vintage Wireless Society Bulletin* 17: 4.
Briggs, Asa (1991), *The Collected Essays of Asa Briggs. Volume 3. Serious Pursuits – Communication and Education* (Englewood Cliffs, NJ: Prentice Hall).
Briggs, Asa (1995), *The History of Broadcasting in the United Kingdom. Volume I. The Birth of Broadcasting* (Oxford: Oxford University Press).
Briggs, Asa (1995), *The History of Broadcasting in the United Kingdom. Volume II. The Golden Age of Wireless* (Oxford: Oxford University Press).
Burns, R. W. (1981), 'Wireless Pictures and the Fultograph', *IEE Proceedings* 128 Pt. A: 1, 78–88.
Burns, R. W. (1986), *British Television: The Formative Years* (London: Peter Peregrinus).
Burns, R. W. (2000), *John Logie Baird, Television Pioneer* (London: IEE).
Burns R. W. (2000), *The Life and Times of A D Blumlein* (London: IEEE).
Bussell, Jan (1950), *The Puppets and I* (London: Faber & Faber).
Caughie, John (2000), *Television Drama: Realism, Modernism and British Culture* (Oxford: Oxford University Press).
Coase, Ronald H. (1954), 'The Development of the British Television Service', *Land Economics* 30: 3, 207–22.

Constantine, Stephen (2006), *Social Conditions in Britain* (London: Routledge).
Curran, James and Seaton, Jean (2018), *Power without Responsibility: Press, Broadcasting and the Internet in Britain*, 8th edn (London: Routledge).
Davis, Wendy (2007), 'Television's *Liveness*: A Lesson from the 1920s', *Westminster Papers in Communication and Culture* 4: 2, 36–51.
Dinsdale, Alfred (1928), *Television* (London: Television Press).
Dowding, G. V. (ed.) (1935), *Book of Practical Television* (London: Amalgamated Press).
Eckerlsey, P. P. (1930), 'The Drama and Television', *Popular Wireless*, 9 August, 583, 588.
Elway, Thomas (1927), 'What Shall We Do with Television?', *Popular Radio* 11: 6, June, 519–22, 579.
Fickers, Andreas (2008), 'Presenting the "Window on the World" to the World. Competing Narratives of the Presentation of Television at the World's Fairs in Paris (1937) and New York (1939)', *Historical Journal of Film, Radio and Television* 28: 3, 291–310.
Fickers, Andreas (2012), 'The Emergence of Television as a Conservative Media Revolution: Historicising a Process of Remediation in the Post-war Western European Mass Media Ensemble', *Journal of Modern European History* 10: 1, 49–75.
Galili, Doron (2020), *Seeing by Electricity: The Emergence of Television, 1878–1939* (Durham, NC and London: Duke University Press).
Gander, L. M. (1939), 'Picture Page', *Radio Times*, 13 January, 6.
Gardiner, Juliet (2010), *The Thirties: An Intimate History* (London: Harper Press).
Gielgud, Val (1957), *British Radio Drama 1922–1956* (London: Harrap).
Gorham, Maurice (1952), *Broadcasting and Television since 1900* (London: Andrew Dakers).
Graves, Robert and Hodge, Alan (1940), *The Long Weekend: A Social History of Great Britain, 1918–1939* (London: Hutchinson).
Hård, Mikael and Jamison, Andrew (2005), *Hubris and Hybrids: A Cultural History of Technology and Science* (London: Routledge).
Harris, Jose (1997), *William Beveridge: A Biography* (Oxford: Oxford University Press).
Hattersley, Roy (2009), *Borrowed Time: The Story of Britain between the Wars* (London: Abacus).
Haynes, Richard (2017), *BBC Sport in Black and White* (London: Palgrave Macmillan).
Hendy, David (2013), 'Painting with Sound: The Kaleidoscopic World of Lance Sieveking, a British Radio Modernist', *Twentieth Century British History* 24: 2, 169–200.
Hennessy, Peter (2006), *Having It So Good: Britain in the Fifties* (London: Penguin).
Herbert, Ray (1997), *Seeing by Wireless: The Story of Baird Television*, 2nd edn ([…]: PW Publishing).

Hickethier, Knut (2008), 'Early TV: Imagining and Realising Television' in Jonathan Bignell and Andreas Fickers (eds), *A European Television History* (Oxford: Blackwell), pp. 55–78.
Hilmes, Michele (1977), *Radio Voices: American Broadcasting 1922–1952* (Minneapolis: University of Minnesota Press).
Hilmes, Michele (2012), *Network Nations: A Transnational History of British and American broadcasting* (London: Routledge).
Honeycombe, Gordon (1984), *Selfridges: Seventy-Five Years. The Story of the Store 1909–1984* (London: Selfridges).
Hubbell, Robert W. (1942), *4000 Years of Television: The Story of Seeing at a Distance* (New York: G. P. Putnams and Sons).
Jacobs, Jason (2000), *The Intimate Screen: Early British Television Drama* (Oxford: Oxford University Press).
Jowett, Garth (1994), 'Dangling the Dream? The presentation of television to the America public, 1928–1952', *Historical Journal of Film, Radio and Television* 14: 2, 121–45.
Kamm, Antony and Baird, Malcolm (2002), *John Logie Baird: A Life* (Edinburgh: National Museums of Scotland).
Koszarski, Richard and Doron Galili (2016), 'Television in the Cinema before 1939: An International Annotated Database', *Journal of e-Media Studies* 5: 1, 1–46.
Langer, Nicolas (1922), 'A Development in the Problem of Television', *Wireless World and Radio Review* 11: 6, 197–201.
Law, Michael John (2018), *1938: Modern Britain. Social Change and Visions of the Future* (London: Bloomsbury).
LeMahieu, D. L. (1998), *Culture for Democracy: Mass Communication and the Cultivated Mind in the Britain between The Wars* (Oxford: Oxford University Press).
Leishmann, Marista (2006), *My Father – Reith of the BBC* (Edinburgh: Saint Andrew Press).
'Letters to the Editor' (1908), *Nature*, 18 June, 15.
Lewis, Jennifer (ed.) (2007), *Starlight Days: The Memoirs of Cecil Madden* (London: Trevor Square Publications).
Martin, Andrew (ed.) (2021), *Sound and Vision: Television from Alexandra Palace (and Some Other Places). A Programme Index 1929–1939* (Birmingham: Kaleidoscope) [pre-published document loaned to author].
McDowell, W. H. (1992), *The History of BBC Broadcasting in Scotland 1923–1983* (Edinburgh: Edinburgh University Press).
McIntyre, Ian (1994) *The Expense of Glory: A Life of John Reith* (London: Harper Collins).
McLean, Donald F. (2000), *Restoring Baird's Image* (London: IEEE).
McLean, Donald F. (n.d.), *The Dawn of Television Remembered – the John Logie Baird years: 1923 – 1936*. Audio CD.
McLean, Donald. F. (2014), 'The Achievement of Television: The Quality and Features of John Logie Baird's System in 1926, *International Journal for the History of Engineering and Technology*, 84: 2, 227–47.

McLean, Donald F. (2018), 'The Great British Broadcasting Competition: A Multi-disciplinary Analysis of the Emergence of BBC television', *Media History* 24: 1, 46–70.

McLean, Donald F. (2019), 'Seeing Across Oceans: John Logie Baird's 1928 Trans-Atlantic Television Demonstration', *Proceedings of the IEEE* 107: 6, 1,206–18.

Medhurst, Jamie (2016), 'Beveridge and Broadcasting in the 1950s' in Medhurst, Jamie, Nicholas, Siân and O'Malley, Tom (eds), *Broadcasting in the UK and US in the 1950s: Historical Perspectives* (Newcastle upon Tyne: Cambridge Scholars), pp. 29–46.

Medhurst, Jamie (2017), '"What a Hullabaloo!" Launching BBC Television Service in 1936 and BBC2 in 1964', *Journal of British Cinema and Television* 14: 2, 264–82.

Medhurst, Jamie (2019), '*Mea Maxima Culpa*: John Reith and Television', *Media History* 25: 3, 292–306.

Moran, Joe (2013), *Armchair Nation: An Intimate History of Britain in Front of the TV* (London: Profile).

Morgan, Charles (1930), 'The Future of Entertainment. Stage: Screen: Wireless: Television', *BBC Yearbook 1930* (London: BBC), p. 41.

Moseley, Sydney, (1952) *John Baird: The Romance and Tragedy of The Pioneer of Television* (London: Odhams Press).

Moseley, Sydney and Barton Chapple, H. J. (1930), *Television To-Day and To-Morrow* (London: Pitman).

Munro, John (1893), *The Romance of Electricity* (London: Religious Tract Society).

Norman, Bruce (1984), *Here's Looking at You: The Story of British television 1908–1939* (London: BBC/RTS).

Overy, Richard (2009) *The Morbid Age: Britain between the Wars* (London: Penguin).

Paulu, Burton (1981), *Television and Radio in the United Kingdom* (Minneapolis: University of Minnesota Press).

Pawley, Edward (1972), *BBC Engineering 1922–1972* (London: BBC).

Pugh, Martin (2009), *We Danced All Night: A Social History of Britain between the Wars* (London: Vintage).

Reith, J. C. W. (1949), *Into the Wind* (London: Hodder & Stoughton).

Report of the Television Committee. Cmd. 4793 (1935) (London: HMSO).

Rieger, Bernhard (2005), *Technology and the Culture of Modernity in Britain and Germany 1890–1945* (Cambridge: Cambridge University Press).

Robinson, Ernest H. (1935), *Televiewing* (London: Selwyn & Blount).

Robson, Neil (2004), 'Living Pictures Out of Space: The Forlorn Hopes for Television in Pre-1939 London', *Historical Journal of Film, Radio and Television* 24: 2, 223–32.

Ross, Gordon (1961), *Television Jubilee: The Story of 25 Years of BBC Television* (London: W. H. Allen).

Sandon, Emma (2003), 'From Vision to Mundanity: Television at Alexandra Palace, London 1936–1952: Memories of Production. An Oral History Approach to the Reassessment of the Early Period of British Television History', Unpublished Ph.D. thesis, University of Sussex.

Sandon, Emma (2007), 'Nostalgia as Resistance: The Case of the Alexandra Palace Television Society and the BBC' in Helen Wheatley (ed.), *Re-Viewing Television History: Critical Issues in Television Historiography* (London: I. B. Tauris), pp. 99–112.

Scannell, Paddy and Cardiff, David (1991), *A Social History of British Broadcasting. Volume One: 1922–1939* (Oxford: Blackwell).

Sendall, Bernard (1982), *Independent Television in Britain, Vol. 1: Origin and Foundation, 1946–62* (London: Macmillan).

Sewell, Philip W. (2014), *Television in the Age of Radio: Modernity, Imagination, and the Making of a Medium* (New Brunswick, NJ: Rutgers University Press).

Shiers, George (1975), 'Television 50 Years Ago', *Journal of Broadcasting* 19: 4, 387–400.

Shiers, George (1997), *Early Television: A Bibliographic Guide to 1940* (New York and London: Garland).

Street, Seán (2006), *Crossing the Ether: British Public Service Radio and Commercial Competition 1922–1945* (Eastleigh: John Libbey).

Stuart, Charles (1975), *The Reith Diaries* (London: Collins).

Swift, John (1950), *Adventure in Vision: The First Twenty-Five Years of Television* (London: John Lehmann).

Taylor, Stephen (1953), 'BBC or Commercial Radio', *Political Quarterly* 24: 4, 357–67.

Television: Collected Addresses and Papers on the Future of the New Art and Its Recent Technical Developments. Volume I July 1936 (New York: RCA, 1936).

Television: Collected Addresses and Papers on the Future of the New Art and Its Recent Technical Developments. Volume II October 1937 (New York: RCA, 1937).

Thorpe, Andrew (1992), *Britain in the 1930s: The Deceptive Decade* (Oxford: Blackwell).

Tiltman, Ronald F. (1933), *Baird of Television: The Life Story of John Logie Baird* (London: Seeley Service).

Trotter, David (2013), *Literature in the First Media Age: Britain between the Wars* (Cambridge, MA: Harvard University Press).

Uricchio, William (1990), 'Introduction to the History of German Television, 1935–1944', *Historical Journal of Film, Radio and Television* 10: 2, 115–22.

Uricchio, William (2008), 'Television's First Seventy-Five Years: The Interpretive Flexibility of a Medium in Transition' in Robert Kolker (ed.), *The Oxford Handbook of Film and Media Studies* (Oxford: Oxford University Press), pp. 286–305.

Walker, James R. (1991), 'Old Media on New Media: National Popular Press Reaction to Mechanical Television', *Journal of Popular Culture* 25: 1, 21–30.

Weber, Anne-Katrin (forthcoming 2022), *Interwar Television Display: New Media and Exhibition Culture in Europe and the USA, 1928–1939* (Amsterdam: Amsterdam University Press).
Wentworth-James, Gertie de S. (1928), *The Television Girl* (London: Hurst & Blackett).
Wheatley, Helen (ed.) (2007), *Re-Viewing Television History: Critical Issues in Television Historiography* (London: I. B. Tauris).
Winston, Brian (1998), *Media, Technology and Society: A History – From the Telegraph to the Internet* (London: Routledge).
Wyver, John (2012), 'Dallas Bower: a Producer for Television's Early Years, 1936–9', *Journal of British Cinema and Television* 9: 1, 26–39.
Wyver, John (2016), 'Middlebrow British Culture Being Mediated', Media history seminar series, University of London School of Advanced Study/Institute of Historical Research, 9 November [unpublished seminar paper].

Websites

http://www.bbc.co.uk/historyofthebbc/research/culture/reith-6 (last accessed 7 July 2016).
http://www.bairdtelevision.com/crystalpalace.html (last accessed 17 July 2018).
https://www.tvdawn.com/background/early-pioneers/ (last accessed 24 October 2019).
https://genome.ch.bbc.co.uk/7481ebc12b4d4d02a0b87c7e33119b3c (last accessed 20 July 2021).
https://genome.ch.bbc.co.uk/8a6e076e63e042f4927ed51b2773bb7d (last accessed 20 July 2021).
https://genome.ch.bbc.co.uk/642708ec0a7f488fbaafbe1561d3355b (last accessed 1 August 2021).
http://www.screenonline.org.uk/tv/technology/technology5.html (last accessed 31 July 2021).
https://www.bbc.co.uk/programmes/p02cjrwb (last accessed 1 August 2021).
https://microform.digital/boa/collections/16/bbc-listener-research-department-reports-1937-c1950/detailed-description (last accessed 1 August 2021).
http://hansard.millbanksystems.com/commons/1938/mar/09/broadcasting (last accessed 1 August 2021).
http://hansard.millbanksystems.com/written_answers/1937/feb/09/television-wales (last accessed 1 August 2021).

Index

Note: *f* after an entry indicates a figure

2LO transmitter, 20, 45, 46, 56, 57
30-line system, 9, 20, 33, 51, 57, 72, 78, 79*f*, 89
   Birkinshaw, Douglas, 103
   closing, 10, 98–9
   Practical Television, 95–6
   Reith, John, 94
   Television Committee (Selsdon Committee), 96
   Television Society, 94
120-line system, 85, 87, 88, 89
180-line system, 90, 109–10, 111
240-line system, 85, 96, 126, 134, 156
405-line system, 103, 126, 134, 138, 156, 158, 159

abdication crisis, 168
Abramson, Albert, 13, 14, 26
   History of Television, 1880 to 1941, The, 4
acting/actors, 77, 141
activity displacement, 10–11
actuality, 166
Adams, Mary, 116
Adventure in Vision: The First Twenty-Five Years of Television (Swift, John), 3
alcohol, 149
Aldridge, Mark, 82, 164
   Birth of British Television: A History, 3
Alexandra Palace, 10, 83, 97–8, 112–13, 119, 135*f*
   grounds, 146
   moral code, 149
Alexandra Palace Television Society archives, 6
Allen, Mary, 116, 117*f*
Allighan, Garry, 169
American Telephone and Telegraph (AT&T), 20, 26, 32, 48
Ampthill, Lord (Arthur Oliver Villiers Russell), 36, 45, 49, 64–5
Angwin, A. S., 37, 87, 93, 97

animals, 79–80
announcers, 116–18, 122
Another Pair of Spectacles (Bridges, Victor), 78
Appleton, Edward, 35
Armchair Nation: An Intimate History of Britain in Front of the TV (Moran, Joe), 4
Arnheim, Rudolf, 165–6
Ashbridge, Noel, 9, 166
   Baird Television Companies, 67–8, 69–70, 71, 88–9, 90–1, 126
   Cenotaph Service, 146, 165
   Cock, Gerald, 113
   EMI, 84–6, 87, 89–90
   radio, 101
   Radiolympia, 119–20, 122
   Television Advisory Committee, 97
   Television Committee (Selsdon Committee), 93
Ashcroft, Peggy, 141
Askey, Arthur, 79, 104n
Astell, Betty, 77
AT&T (American Telephone and Telegraph), 20, 26, 32, 48
Attlee, Clement, 46
audiences, 121–2, 145, 150–2, 166–7
   increasing, 156–8

Baird, John Logie, 1, 2, 8, 19–28, 35, 36, 44, 138–9
   achievements, 48
   BBC, 33, 34, 43, 44, 72, 77, 99
   BBC service opening ceremony, 129
   British Association lecture, 27
   Dinsdale, Alfred, 105n
   EMI, 86–7
   experimental broadcast, 56
   funding, 70–1
   government, 58–9
   Lees-Smith, Hastings B., 65–6

INDEX

London to Glasgow demonstration (1927), 26–7
as lone inventor, 57
MacDonald, Ramsey, 58–9, 67
Man with the Flower in His Mouth, The (Pirandello, Luigi), 61
media, the, 50
Royal Institution demonstration (January 1926), 1, 8, 22–3, 27
Selfridges demonstrations (1925), 20–1
Soho demonstration (April 1926), 23
television in cinemas, 159
television, first to demonstrate, 47
Baird, Malcolm and Kamm, Antony, 128, 164, 165, 166
Baird Television Companies, 1, 24, 26, 32, 36, 134
 BBC, 9, 32, 33–5, 37–47, 50, 51, 64–9, 70–1, 72
 BBC, broadcasting with 56–63, 85–91, 99
 BBC service opening ceremony, 129
 Britishness, 93, 102–3
 EMI, 84, 85, 86–7, 103
 funding, 70–1
 GPO, 22, 32–3, 36, 37, 41–4, 66, 70, 88
 high-definition television service, 119, 120, 122, 127
 IFS, 110, 119, 122, 123, 126, 128, 134, 135*f*, 137
 Murray, W. Gladstone, 37, 39–40
 overseas options, 32, 45, 65, 72
 pride, 48
 problems, 136–8
 programming, 78
 Radiolympia, 119, 120, 122
 Television Committee (Selsdon Committee), 93
 ultra-short waves, 85
Baker, Josephine, 79, 92*f*
Balbi, Gabriele, 10
Baldwin, Stanley, 59
ballet, 150
Ballet Rambert, 150
Barry, Michael, 115, 116, 118, 141
Bax, Peter, 116
BBC (British Broadcasting Corporation), 8, 9, 32–3, 99–100
 2LO transmitter, 20, 45, 46, 56, 57
 30-line system, closing 98–9
 Baird Television Companies, 9, 32, 33–5, 37–47, 50, 51, 64–9, 70–1, 72
 Baird Television Companies, broadcasting with 56–63, 85–91, 99, 119

Brookman's Park transmitter, 9, 47, 58
 creation, 17–18
 criticism, 42, 50, 51
 duties, 41
 economy, 99–100
 EMI, 84, 85–90
 GPO, 33, 35, 36, 37, 39, 41, 42, 43–4, 46–7, 50, 85, 86–8, 153
 monopoly, 58
 programmes, 77–80
 radio, 101–2
 Reith, John, 36
 reputation, 36, 51
 staff (announcers), 116–18, 122
 staff (production and engineers), 80–3, 113–16
 Swift, John, 166
 'Television', 89
 television broadcasting service, 68–73
 Television Committee (Selsdon Committee), 93–4, 95, 96
 television debates, 9–10
 television, arguments against, 40–1
 ultra-short waves, 85
 see also BBC Television Service *and* high-definition television service
BBC Oral History Collection, 6
BBC Television Orchestra, 121, 127
BBC Television Service, 71–3, 134
 audience, increasing, 156–8
 cinema and television, 159–60
 closedown and war, 153–5
 expansion, 158–9
 finance, 155–6
 opening ceremony, 125–30
 programmes, 139–50
 radio and television, 160–1
 Reith and television, 163–9
 theatre and television, 161–3
 trial period, 134–9
 viewers, 150–2
 see also high-definition television service
Beadle, Gerald, 168
Bell, Alexander Graham, 14
Bell/AT&T demonstration (1927), 26
Bell Telephone Laboratories, 26
Birkinshaw, Douglas, 83, 103, 116
Birmingham Repertory Theatre, 143
Birth of British Television: A History (Aldridge, Mark), 3
Bishop, Harold, 86–7, 153
Black, George, 162–3
Bligh, Jasmine, 116, 117, 135*f*, 138, 157

Bliss, John, 104n
Blue Peter television programme, 146
Blumlein, Alan, 84
Boat Race (Oxford–Cambridge), 10, 148, 157
Bolton, Betty, 77, 79
Book of Practical Television (Dowding, G. V.), 78
Boon, Eric, 159
Bosham, L. 147
Boulestin, Marcel, 148
Bower, Dallas, 114, 116, 141, 142
    ballet, 150
    Coronation of King George VI and Queen Elizabeth, 144
Box and Cox (Morton, John Maddison), 74n
boxing, 147, 157, 159–60
Boyle, Andrew
    Only the Wind Will Listen: Reith of the BBC, 5
Bradly, Harold, 78
Branston, Gill, 7
Bray, Alan, 136
Bray, John, 138
Bridges, Victor
    Another Pair of Spectacles, 78
Bridgewater, Tony H., 22, 47, 72, 116, 123
    BBC, 78, 83
    Baird, John Logie, 22, 26, 47
    'Coal Comfort' sketch, 71
    Robb, Eustace, 80
    Studio BB, 78
Briggs, Asa, 2, 3–4, 16, 33, 123
    Baird, John Logie, 21
    Baird Television Companies, 34, 167
    BBC funding, 155
    Cock, Gerald, 175n
    EMI, 103, 167
    Robb, Eustace, 82
Bristol and West of England Radio Traders Association, 101
Britain, inter-war years, 16–17
British Association lecture, 27
British Broadcasting Corporation (BBC) *see* BBC
British Empire, 48, 49, 59, 144
British Television: The Formative Years (Burns, Russell), 4
Britishness, 93, 102; *see also* national pride
Brittain, Harry, 6, 26, 35
Broadcast Over Britain (Reith, John), 163
broadcasting
    agreements, 68, 69
    experimental 8, 32–3, 45, 46–7, 56–7

first television drama, 9
funding, 18, 68, 70–1, 72
Man with the Flower in His Mouth, The (Pirandello, Luigi), 59–64
national programme, 18
outside broadcasts, 66
public service, 18
regional programme, 18
Reithian approach, 18
universal service, 18
see also demonstrations *and* programming
Broadcasting and Television since 1900 (Gorham, Maurice), 3
Broadcasting House, 9, 73, 78, 87
    moral code, 149
Brookman's Park transmitter, 9, 47, 58
Brown, James, 48
Brown, O. F., 93, 97
Buck and Bubbles, 127
Burns, Russell, 13, 19, 50, 126, 150
    British Television: The Formative Years, 4
Bussell, Jan, 141, 169

Cadman, John, 93
Campbell, Desmond, 61, 83, 98, 116, 139
Campbell-Swinton, Alan Archibald, 15, 36–7, 38
    television, arguments against, 41, 46, 57
Cardiff Times
    'Marvels of the Future', 15
Carpendale, Charles, 41, 45, 166
    30-line system, closing, 98–9
    BBC service opening ceremony, 129
    EMI, 87
    finance, 155
    Robb, Eustace, 80, 82
    Television Committee (Selsdon Committee), 93, 94
'Case for Wireless Drama, The' (Baddeley, V. C. Clinton), 60
Caughie, John, 7, 142
Cenotaph Service, 145–6, 165
Chamberlain, Neville, 146
Church, A. G., 68
cinema, 17, 52, 94, 122, 142
    television in, 159–60
Clarendon, Earl of (George Herbert Hyde Villiers), 41
Clark, Alfred, 126, 127, 129
Clarke-Smith, D. A., 141
'Classification of Emitron Shots' (Madden, Cecil), 114–15
Clinton-Baddeley, V. C., 60

INDEX

'Case for Wireless Drama, The', 60
clothing, 117, 118
'Coal Comfort' sketch, 71
Coase, Ronald, 56
Cock, Gerald, 82, 83, 113–14, 136–7
   BBC service opening ceremony, 129–30
   Black, George, 163
   Briggs, Asa, 175n
   Coronation of King George VI and Queen Elizabeth, 144
   finance, 160–1
   Madden, Cecil, 115, 119, 143
   moral code, 149–50
   More O'Ferrall, George, 116
   Ogilvie, Frederick W., 168–9
   outside broadcasts, 146
   promotion of television on radio, 160–1
   Radiolympia, 119, 123
   Reith, John, 168–9
   Sunday Night Play, 143
   television sets, 156, 160
Columbia Graphophone, 84
Come and Be Televised television programme, 153, 157
Constantine, Stephen, 16
cookery, 148–9
Coronation of King George VI and Queen Elizabeth, 5, 10, 144–5
Cossor, 91, 119
Cover to Cover (Rotha, Paul), 120
Cowell, Elizabeth, 116, 117*f*, 136, 153, 154
Craggy, Cyril Andrew, 42–3
Crawford, Earl of (David Lindsay), 92
cricket, 148
Crimson Caresses (Wentworth-James, Gertie de), 52
culture, 16–17, 52

Daily Mail, 17
Danahar, Arthur, 159
dance, 77, 78–9, 150
Dance Orchestra, 73
Dare, Joan, 71
Dawn of Television Remembered – the John Logie Baird Years: 1923–1936, The (McLean, Donald F.), 12n
Day, Wilfred, 19
Dean, Basil, 142–3
demonstrations, 33, 34, 36, 37–8
   Baird 180-line system demonstration (1934), 90
   Baird demonstrations for the BBC (1928), 38–9, 42

Baird London to Glasgow demonstration (1927), 26–7, 48
Baird Long Acre demonstration (1931), 69–70
Baird Long Acre to Engineers' Club demonstration (1928), 37
Baird Royal Institution demonstration (1926), 1, 8, 22–3, 27
Baird Selfridges demonstrations (1925), 20–1
Baird Soho demonstration (1926), 23
EMI demonstration (1934), 89–90
EMI/Baird demonstrations regarding Broadcasting House installation (1933), 87–8
first, 47
GPO, 44
IFS, 126
national pride, 48
Radiolympia, 120–2
secret, 42, 43, 44
visitors, 48–9
depression, 16, 99–100
Derby, the, 66, 147, 148
Dimbleby, Richard, 146
Dinsdale, Alfred, 33, 52, 105n
Disney, Walt, 160
Dixon, Adele, 127, 128
Dorté, Philip, 152
'Double Cross, The' (Stayton, Frank), 71
Douglas, Fred, 77, 79
Dowding, G. V.
   Book of Practical Television, 78
drama, 143
Drummond, Flora, 123

Eccles, William, 35
Eckersley, Peter, 9, 33–5, 36, 51, 57, 77
   'Suggested attitude towards Television', 38–9
   'Terms of Reference', 33–4
   Robb, Eustace, 80, 81
   EMI, 87
   Man with the Flower in His Mouth, The (Pirandello, Luigi), 63–4
economy, 16, 49, 99–100
Edison, Thomas, 21
Ediswan, 119
Edward VIII (King of the UK, formerly Prince of Wales), 87, 168
Edwards, Norman, 38
Electrical and Musical Industries Ltd (EMI) *see* EMI

Eliot, T. S.
   Murder in the Cathedral, 141
Elizabeth (Queen Mother of the UK), 5
Elstree Calling (Charlot, André; Hulbert, Jack; Murray, Paul; Hitchcock, Alfred), 6
Elvey, Maurice
   High Treason, 52
Elway, Thomas, 27
EMI (Electrical and Musical Industries Ltd), 9, 84, 85–90, 91, 103; *see also* Marconi-EMI
Emitron camera, 111–12, 135*f*, 144–5*f*
Evans, Arthur, 158
Eversley, Mary, 62*f*
Everson, 8
Expense of Glory: A Life of John Reith, The (McIntyre, Ian), 5
'Experimental Television Transmission by the Baird Process', 56

FA Cup Final, 10, 148
Farnsworth, 8
fears, 10
Ferranti, 119
Fickers, Andreas, 50
finance, 18, 68, 70–1, 72, 94
   BBC Television Service, 155–6
   Cock, Gerald, 160–1
   Reith, John, 70, 155, 167
   Robb, Eustace, 80–1
First Aid 3: Accidents in Sports television programme, 147
Fleming, Ambrose, 51, 56, 57, 69
football, 10, 148
Freeman, C. Denis, 62*f*
Fugue for Four Cameras (Tudor, Antony), 150
Fultograph, 37

Gainford, Lord (Jack Pease), 64–5, 101
Galili, Doron
   Seeing by Electricity: The Emergence of Television, 1898–1939, 4
Gander, L. Marsland, 145
Garson, Greer, 141
Gaumont-British, 52
GEC (General Electric Company), 17, 24, 119
General Post Office (GPO) *see* GPO
General Theatre Corporation, 162–3
George VI (King of the UK), 5, 10
Germany, 45, 49, 64, 66, 68, 109–11

Gielgud, Val, 59–60, 61*f*, 79–80, 169
   Robb, Eustace, 80, 81, 82
Goebbels, Joseph, 131n
Goldie, Grace Wyndham, 121–2, 140, 142, 148
   Reith, John, 165, 168
Gorham, Maurice, 3, 19
   Broadcasting and Television since 1900, 3
government, the, 9, 35–6, 43–4, 58–9; *see also* GPO
   funding, 70
   industry, 103
   Television Committee (Selsdon Committee), 10, 91–9, 101–2, 103, 126
GPO (General Post Office), 5–6, 8, 9, 17
   30-line system, closing, 98–9
   Archives, 5–6
   Baird Television Companies, 22, 32–3, 36, 37, 38, 41–4, 66, 70, 88
   BBC, 33, 35, 36, 37, 39, 41, 42, 43–4, 46–7, 50, 85, 86–8, 153
   EMI, 85, 86–8
   government discussions, 35–6, 59
   Reith, John, 36, 37
   Television Ltd, 22, 24–5
Graham, William, 56
Gramophone Company, 84
Graves, Cecil, 73, 90–1, 114
   BBC service opening ceremony, 129–30
   'Television', 72–3
   television in cinemas, 159
Gray, Frank, 26
Greenbaum, Hyam, 121, 127
Greer, Harry, 89, 129
Grey, Earle, 60, 62*f*
Grierson, John, 150
Grisewood, Freddie, 144, 146

Hall, Henry, 73
Hansard, 6
Hansel and Grete (Humperdinck, Engelbert), 150
Hård, Mikael and Jamison, Andrew, 7
Harvey, Len, 157
Hattersley, Roy, 106n
Haynes, Richard, 146–7
Here's Looking at You (Hill, Ronald), 120
Here's Looking at You: The Story of British Television 1908–1939 (Norman, Bruce), 4
Hickethier, Knut, 14, 110
high-definition television service, 1, 10, 89, 95, 98, 114
   Alexandra Palace, 10, 112–13, 120, 135*f*

Baird Television Companies, 119, 120, 122, 127
launch, 125–30
Marconi-EMI, 119, 126–7
preparations, 98, 118, 119
Radiolympia, 116, 118–25
staff, 113–18
see also BBC Television Service
High Treason (Elvey, Maurice), 52
Hill, Ronald
Here's Looking at You, 120
His Master's Voice (HMV), 84
history, 7
History of Television, 1880 to 1941, The (Abramson, Albert), 4
HMV (His Master's Voice), 84
Honeycombe, Gordon, 21
Hoover, Herbert, 26
horse racing, 66, 147, 148
How He Lied to Her Husband (Shaw, George Bernard), 141
'How I Planned my Kitchen' radio porgramme, 56
Howard, Sydney, 56
Howard, Trevor, 141
Hubbell, Richard W., 14
Hulbert, B. J., 149
Humperdinck, Engelbert
Hansel and Gretel, 150
Hunt, K. P., 121, 128
Hutchinson, Oliver, 9, 33, 36
Baird Television Companies, 45, 46
BBC, 41–2, 45
GPO, 22, 24–5, 32, 42, 46, 49
media, the, 50–1
overseas options, 32, 45
television sets, 23–2, 25, 44–5

iconoscopes, 111
Ideal Home Exhibition, 157
IFS (Intermediate Film System), 119, 126, 128, 135*f*, 137
Ashbridge, Noel, 122, 126
Cock, Gerald, 123, 137
Germany, 110
Pawley, Edward, 134
In Town Tonight radio programme, 124
Independent Television (ITV), 1
industry, 16, 65, 67, 103, 159
Moseley, Sydney, 69–70
L'inhumaine (L'Herbier, Marcel), 52
Inns, George, 62*f*
interference, 147

Intermediate Film System (IFS) *see* IFS
Intimate Screen: Early British Television Drama, The (Jacobs, Jason), 4
Into the Wind (Reith, John), 5
Isaacs, Rufus *see* Reading, Lord
ITV (Independent Television), 1
Ives, Herbert E., 26, 27

Jacobs, Jason, 141
Intimate Screen: Early British Television Drama, The, 4
Jenkins, Charles F., 27, 47
Johnson, Alva, 50
Johnston, Denis, 141
Journey's End (Sheriff, R. C.), 142
Jowitt, William, 92
Julius Caesar (Shakespeare, William), 142

Kamm, Antony and Baird, Malcolm, 128, 164, 165, 166
Kennedy, Angus, 59
King, Connie, 56
Kirke, H. W. L., 84, 86, 89–90
Korn, Arthur, 15

Lang, Fritz
Metropolis, 52
Law, Michael, 16, 157–8
'Learn to Televise' courses, 78
Lees-Smith, Hastings B., 45, 46, 65–6
LeMahieu, D. L., 163
Lewis, Cecil, 116, 122*f*, 125, 139
Coronation of King George VI and Queen Elizabeth, 144
licences, 18, 22, 24, 25, 66, 70, 97
Lindsay, David *see* Crawford, Earl of
Listener, The, 139
literature, 52
Lloyd, Maude, 150
Lodge, Oliver, 41, 46
London to Glasgow demonstration (1927), 26–7, 48
Looking In (Watt, John), 80

McAvoy, Jock, 157
MacDonald, Ramsey, 58–9, 67
Television Committee (Selsdon Committee), 92
McDowell, Bill, 165
McGee, J. D., 84
McIntyre, Ian
Expense of Glory: A Life of John Reith, The, 5

McKay, Helen, 120
McLean, Donald F., 7, 13, 16, 126
   Baird, John Logie, 48
   Baird Television Companies, 93
   Dawn of Television Remembered – the John Logie Baird Years: 1923–1936, The, 12n
   Looking In (Watt, John), 80
   national pride, 47
   Royal Institution demonstration, 23
   television quality, 78
Madden, Cecil, 5, 114, 136, 162
   'Classification of Emitron Shots', 114–15
   closedown and war, 154–5
   Coronation of King George VI and Queen Elizabeth, 144
   drama, 140–1, 143–4
   Picture Page, 123–4
   Radiolympia, 119, 120
   Starlight Days: The Memoirs of Cecil Madden, 4
   'Television Ideas', 114
make-up, 73
Malone, Cecil, 35, 36
Man with the Flower in His Mouth, The (Pirandello, Luigi), 59–64
Manville, Edward, 26, 45, 49
Marconi Archive, 6
Marconi-EMI, 93, 102, 129, 134, 136–8; *see also* EMI *and* Marconi Wireless Telegraph Company
   high-definition television service, 119, 126–7
   Radiolympia, 119
Marconi Wireless Telegraph Company, 17, 20, 57
Marigold (Abbott, Allan, F. and Garvice, Charles), 141
Marshall, Howard, 148, 161
Martin, Andrew
   Sound and Vision: Television from Alexandra Palace, 4–5
'Marvels of the Future' (*Cardiff Times*), 15
Masefield, John, 144
media, the, 38, 41, 50–1, 73, 139–40
   Alexander Palace, 113
   Baird Television Companies, 40, 50, 51
   BBC, attacks on, 40, 42
   BBC anniversary, 168
   BBC programming, 77
   BBC service opening ceremony, 128, 129
   Coronation of King George VI and Queen Elizabeth, 145
   Germany, 45, 66, 110

GPO, 25
   interest, 27
Listener, The, 139
live television, 146
Man with the Flower in His Mouth, The (Pirandello, Luigi), 60, 62–3
public relations, 150–1
Radio Times, 34–5, 40, 56, 73, 141, 161
Radiolympia, 121–2
Royal Institution demonstration, 23
sports programmes, 147
Television Committee (Selsdon Committee), 97
television potential, 15–16, 139–40
television uses, 27, 139–40
Times, The, 8, 23
USA, 111
uses of television, 99f–100
Meighn, Moira, 148
Melba, Nellie, 17
Metropolis (Lang, Fritz), 52
Metropolitan-Vickers, 17
Mickey Mouse, 153, 154, 160
Middleton, C. H., 146, 157, 158f
Millard, Lionel, 60, 62f
Miller, Joan, 123, 125, 150
mirror drum system, 66, 78, 90
Mitchell, Leslie, 116–18, 120, 127, 128, 136
   Picture Page, 124
Mitchell, W. G. W., 27, 43
Mitchell-Thomson, William *see* Selsdon, Lord
Modern Pastoral, A radio programme, 161
moral code, 149–50
Moran, Joe, 2
   Armchair Nation: An Intimate History of Britain in Front of the TV, 4
Morbid Age: Britain Between the Wars, The (Overy, Richard), 16
More O'Ferrall, George, 116, 120, 141, 142
   Picture Page, 123–4
Morgan, Charles, 58
Morley, Royston, 141
Moseley, Sydney, 5, 9, 33, 64
   BBC, 37, 40, 41–2, 43, 67, 64, 69, 70
   EMI, 84, 86
   experimental broadcast, 56
   industry, 69–70
   Man with the Flower in His Mouth, The (Pirandello, Luigi), 59, 61
   media, the, 51
Moss Empires, 162–3
Muggeridge, Malcolm, 165

INDEX

Munro, D. H., 116, 138, 151–2
Munro, John, 14–15
Murder in the Cathedral (Eliot, T. S.), 141
Murray, Evelyn, 33, 42, 71
Murray, W. Gladstone, 37, 39–42, 43, 51, 66–8, 71
   radio, 101–2
Music Hall Cavalcade, 144
My Father: Reith of the BBC (Leishman, Marista), 5

National Archives, Kew, 6
national pride, 47–8, 49, 59, 65, 102, 110, 127, 148
Netherlands, 36
Nevinson, C. R. W., 60
'Newcomer to Viewing, A' radio programme, 161
news programmes, 107n
Nicholls, Basil, 82, 113
Nipkow, Paul, 20, 47
Nipkow system, 20, 26, 47
Norman, Bruce, 164
   Here's Looking at You: The Story of British Television 1908–1939, 4
Norman, R. C., 127, 128

O'Donovan, Fred, 116
Ogilvie, Frederick W., 153, 168–9
Oliver, Vic, 163
Olivier, Laurence, 141
Olympia Radio Exhibition (1936), 10, 11
Olympic Games (1936), 110
Only the Wind Will Listen: Reith of the BBC (Boyle, Andrew), 5
opera, 150
Orr-Ewing, Ian, 116
Ostrer, Isidore, 159
outside broadcasts, 66, 143–6, 147, 157
Overy, Richard
   Morbid Age: Britain between the Wars, The, 16

Pain, Daisy, 140, 151
Palmer, Roundell Cecil *see* Wolmer, Viscount
Paramount Astoria Girls, 80
Parnell, Val, 163
Paulu, Burton, 49
Pawley, Edward, 71–2, 134, 136
Pear, T. H., 139
Pease, Jack *see* Gainford, Lord
perception, 10–11
Percy, J. D., 154

Phillips, 119
Phillips, F. W., 32–3, 68–9, 86–8, 93
   30-line system, closing 98–9
   Alexandra Palace, 98
   Television Advisory Committee, 97
   television sets, 156
Picture Page, 123–5, 148
Pink Purity (Wentworth-James, Gertie de), 52
Pirandello, Luigi
   Man with the Flower in His Mouth, The, 59–64
Pogo, 121
popular culture, 52
Post Office *see* GPO
Priestley, J. B., 143
   When We Are Married, 142–3
Prince, Arthur, 163
Pringle, Harry, 116, 120
programmes/programming, 53, 68, 71, 167
   ambitious, 80
   American influences, 149
   Baird Television Companies, 78
   BBC, 71, 77–80
   BBC Television Service, 139–50
   Birkinshaw, Douglas, 103
   cars, 125
   drama, 140–3
   finance, 71
   importance of, 123
   loss of, 6–7
   Murray, W. Gladstone, 67
   news, 107n
   outside broadcasts 66, 143–6, 147, 157
   Picture Page, 123–5
   potential speakers, 140
   Radiolympia, 122–5
   RMA, 156
   Selsdon, Lord, 155
   sport, 10, 66, 110, 140, 146–8, 157
   Television Committee (Selsdon Committee), 95, 96
   variety, 148–50
'Programmes as Broadcast' (Ps-as-Bs) records, 153–4
public relations, 150–1
public service, 18, 24, 39–40, 71–3
   opening ceremony, 125–30
   see also BBC Television Service *and* high-definition television service
Pugh, Martin, 16

Quayle, Anthony, 141
Quigley, Janet, 140

radio, 17–18, 49, 51
  decline, 103
  Radiolympia, 116, 118–25
  television, relationship with, 160–1
  television as threat, 101–2, 160
  Television Committee (Selsdon Committee), 96
Radio Corporation of America (RCA), 20, 84, 86, 111–12
Radio Manufacturers Association (RMA), 101–2, 156, 158–9
Radio Times, 34–5, 40, 56, 73, 141, 161
Radiolympia, 116, 118–25, 157–8*f*
railways, 100
Rambert, Marie, 104n
Rau, Rama, 140
RCA (Radio Corporation of America), 20, 84, 86, 111–12
Reading, Lord (Rufus Isaacs), 92
Redgrave, Michael, 141
Reichs-Runkunk-Gesellschaft (Reich Broadcasting Service), 45
Reith, John, 1–2, 3, 18, 50, 68, 69, 130, 163–9
  audiences, 150
  Baird Television Companies, 38, 43, 46–7, 86, 88
  BBC service opening ceremony, 128–9
  biographies, 5
  Broadcast Over Britain, 163
  Cock, Gerald, 113–14
  Derby, the, 148
  diaries, 5
  EMI, 86, 87, 88
  finance, 70, 155, 167
  GPO, 36, 41, 46
  Into the Wind, 5
  moral code, 150
  Murray, W. Gladstone, 40
  opera, 150
  sports, outside broadcasts, 147
  technology 136, 137–8
  'Television', 69
  Television Committee (Selsdon Committee), 93–4, 103
  television in cinemas, 159
Reith Diaries, The (Stuart, Charles), 5
Rendall, R. A., 151
Reynolds, N. B., 48
Richardson, Ralph, 141
Rieger, Bernhard, 110
RMA (Radio Manufacturers Association), 101–2, 156, 158–9

Robb, Eustace, 71, 76n, 78–9, 80–3, 113, 147
  theatre, 162
Roberts, J. Varley, 93, 97, 102, 126–7
Robinson, Ernest H., 139
Robson, Neil, 139
Rogers, Maclean
  Third Eye, The, 52
Rotha, Paul
  Cover to Cover, 120
Roy, Harry, 163
Royal Institution demonstration (January 1926), 1, 8, 22–3, 27
Royal Television Society, 6
  Archive, 6
rugby, 157
Ruhmer, Ernest, 15–16
Russell, Arthur Oliver Villiers *see* Ampthill, Lord
Ryan, A. P., 122, 125

sabotage, 120
Sandon, Emma, 164
Sarnoff, David, 18, 111, 112
Scannell, Paddy and Cardiff, David, 7
Scophony Ltd, 91
Seccombe, Lionel, 157
Second World War, 2
Seeing by Electricity: The Emergence of Television, 1878–1939, (Galili, Doron), 4
Selfridge, George, Jr, 20–1
Selfridges Archive, 6
Selfridges demonstrations (1925), 20–1
Selsdon, Lord (William Mitchell-Thompson), 35, 92–3, 96–7, 126–7, 155
Selsdon Committee, 10, 91–9, 101–2, 103, 126
Sewell, Philip, 14
Shaw, George Bernard, 141
  How He Lied to Her Husband, 141
Sheridan, Dinah, 123
Sheriff, R. C.
  Journey's End, 142
Shiers, George, 25
Shoenberg, Isaac, 84, 102
Sieveking, Lance, 60–1*f*, 62*f*
Silvey, Robert J., 150
Simmonds, Oliver, 156
Simon, John, 159
Simon, L., 88
Simpson, F. J., 147
Simpson, Wallis, 168
16 Portland Place, 90*f*–1*f*
Smith, Frank, 97, 155

INDEX

Smith, Willoughby, 14
Snuggs, John, 124
society, 16, 41
Soho demonstration (April 1926), 23
Sorter, Frank, 49
sound, 9
   synchronised with vision, 57–8
Sound and Vision: Television from Alexandra Palace (Martin, Andrew), 4–5
sport, 10, 66, 110, 140, 146–8, 157
spotlight system, 71, 126
Stanley, Lulu, 56
Starlight Days: The Memoirs of Cecil Madden (Madden, Cecil), 4
Stayton, Frank
   'Double Cross, The', 71
Stewart, E. G., 23–4
'Stookie Bill', 22, 27
Strachan, D. Grant, 102
Streeton, William, 162–3
Stuart, Charles
   Reith Diaries, The, 5
Studio BB, 73, 78, 79*f*
'Suggested attitude towards Television' (Eckersley, Peter), 38–9
Sunday Night Play, 143
Swift, John, 3, 33, 71, 101, 103, 166
   Adventure in Vision: The First Twenty-Five Years of Television, 3
   Alexander Palace, 112

TAC (Television Advisory Committee), 97–8, 126–7, 129, 138, 155–6
   national expansion, 158
Tallents, Stephen, 130, 150
technology, 13, 14–16, 134–8
   120-line system, 85, 87, 88, 89
   180-line system, 90, 109–10, 111
   240-line system, 85, 96, 126, 134, 156
   405-line system, 103, 126, 134, 138, 156, 158, 159
   American, 26
   benefit of 17
   Birkinshaw, Douglas, 103
   Coronation of King George VI and Queen Elizabeth, 144–5
   EMI, 84
   Emitron camera, 111–12, 135*f*
   Fultograph, 37
   Germany, 109–11
   iconoscopes, 111
   IFS, 110, 119, 122, 123, 126, 128, 134, 135*f*, 137

interference, 147
investment, 16
mirror drum system, 66, 78, 90
national pride, 110
Nipkow system, 20, 26, 47
Nipkow, 20, 26
outside broadcasts, 66
quality, 77–8
railway experiment, 100
Reith, John, 167, 168
spotlight system, 71, 126
Studio BB, 78, 79*f*
Television Committee (Selsdon Committee), 96
Television Society, 95
ultra-short waves, 84, 85, 89, 90, 95
USA, 109, 111–12
see also high-definition television service *and* 30-line system
telecine, 134
teleology, 7
telephones, 14–15
telephony, 10
television, 20, 166
   appeal of, 130
   arguments against, 40–1, 46, 60, 64, 165–6
   dominance, 1
   entertainment, 58
   etymology, 1, 28n
   as institution, 2
   live, 134, 142–7
   national pride, 47–8
   origins, 14–16
   potential, 63, 79, 81, 83, 123, 139–40
   power of, 58
   race for, 22, 48, 49–50
   Reith, John, 164–5
   standards, 138, 156
   uses, 27, 51–2, 99*f*, 100
   see also Baird, John Logie
'Television' (BBC), 89
'Television' (Graves, Cecil), 72–3
'Television' (Reith, John), 69
Television (journal), 33, 48, 77
'Television on an Express Train; A novel experiment', 100
Television Advisory Committee (TAC) *see* TAC
Television Committee (Selsdon Committee), 10, 91–9, 101–2, 103, 126
Television Exhibition (Berlin, 1929), 49
'Television Exhibition' (London, 1937), 157

Television Girl, The (Wentworth-James, Gertie de), 6, 10
'Television Ideas' (Madden, Cecil), 114
'Television in emergency period', 153
Television Ltd, 21, 22
　GPO 24–5
'Television on an Express Train: A novel experiment' (*Television*), 100
television programmes *see* programmes/programming
'television scare', 101, 113
television sets, 22, 23, 38, 50, 65, 88
　Baird Television Companies, 24, 33, 44, 50, 70, 85
　Cock, Gerald, 156, 160
　competitive market, 158
　cost, 118–19, 151, 156, 166–7
　EMI, 85
　Germany, 109–10, 111
　Hutchinson, Oliver, 44–5
　Ideal Home Exhibition, 157
　incentive for, 57, 155–6
　obsolescence, 89, 94
　Radiolympia, 118–19
　recording owners, 152
　RMA, 156
　Stewart, E. G., 24
　switching systems, 133n
　TAC, 129
　see also televisors
'Television Show' (Selfridges, 1938), 157
Television Society, 27–8, 59, 94–5
televisors, 25, 33, 36, 38; *see also* television sets
tennis, 10, 147
'Terms of Reference' (Eckersley, Peter), 33–4
theatre, 142–3, 161–3
Third Eye, The (Rogers, Maclean), 52
Thomas, Godfrey, 87
Thomas, Stephen, 116
Thorndike, Sybil, 141
Times, The, 8, 23
transmitting stations, 25
Trotter, David, 52
Tryon, George, 127, 156
Tudor, Antony
　Fugue for Four Cameras, 150
Turner, L. B., 34–5

Up from the Country television programme, 161
Uricchio, William, 14, 110
USA, 18, 65, 66, 67, 72
　AT&T, 20, 26, 32, 48
　EMI, 84
　programmes, influence on, 149
　RCA, 20, 84, 86, 111–12
　technology 109, 111–12
　see also RCA

Van Dyck, Arthur, 112
Vic-Wells Ballet, 150
'Viewers and the Television Service', 151
Villiers, George Herbert Hyde *see* Clarendon, Earl of
vision, synchronised with sound, 57–8

Wakelam, Henry B. T. (Captain), 148
war, 153–5
Weber, Anne-Katrin, 110
Wentworth-James, Gertie de, 51
　Crimson Caresses, 52
　Pink Purity, 52
　Television Girl, The, 6, 10
West, A. G. D., 88–9
Western Electric Company, 17
Wheatley, Helen
　Re-Viewing Television History: Critical Issues in Television Historiography, 7
When We Are Married (Priestley, J. B.), 142–3
Williams, Derek, 141
Wimbledon Tennis Championships, 10, 147
Winston, Brian, 4, 13, 14, 33
Wireless Pictures Ltd, 37
Wireless Telegraphy Acts, 5, 22, 97
Wireless World and Radio Review, The, 19, 20
Wolmer, Viscount (Roundell Cecil Palmer), 26
Wood, Howard Kingsley, 69, 70, 92–3, 96–7
Wyver, John, 141, 166

Yearbook, 8
Young, Gladys, 60, 62f

Zoo, The television programme, 154f
Zworykin, Vladimir, 111

EU representative:
Easy Access System Europe
Mustamäe tee 50, 10621 Tallinn, Estonia
Gpsr.requests@easproject.com

www.ingramcontent.com/pod-product-compliance
Lightning Source LLC
Chambersburg PA
CBHW070356240426
43671CB00013BA/2523